Arno Böhler, Susanne Valerie Granzer (eds.)
The Flavor of Thinking

Arno Böhler teaches philosophy as a faculty member at the Department of Philosophy at the University of Vienna, and he also teaches aesthetics at the mdw – University of Music and Performing Arts Vienna, Austria. He serves as the Principal Investigator of the PEEK research project "Philosophy in the Arts : Arts in Philosophy. Cross-Cultural Research on the Significance of the Heart in Artistic Research (AR) and Performance Philosophy (PP)", conducted at ARC-mdw and funded by the Austrian Science Fund (FWF). He has been a visiting research fellow at the University of Bangalore, the University of Heidelberg, New York University, and Princeton University, as well as a visiting professor at the University of Applied Arts Vienna, the University of the Arts Bremen (HdK Bremen), the University of Vienna, and the Berlin University of the Arts (UdK Berlin).

Susanne Valerie Granzer, also known as Susanne Valerie, is a professor emeritus of acting at the Max Reinhardt Seminar at the University of Music and Performing Arts in Vienna, Austria. As an actress, she has performed at state theatres across the German-speaking world. Alongside her acting career, she earned a PhD in Philosophy from the University of Vienna in 1995. Together with the philosopher Arno Böhler, she established the Vienna-based cultural factory *baseCollective* and the festival *Philosophy on Stage*. She is currently a key researcher on the research project "Philosophy in the Arts : Arts in Philosophy. Cross-Cultural Research on the Significance of the Heart in Artistic Research and Performance Philosophy", conducted at ARC-mdw and funded by the Austrian Science Fund (FWF).

Arno Böhler, Susanne Valerie Granzer (eds.)

The Flavor of Thinking

Philosophy in Artistic Research - Artistic Research in Philosophy

mdwPress

[transcript]

This research was funded in whole or in part by the Austrian Science Fund (FWF) [10.55776/AR822] and the Open Access Fund of mdw – University of Music and Performing Arts Vienna.

Österreichischer
Wissenschaftsfonds

Bibliographic information published by the Deutsche Nationalbibliothek
The Deutsche Nationalbibliothek lists this publication in the Deutsche Nationalbibliografie; detailed bibliographic data are available online at https://dnb.dnb.de

First published in 2026 by mdwPress, Vienna and Bielefeld
2026 © Arno Böhler, Susanne Valerie Granzer (eds.)

The automated analysis of the work in order to obtain information, particularly concerning patterns, trends, and correlations as defined in § 44b (text and data mining) of the German Copyright Act (UrhG) is prohibited without the written consent of the rights holders.

transcript Verlag | Hermannstraße 26 | D-33602 Bielefeld | live@transcript-verlag.de

Cover design: bueronardin/mdwPress
Cover illustration: Eva-Maria Jägle, Christoph Müller
Layout: Jana Diewald
Copyediting: Eva-Maria Jägle, Christoph Müller
English translations: Mirko Wittwar
https://doi.org/10.14361/9783839472118
Print-ISBN: 978-3-8376-8119-2 | PDF-ISBN: 978-3-8394-7211-8 |
ePUB-ISBN: 978-3-7328-0016-2

Contents

Introduction: Arts-Based-Philosophy
Towards an Aesthetic Image of Thought

Arno Böhler

The problem...

June, 2023. Again I am sitting at my computer and writing a research proposal for the Austrian Science Fund (FWF) in the framework of the program for arts-based research and development (PEEK), this time with the title "Art in Philosophy: Philosophy in the Arts. The Significance of the *Heart* in Artistic-Research (AR) and Performance Philosophy (PP)."[1] The relation of art and philosophy has kept fascinating me for many years. Tenaciously. Insistently. Still. Just *as-if* it was—freely paraphrasing Kafka—"made only for me".[2]

Even though I found myself personally in the wake of this question, the problematic relation between art and philosophy simultaneously gave me a distinct feeling of having come across something that was of general, even historical interest. Because the formula art (and/or/versus) philosophy seemed to respond to a long intellectual history that *again* became highly problematic and questionable today—even

---

1   The proposal has finally been approved by the Austrian Science Fund (FWF): Grant-DOI 10.55776/AR822. https://www.mdw.ac.at/the.heart/ (last accessed: 12 June 2025). The word "again" refers to a second research proposal I wrote in 2012, in which I was overwhelmed by the same feeling. Namely, that the relationship between art and philosophy "has kept fascinating me for many years. Tenaciously. Insistently. Still. Just as if it were—freely paraphrasing Kafka—'a research question, made for me.'" (Böhler 2019b, 240)

2   "No one else could ever be admitted here, since this gate was *made only for you*." (Kafka 2009, 152)

though not many people yet have accepted it as a top priority issue. Though it strikes us all, it hits us *in secret*, still; in a sublime manner operating below the threshold of our common public awareness; below the threshold of our shared public interests; below the threshold of our public everydayness. As-*if* it would not strike us at all.

Initially, aesthetic troubles of this sort probably always matter for 'all and none,' to indirectly quote the subtitle of Nietzsche's book *Thus Spoke Zarathustra*. They shake us all, but almost nobody seems to register their sublime (*sūkṣma*) vibes (*vṛtti*),[3] precisely due to the subtleness of the matter at stake. This also seems to be the reason why the historical need of a new aesthetic image-of-thought[4] is still not broadly discussed. It seems better to not touch such vague grounds. Better to silence them. Better to let them vibrate unanswered in the depth of one's soul—unheard, without anybody consciously recognizing them, taking care of them, imagining them.

For, from the viewpoint of a psychology built from anima what we are doing when deeply engaged in imagination is indeed aesthetic. Depth psychology *is* depth aesthetics, and the task of psychology from that date on would have been laying out the aesthetic modes of the deep imagination... (Hillman 1981, 36)

Indeed, the matter is sublime and cryptic ...

This book claims to exemplarily show that the relation of art and philosophy *currently* undergoes a sublime but crucial historical transformation. There are more than enough signs which indicate that the alteration of the historically handed down relatedness of art *and*

---

3   In Sanskrit, *sūkṣma* means energy-matter that vibrates (*vṛtti*) so smoothly that our sense organs are hardly able to register and grasp such subtle vibes.

4   According to Deleuze, an *image-of-thought* is a historical configuration of how thinking itself imagines the performance of thinking. Descartes' "ego cogito", for instance, did create a historical image of what thinking means in modern European times. Nietzsche, for instance, questioned this image-of-thought in *Beyond Good and Evil*, in an aphorism on "the superstitions of the logicians" by stating "that a thought comes when 'it' wants, not when 'I' want." (Nietzsche 2002, 17)

philosophy is already in the making, at least at the margins of contemporary philosophy and contemporary arts.[5]

First signs...

First and foremost, I suggest to read Nietzsche's vision of a new species of philosophers, "whose taste and inclination are somehow the reverse of those we have seen so far" (Nietzsche 2002, 6) as a prelude to a philosophy of the future[6] in which a new way of doing philosophy in alliance with the arts has started to incubate. What distinguishes the day-break of these new artist-philosophers[7] from their ancestors is primarily their reversed sense of taste, says Nietzsche. They *feel* different from their ancestors. They *sense and taste* the world differently and even *think* qualitatively differently, due to the aesthetic image-of-thought they perform while thinking in strong opposition to the handed down tradition of the ascetic image-of-thought of their forefathers who regularly imagined the performance of thinking to be an action performed entirely separate from the rest of their body on an ideal, non-sensual plane-of-being. As a rule, their ancestors just seemed to want one thing only, says Nietzsche. Namely, "repose in all cellar regions" (Nietzsche 1989, 108). If a philosopher lacked this ascetic appetite in the souterrains of his or her body, one could be sure that s/he was called merely a so-*called* philosopher. "A philosopher in quotation marks who lacked decisive features to be called a genuine, true, serious philosopher ..." (Böhler 2014, 242)

To rescue the dominant meta-position of the mental performance of thinking in the life of one's lived-body, the performance of think-

---

5   Philosophizing on the margins of philosophy is precisely the way of doing philosophy, once philosophy has started to accept its fictional character. (Derrida, 1982).

6   *Prelude of a Philosophy of The Future* is the subtitle of Nietzsche's book *Beyond Good and Evil.*

7   Nietzsche uses the term artist-philosopher (Künstlerphilosoph) in his late writings, in order to signify that the forthcoming generation of philosophers will be both, artists and philosophers, at once. (Böhler 2015). Mediathek PEEK-Project (FWF): AR 275-G21 https://homepage.univie.ac.at/arno.boehler/php/?p-7913 (last accessed: 12 June 2025).

ing had to be imagined in classical times to be a kind of *disinterested* performance. That is to say, an action that is entirely grounded in itself (*cogito*). Autonomous thinking, not at all influenced by the souterrains of one's lived-body, this seemed to be their special matter. As-*if* one's thoughts would not at all be influenced by one's appetite, one's drives, instincts, feelings, aspirations, longings, inclinations, intuitions, as well as by the external atmosphere, circumstances and discursive contextuality in which a lived-body actually finds itself embedded in its being-in-the-world.

Nietzsche's assumption that consciousness is not "*opposed* to instincts in any decisive sense" actually raised a new level concerning the question "What is called thinking?" by assuming that "most of a philosopher's conscious thought is secretly directed and forced into determinate channels by the instincts" (Nietzsche 2002, 7). For classical philosophers, still today it is probably this assumption which is the most shocking aspect of Nietzsche's new aesthetic image-of-thought (Böhler 2017, 580).

The ascetic versus the aesthetic image-of-thought...

Imagining the act of thinking as it would take place entirely detached from the rest of one's body on an immaterial, ideal plane of being—disinterested and entirely separated from the 'lower' planes of one's lived-body—is the typical way of characterizing the performance of thinking trapped by the ascetic ideal (Nietzsche 1998, 97-163) and the ascetic image-of-thought that follows the ascetic ideal. In the course of such a view, the head (*caput*)[8] actually becomes the incorporated capitol and ruling regime of one's entire body.

Such an ascetic image-of-thought goes hand in hand with a contemplative interpretation of the arts, in which they are appointed the role of a sedative (Schopenhauer); or, at least, of a sort of 'disinterested intuition' (Kant). In both instances, the task of the arts lies either in silencing the restless forces operative in the cellar regions of one's lived-bodies (Schopenhauer) or, more modestly, in praising art as a

---

8   On the relation of the head (caput) with the cape and capitalism see Derrida 1992.

form of contemplation (Nietzsche 1989, 103-106) in which one's aesthetic judgment reflects the aesthetic value of things in a mindful, conceptual manner.

What such aesthetics-of-reception are missing, according to Nietzsche, is the very experience of the artist him- or herself. Namely the one who is producing and not just consuming art. Or more precisely, the one who is artistically *consuming the production of art* in a sort of self-affection that is stimulated by an artistic research process within the artists themselves. Ascetic aesthetics, the aesthetics of European classical times, actually ignored this fact that the arts are, in the first place, *a research process that stimulates artists while they create art.*

The classical ascetic image of the arts stands in a strong contrast to Nietzsche's own view on aesthetic matters. First of all because he, being himself an artist-philosopher, was intimately familiar with artistic research processes, due to the many styles of writing he was experimenting with while he was generating his philosophy–writing aphorisms, treatises, poems, epics, letters and even musical compositions which afterwards he himself played and interpreted on the piano.

Artistic experiences which Nietzsche, by the way, shared with his greatest antagonist Plato, who in the first place also was an artist before he met his teacher Socrates and started to become a Socratic philosopher. The tradition of philosophy even claimed that in a highly symbolic scene Socrates recommended his aristocratic master student Plato to burn his art work before entering the realm of philosophy and becoming a *serious* Socratic philosopher (Böhler 2019c). As-*if* for artists the gate was from then on be closed to enter the temple of Socratic philosophy and serious academic scholarship. From now on one had to choose, *either* to become a Socratic philosopher *or* an artist. To be or become both, to be and become a hybrid *philosopher-artist* and/or an *artist-philosopher* is considered to be contradictory in itself since then. And, honestly: It still appears to be contradictory today for most classical philosophers and classical artists, at least in Continental Europe and those non-European cultures which are academically trained by such a Socratic Episteme.

At least since Hellenistic times, when philosophers were starting to attack their ancestors' mythological style of doing philosophy by criticizing their way of doing 'philosophy' as a form of thinking based on arbitrary imaginations which did miss any reasonable argumentation, precisely since then the fusion of art *and* philosophies does not appear as a reasonable academic enterprise anymore for most academic scholars. Still today. Arts-based-Philosophy, Philosophy-based-Arts is actually nothing serious academic researchers would generally recommend their students to strive for.

But even though in the meantime the Socratic way of doing philosophy has become the standard model of what it means to do academic philosophy, even on a global scale, the situation seems to have changed since Nietzsche entered the stage of continental philosophy and started to challenge precisely the Hellenistic assumption that art and philosophy have per se to be considered antagonistic forces.

It is worth mentioning that the Socratic way of doing philosophy, which Socrates' master student Plato institutionalized for the first time in his Platonic Academy, probably would have never survived if Socrates' master student had not possessed such brilliant artistic writing skills. Socrates, who had not written any text, was obviously in need of the artist-philosopher Plato, who dramatized the oral teachings of his master in an artistic manner in such an elegant way that Socrates' teachings survived historically. Is this not Socratic irony? Plato's teacher advised him to burn his artworks in order to become a serious Socratic philosopher. But in the end the Socratic way of doing philosophy probably only survived due to the artistic skills of Socrates' aristocratic student who was trained in the arts and finally founded the first academia?

One has to have this entire primal scene in mind in order to understand the weight and depth of the following propositions by artist-philosopher Friedrich Nietzsche who was also an academically trained philologist of ancient Greek and Roman culture: "My Philosophy is reversed *Platonism*."[9] And more than 16 years later, in a letter

---

9   "Meine Philosophie umgedrehter Platonismus: je weiter ab vom wahrhaft Seienden, um so reiner schöner besser ist es. Das Leben im Schein als Ziel." (Nietzsche 1967–1977, 7 [156])

to his friend Paul Deussen of November 16, 1887, he appends the following remark to this early posthumous fragment, "perhaps this old *Plato* is my actual great opponent? But how proud I am to have such an adversary!" (Nietzsche 2003, 200; Translation A. B.)

Nietzsche actually developed his own *aesthetic* image-of-thought in strong opposition to the other artist-philosopher, the divine and most esteemed Plato, who finally followed Socrates' *ascetic* image-of-thought by banning the poets from his ideal state, arguing that they were just imitating reality and thus following an aesthetic rather than an idealistic form of imagination which was still trapped in sensual affections and not in the sober, non-sensual thinking of ideas. "The Socratic disregard of the instinctive ... The divine *Plato*, too, has fallen prey to Socratism in this instance ..." (ibid., 542)

Nietzsche's reversal of Platonism historically *resists* this ascetic image-of-thought, by claiming that the performance of thinking is, in-itself, a sensual activity in resonance with all the other parts of one's lived-body. Consequently, the function of philosophy cannot lie in the ascetic enterprise to leave the sensual realm of affections behind in order to enter an immaterial realm of pure ideas, freed from any affect. Sober thinking was precisely the kind of thinking Socrates was longing for. And the modern versions of the ascetic image-of-thinking, the so-called 'objective' sciences, still today follow this Socratic approach, according to Nietzsche. Think sober! This is just the modern mask of the old ascetic ideal (Nietzsche 1989, 146-154).

Nietzsche, on the contrary, reversed this ascetic image-of-thought by actually calling the arts "the greatest stimulus to life".[10] The beauty of art consists in the "promise to happiness",[11] as Stendhal

---

10 In his lecture course on Nietzsche during World War II, Martin Heidegger read this proposition as the very foundation of Nietzsche's aesthetic position. Cf. Heidegger 1996.

11 In the third book *On the Genealogy of Morals*, Nietzsche takes Stendhal's definition of beauty, "beauty is a promise of happiness", as the counter position to Kant's aesthetic of disinterestedness and Schopenhauer's aesthetic quietism. "That is beautiful," said Kant, which gives us pleasure *without interest*. Without interest! Compare with this definition one framed by a genuine 'spectator' and artist—Stendhal, who once

once said, in accordance with Nietzsche's own aesthetic view. Art not only promises happiness in a future to come, but also *awakens* passionate feelings (Derrida 2000, 26-29) here and now by virtue of *doing* art, *processing* art, *performing* artistic research. The arts *currently stimulate*. They are *activating* in particular the virtual planes of beings; not just those planes which have already been active and activated in a soul but also, and primarily, those planes of being which so far have not yet been animated in one's anima. Virtual planes, which until now were resting secretly in the background of somebody's psycho-mental awareness; hidden, cryptic, latent, calm, unanimated, occult, virtual. There they were waiting for their dawn to matter once by virtue of an artistic stimulation, capable of animating them. For Nietzsche, as for Stendhal, art seems to be precisely the force that is capable to *animate one's being-in-the-world* (zōē).

Nietzsche's overall mantra, "my Philosophy is reversed *Platonism*", signifies precisely the historic turning point in which the ascetic image-of-thinking will have been metonymically replaced by the aesthetic image-of-thought which is the reversal of the first. Art is no sedative, on the contrary, it is the stimulating force (zōē) that intrinsically characterizes the very meaning of life-itself (zōē). Being stimulated means being alive. In the course of this aesthetic revolution notions such as the lived-body, the notion of life as such (Agamben 1999), and in particular the animating force of life (zōē) will have to be reevaluated, reconceptualized and transformed as core issues at stake in the wake of an altered relation between philosophy and the arts.

Zōē, the animating force of life...

The force capable of stimulating one's anima, of activating and animating oneself, is the force which ancient Greek language called Zōē. Understanding artistic research as Zōē—which is an exemplary

---

called the beautiful *une promesse de bonheure*. At any rate he *rejected* and repudiated that one point about the aesthetic condition which Kant had stressed: *le désintéressement*. Who is right, Kant or Stendhal?" (Nietzsche 1989, 104)

attempt of this book—not just considers the arts to be a kind of ani-malistic or even beastly force of life. In ancient Greek times one can find Zōē in all forms of life, even in the life of the Gods, probably even in physical matter.[12] This becomes conceivable once one considers all forms of beings, from a genealogical perspective, as something which has been activated already by a force that gave birth to their appear-ance (natality). Insofar as every single being is considered to be al-ready the result of a generative process of becoming, it can be said to be an offspring of a primordial ontological activity (zōē) which is secretly operative in letting something come into being. And as far as all forms of beings are brought into being, their mattering constitu-tively implies a virtual dimension in which they actually were not yet constituted but absent. Before they came into being, they were vir-tually real in the very sense in which Gilles Deleuze defined this term in his philosophy: "the virtual is opposed not to the real but to the actual. The virtual is fully real in so far as it is virtual." (Deleuze 1994, 208) Every single being which comes into being is already an activa-tion of the virtual plane of being. And the ontological performance of being-itself, its univocal verbal sense (zōē), consists precisely of the mattering of possibilities which so far have not yet mattered. Being's zōē, the verbal performance of being-itself, is actually operative in activating, stimulating, animating and awakening the virtual planes which life, Zōē, finds in *herself*: dormant, sleeping, not yet alive, in a void, full of potentials, ready to matter once. Successively activat-ing the posse-esse which was resting in *her* virtual plane from the very beginning, the Zōē, operative in the evolutionary wake of nature, actually unfolds, step by step, the possibilities which are about to matter and enter the realm of manifest (vyakta) nature once.

It is precisely the promise (Nietzsche 1989, 57; De Man 1979, 246-277) of such a *reversed sense of taste* that historically will have re-placed the ascetic taste, which will pave the way toward the aesthetic revolution which Nietzsche envisaged in *Beyond Good and Evil*. A re-volt in which one finally will be ready to sense the arts as life-ani-

---

12   Leibniz, Nietzsche, but also contemporary research on animism, pan-psychism and new materialism claim that even particles are already modes of a physical form of life (Zōē).

mating forces (zōē), capable of activating virtual planes of existence which so far did rest in the background of one's psycho-mental awareness in hidden planes of nature. It is this *new taste* that will differentiate the new post-Socratic and post-Platonic species of philosophers from their forefathers, according to Nietzsche. The epochal revolution which he announced in *Beyond Good and Evil* was therefore thought to be, in the first place, an *aesthetic* one. A revolution of one's heart.

> Whatever value might be attributed to truth, truthfulness, and selflessness, it could be possible that appearance, the will to deception, and craven self-interest should be accorded a higher and more fundamental value for all life.... But who is willing to take charge of such a dangerous Perhaps! For this we must await the arrival of a new breed of philosophers, ones whose taste and inclination are somehow the reverse of those we have seen so far – philosophers of the dangerous Perhaps in every sense. – And in all seriousness: I see these new philosophers approaching. (Nietzsche 2002, 6)

Experimental labs...

But it was not only Nietzsche, the untimely artist-philosopher and philologist (cf. Hamacher 2015) of 19th century continental Europe, whose philosophy indicates a radical shift in the relation of art *and* philosophy. Contemporary formats such as performance-philosophy (cf. Cull and Lagaay 2020), philosophy-on-stage (Böhler and Granzer 2018; Böhler 2019b; Böhler and Granzer 2020; Böhler, Schäfer and Aigner 2017a), artistic research (cf. De Assis, Giudici 2017; De Assis, Giudici 2019; Badura, Dubach, Haarmann, Mersch, Rey, Schenker, Pérez 2014), arts-based-philosophy, the sense-lab,[13] and similar

---

13   What Erin Manning and Briam Massumi called "Sense-Lab" is precisely such an experimental approach toward an aesthetic image-of-thought. Erin Manning 2004, SenseLab, http://erinmovement.com/about-sense-lab (last accessed: 12 June 2025).

initiatives[14] are clear signs indicating the altering of the classical handed down relation of art *and* philosophy. It is already a historical fact that their relatedness is *experimentally* under investigation today. Not just theoretically, but practically *and* theoretically. Insofar as all around the globe artistic researchers, philosopher-artists and artist-philosophers have started to experiment with *new possibilities to connect* philosophy and the arts in order to generate, as one might say, aesthetic images-of-thinking; thought-images in which the performance of thinking is no longer experienced *as-if* it would be a non-sensual performance but, on the contrary, as a sensitive activation of one's mind in alignment with the cellar regions of one's body which are allowed to speak up, utter their voice, tune our judgments, or instinctively channel our thoughts into certain directions in an associative manner. Even the philosopher's conscious thoughts are now taken to be "secretly directed and forced into determinate channels by the instincts," to recall Nietzsche again.

According to this post-Socratic species of philosophers, the thinking performance which takes place in a lived-body as a sublime body of thoughtful 'matterings' is never just tuned by interior bodily processes only. Because a body does never exist in-itself, separated from the relational affairs with the world it finds itself in. These relational affairs are not just external causes at a certain distance, because they affect a lived-body first hand—at its bodily-surface and even under its skin.

Every single body, and in particular every lived-body, is therefore never a wordless individual being that would exist entirely in-itself, separated from the relational affairs it inhabits. Not at all are lived-bodies isolated things-in-themselves.[15] They are rather centers (sensitive-agential-knowing beings) of an entity that finds itself exposed[16] into worldwide relations which co-constitute its *monadic*

---

14   Performance Philosophy is a global network of initiatives working in this research field: https://www.performancephilosophy.org/ (last accessed: 12 June 2025).

15   Jean-Luc Nancy put this matter in a nutshell by claiming that "psyche is extended. It knows nothing of it" (Nancy 2008, 21).

16   On the concept of lived-bodies as worldwide expositions, cf. Nancy 2008.

being-in-the-world. Hence the corporeal Da-sein (being-there) of a lived-body, its local appearance, should be considered the feeling, acting and knowing *center of a monad* which constitutes its worldwide periphery. All the relational affairs the corporeal center of a lived-body actually inhabits are *co-extensive dimensions* of its corporeal being-in-the-world. Its environment is therefore not just an external area that surrounds it but an *intimate, constituting co-dimension* of its being-in-the-world. From the very beginning when a body comes into being, it will always already have been a relational affair, since it appears in a field of relations which has already been there before it appeared and which allowed it to appear as its sufficient reason.[17] This is true for a lived-body, but also for material particles, which always appear in relation to other particles and only show the attributes they actually possess in relation to others, which allow them to show up with these attributes.

This is also the reason why a body does never end at its three-dimensional surface but extends from there into worldwide relations which are an integral part of its own corporeal *Da-sein*; even though these relational affairs are external to the volume of its three-dimensional body.

A lived-body *intimately feels* the so-called external vibes of all the other bodies which touch the flesh of its own body. It *intimately tastes* them, tries to understand *their* significance and affordances from the very center of its local center within the relational affairs it is actually embedded in and in touch with in a worldwide manner.

To question the relational affair between philosophy and the arts *experimentally* in lab-situations therefore implies that artist-philosophers and philosopher-artists[18] who are engaged in artistic research processes are not just intellectually but also physically and

---

17   In German, sufficient reason literally means "der zu-reichende Grund," the ground of being that grants and allows you to exist by entering the relational field of a world, that welcomes you and lets you be and become.

18   The philosopher-artist and artistic researcher Nikolaus Gansterer, for instance, has developed the format of trans-lectures, by which in his paintings he responds artistically to written texts or live talks of philosophers, in order to realize the atmosphere of their talks by painting.

sensually engaged and stimulated in the research they explore within their concrete research field. The entire *apparatus*, to use a term from philosophy-physics,[19] which researchers inhabit during their research performance does actually *tune* their research in a sensual manner, so that everybody engaged in the research can actually sense the flavor of the atmosphere in which they are doing their research. The light-situation, the socio-political relational affairs among the researcher, the contemporary discourses circulating in their research fields etc. All of them are constituting factors of the experimental apparatus which can alter the output of one's research. Sometimes smoking a cheap cigar (Barad 2007, 161-168) can alter the outcome of an experimental apparatus. The attempt to alter the relation between artistic practices and the performance of thinking, which is contemporarily under investigation in such research labs, therefore has to consider their *intellectual*, but also their *vital, sensual* and *physical* relatedness toward the world which researchers inhabit during their research-performance (Böhler 2019a; Böhler, Schäfer and Aigner 2017b).

Sense-Lab...

The heterogeneity of all these approaches which in actu do emerge at the margins of philosophy and the arts clearly exhibits the still instable character of this entire research field. The new intra-action among philosophy and the arts is apparently still in the making and therefore necessarily vague and experimental. The emergence of the conceptual persona of the artist-philosopher, the incubation of an aesthetic image-of-thought and the constitution of a new taste that opposes the ascetic ideal, these matters have not yet gained a stable form and definite sense so far, they have not yet *mattered.* Their *worlding* is still in the making, vague, experimental, associative-precise in their playful be-coming.

Gansterer, Nikolaus, https://www.gansterer.org/ (last accessed: 12 June 2025).

19   On the concept of the apparatus in the context of philosophy-physics see Barad 2007.

But even though the historical outcome of this emergent research field is in statu nascendi today, the offspring of formats as performance philosophy, philosophy on stage, artistic research, arts-based-philosophy, the sense-lab and similar approaches are clearly indicators as well as precursors of a crucial shift in the classical handed down relation between the arts and philosophy.

Mnemosyne, the womb…

Even though the attempt to matter a new connectedness among philosophy and the arts does not show one single but many faces today, it is worth remembering that in ancient Greek mythology philosophy and the nine muses were descendants of the same mother, *Mnêmosynê* (Böhler 2016). She has been considered mythologically to be the one common root of philosophy and the arts. A *productive womb* from which a *generative* form of memory emerges which is operative in her children once they are actually in the vibrant state of *remembering a future to come*. In *Mnemosyne*, remembering emerges as a visionary form of imagination in which the arts and philosophy have started to imagine, envision and intuit a virtual state of being. Thereby her off-springs are actually operating in the wake of a "Memory of the Future" (cf. Derrida 1989; Böhler 1996; Aurobindo 1999, 312, 524). It draws her children toward the *virtual plane of possibilities* which are ready to dawn and matter. But the virtual cloud of possibilities, which constitutes an inherent zone of their mother's womb, on the other hand actually needs the activities of philosophy and the arts to stimulate *her* potentials. It is up to her children to make the virtual cloud of her womb collapse, to use a terminology from quantum physics again. She feeds her children by rendering them her virtual matter which they are about to accept, affirm, taste, digest or refuse. Thereby she is able to provide the growth of her children as the nurse of *their* becoming.[20]

---

20   In *Timaios*, Plato calls Khora the nurse of becoming (Böhler 2025).

The South-Asian Perspective...

Perceived from a cross-cultural South-Asian perspective, it seems *as-if (iva)*[21] a *tantric* approach toward philosophy would reappear again in the context of this research field, and in particular from the Nietzschean perspective concerning this matter.[22]

Tantrism, one of the main spiritual traditions in South-Asian thought, was precisely that *darśana*[23] in the history of South-Asian philosophies that historically shows the most intensive interest in matters of aesthetics. From this it comes with no surprise that Abhinavagupta (~950-1020 CE), the tantric mastermind of Kashmir Shaivism, delivered us one of the most refined interpretations of Indian aesthetics in the entire history of South-Asian thinking (Gnoli 1985; Deshpande 1989; Bäumer 1992; Dyczkowski 1992b; Lakshmanjoo 2015; Böhler 2019d).

Similar to the experimental labs we have mentioned above, the tantric laboratories of ancient Indian times too resisted the ascetic ideal of their times[24] by actually introducing a spirituality that was based on a conception of consciousness (*cit, puruṣa*), moved by blissful vibes (*spanda*) which successively unfold, step by step, the 36 principles (*tattvas*) of tantric philosophy in the evolutionary unfolding of time (*kāla*). (Lakshmanjoo 2015, 1-10, Dyczkowski 1992)

If one translates *tattva* with the Latin word principle, it is worth mentioning that *tattvas* can either be actively awake in nature (*vyakta*), or they can sleep and therefore be non-manifest (*avyakta*) in nature. If *tattvas* sleep, *as-if* dead, they are actually in the hold of grav-

---

21   On the fiction, that something is not there even though it is there, see Derrida (1995). On the Sanskrit term *iva* (*as-if*) see also Böhler, A., Granzer, S., Loughnane, A. and G. Parkes (2016).

22   Concerning this South-Asian Perspective on this historical move, see my article in this volume on "Poets of the Heart. Friedrich Nietzsche and Sri Aurobindo".

23   *Darśana* is usually translated as philosophical view, philosophical intuition, philosophical vision. It derives from the root seeing, intuit, vision, envisioning and thus resonates with the Greek word *theoria*.

24   The main ascetic traditions, tantric philosophies were arguing against, were Vedanta and Buddhist philosophies (Lakshmanjoo 2015, 101-106).

ity (*tamas*), which keeps them trapped in a state of deep sleep in the lower ocean of the subconscious (cf. Aurobindo 1998, 106-108). Once the psychic-being awakes in nature, the cosmic heart, which until then has been sleeping wrapped in the lower ocean of the unconscious, erects from there as the life-force, operative in a lived-body. This ascent of the cosmic heart in the wake of a lived-body actually unfolds, step by step, until the life force has activated its full potential.[25] Each of these evolutionary steps marks the unfolding of a new center of the heart in which the cosmic heart successively activates all the capacities which were locked within root matter (*mūla prakṛti*) from the very beginning of creation. For instance, the activation of the lowest, the physical plane-of-being (*annamaya*), actually induces the mattering of physical particles in nature.[26] They are the first manifestations in the process of creation which come out of the root matter (*mūla prakṛti*). The activation of the vital plane-of-being (*prāṇamaya*) actually *stimulates* the bodily appearance of plants and animals which now show up in nature. The activation of the mental plane-of-being (*manomaya*) actually *animates* the evolutionary day-break of the human race; and the activation of the supra-mental (*unmanā*) planes-of-being, *vijñānamaya*, *ānandamaya* and *sat-cit-ānanda* finally *awaken* supra-human beings, which now start to bodily appear in nature. In *sat-cit-ānanda*, the habitat of Śiva, finally all 36 principles will have been activated in the evolutionary course of time, according to most tantric philosophies. The lowest plane of being at the very beginning, the highest plane of being at the very

---

25   "The emptiness (vyoman) of deep sleep is technically called the 'Heart' because it resides in the centre." (Dyczkowski 1992, 42)

26   The doctrine of the five sheaths (*pañcakośa*) usually distinguishes between the physical (*annamayakośa*), the vital (*prāṇamayakośa*), the mental (*manomayakośa*) and the supra-mental sheaths (*vijñānamayakośa*, *ānandamayakośa* and *sat-cit-ānanda*). It is said that the psycho-mental awareness of a fully awakened (Prabuddha) would move and live in the activation of all five sheaths which constitute the physical (*sthūla*) and the sublime (*sūkṣma*) body in a state of *sat-cit-ānanda* (Aurobindo 1999, 10-19).

end of the evolutionary ascent of matter that actually goes hand in hand with the descent of the spirit (sat-cit-ānanda) into matter.[27]

It is remarkable that in tantric contexts, as in Nietzsche, the arts are primarily considered as *animating forces* (śaktis). Tantric arts, which were conceived to be sacred at their times, finally aimed to induce the spiral upward movement of one's life-forces (praṇa-kuṇḍalinī-śakti) in order to successively unfold all the hidden stages of consciousness (cit-śakti) at once (Deshpande 1989). A journey in which one's psycho-mental awareness unfolds into higher and higher stages of self-awareness through the successive activation of the 36 principles-of-being. The stimulation of these principles will finally have activated the *gnostic-heart* (vijñāna, kavi-hṛdi) that, from the very beginning of our cosmic creation in the lower ocean of the subconscious, was resting in deep sleep at the very bottom of one's heart (Aurobindo 1998, 42-43; cf. Muller-Ortega 1989; Skora 2007). And since the activation of the *gnostic-heart* belongs to the supra-mental planes-of-beings (unmanā), most human beings so far felt *as-if* it would be out of their reach.

When Nietzsche defined the performance of art as the greatest stimulus to life in the wake of a blissful promise (ānanda), his Dionysian view of the arts as an elementary form of intoxication resonates so strongly with tantric aesthetics that without harm one could easily call him a tantric philosopher born in 19th century continental Europe.

It is core for such a Dionysian-Saivite perspective on the arts to understand that the intoxication that takes place in artistic research is not just a sensual stimulation by things which have been activated and are active already but a stimulation that derives from *virtual planes of being* in which all the possibilities of being reside in a virtual cloud of unformed matter, ready to matter. One has to go beyond heaven, into a realm higher than heaven, as the Ṛg-Veda beautifully

---

27 The always active plane of sat-cit-ānanda shows striking similarities with Aristotle's concept of the *actus purus* (Aristotle 1989, Metaphysik XII 7, 1072b): a (substantial) form-of-being in which all 36 planes-of-being have already been activated from the very beginning, even before the genesis of things started.

says in poetic terms (cf. Aurobindo 1998, 150), when someone aims to touch the virtual plane-of-being in which precisely those possibilities reside which have not yet mattered but are about to matter. The critique which Socrates utters in Plato's ideal state, that the arts are just mimetically reproducing sensual images of an already given (sensual) reality, does not apply here because the sacred arts of ancient times were sensually attracted by the *virtual* plane-of-being which they experienced as a void, full of possibilities, ready to matter once. Artistic research, drawn toward the virtual plane-of-being, therefore does not just duplicate reality. On the contrary. It releases virtual possibilities which were resting in the dormant chambers of one's *gnostic-heart-mind* (gnostic intellect; *vijñāna*). They were there from the very beginning, but they were resting on a virtual plane of being in the unanimated background of our human intellect (mental mind): hidden, veiled, covered, dormant, cryptic, occult, not active and activated at all. By the performance of the tantric sacred arts, the deepest, most occult chambers of one's *buddhi* (intellect/reason)[28] are actually stimulated to awake.

According to the tantric master *Abhinavagupta*, the most hidden chambers of one's intellect harbor not just mental, but supra-mental (*unmanā*) capacities. As a rule, they are usually inactive in humans, but basically (in principle) they can awake in humans in the wake of intellectual capacities (*siddhis, vibhūtis*) which transgress the ordinary mental plane of mental judgements by the activation of an intuitive kind of reasoning (*pratibhā*), inspired by the dawn of possibilities, which have not yet dawned and mattered. The event of their realization makes one wonder (*camatkāra*). And even *Patañjali*, the author[29] of the Yoga-Sūtra (Desikachar 1995; Larson 2014; White 2014), one of the most orthodox schools of Yoga in the South-Asian tradition with strong ascetic tendencies, became the subject of a popular legend, *The legend of Sage Patañjali* (Jayaraman 2004), which holds that *Patañjali* received his enlightenment by virtue of watching

---

28   In South-East philosophies, the Sanskrit term *buddhi* means the intellect which can awake (*buddha*). In Buddha, the buddhi is awake (buddha) and active.

29   On the question of his authorship see White 2014.

a sacred performance of Śiva in the golden temple of Cidambaram. Not only the performer, but also the audience seems to be able to be stimulated in their highest yogic potentials, just by watching a sacred performance.

To think philosophically and do aesthetics within the emergent apparatus of such tantric labs did obviously not just mean to conceptually reflect matters of the arts in the modern European sense of aesthetics. Rather, it meant the step by step actualization, stimulation, animation and awakening of the physical, vital, mental and even the supra-mental planes-of-being *through artistic research.*

Before the axis age...

Once we open ourselves towards such archaic concepts of the (sacred) arts, we face a struggle which Europeans know from the study of ancient Greek history: The struggle between Mythos & Logos. This struggle was not limited to the ancient Greek culture. A similar struggle can also be found in the history of South-Asian cultures.

If one goes back to the oldest Veda, the Ṛg-Veda (probably 1500 BCE), the vision (*darśana*) of knowledge (*veda*) explored in this text was still presented in a poetic, mythological form. It narrates the cosmogenesis of our world in hymns which were explicitly written by poets (*Kavis*). The Vedic poems were studied by heart, but also chanted, to share them with the people in public (Gonda 1977).

Before the Axis Age (~800-200 BCE), to envision Vedic-knowledge (*darśana*) obviously meant to intuit it *artistically* among the people. As-*if* only artistic methods would be able to stimulate and awake the highest degrees of (gnostic) knowledge, accessible to human beings, engaged in doing and consuming the arts simultaneously in a commonly shared public field.[30] As-*if* only the artistic instrumentation of one's thoughts, feelings and behavior would be able to trigger the intuitive, supra-mental planes-of-being.

---

30   On the question whether poetry is able to trigger a higher form of knowledge than argumentation and reasoning see article four by Soumyabrata Choudhury in this volume, 123-139.

In Vedic times, the poets (*Kavis*) were obviously considered artist-philosophers, not because they wanted to decorate their highest-planes-of-knowledge with an artistic make-up and beautiful cosmetics, but in order to awake and invoke the highest planes of being by virtue of artistic practices, which allow these higher realms to emerge and descend.

Later, when the so-called Axis Age approached and Vedānta entered the stage of our world-history (probably 7th–0th BCE), a transformation in the style of writing and doing philosophy took place, in which philosophy more and more assumed a philosophical style. With Debashish Banerji one might argue that

> the comparison of Greek wisdom sources is interesting and instructive, since we may see similarities in language use between the Upaniṣads and pre-Socratic wisdom literature. The modern philosophical interest in this style of Greek expression may be found to begin with Nietzsche, later reopened by Martin Heidegger, a contemporary of Sri Aurobindo, and in times closer to ours own, by Gilles Deleuze. What these philosophers saw in pre-Socratic Greek wisdom literature was a proto-philosophy, a poetic or mystic use of logic at the service of ontological experience, and prior to its epistemological objectification. Sri Aurobindo's interest in and interpretation of the Upaniṣads follow similar lines, drawing attention to a language which works simultaneously at visionary, experiential, praxical and logical levels of awareness. (Banerji 2020, xxiii-xxiv)

The interest in pre-Socratic philosophy, which started with Nietzsche and his critique of the Socratic way of doing philosophy, seems to reanimate a proto-philosophy which was artistic in its methods, style and instrumentation. As-*if* the pre-Socratic wisdom-literature would awake anew, not just with Nietzsche in the European context but with Sri Aurobindo Ghose also in the South-Asian context.[31]

---

31   Concerning this issue see the article *Poets of the Heart. Friedrich Nietzsche and Sri Aurobindo* in this volume, 32-68.

Truth in Post-Truth times

"The earliest matter I became serious about is the relation between art and truth: and even now I stand before this dichotomy with a sacred shiver of horror." (English translation A. B.)[32]

I would like to repeat my claim that the issue Nietzsche broaches in this late, unpublished note from summer 1888 is in fact "a résumé of his entire path of thinking."[33] What had shaken him to the core from the very beginning of his mature life was the dubious relation between art and truth. And even now, about 20 years later, in the fall of his life, this question still triggered a sacred shiver of horror ("heiliges Entsetzen") in the heart of his soul. The relational affair between the arts and philosophy obviously occupied him throughout his entire life, from the very beginning until its very end. The seemingly antagonistic relation between truth and art, truth and philosophy, philosophy and art made him shiver and tremble. Sacredly, horribly, uncannily, seriously, ironically. For him, it apparently became the most serious matter which haunted him through his entire life and sometimes made him laugh.[34]

We seem to share the same problem...

While reading this unpublished note from 1888 it became clear to me that 'my' question concerning the relation of art *and* philosophy, art *in* philosophy, and philosophy *in* the arts articulated a problem that was not just 'my' personal problem but one that appears to be deeply rooted in the history of continental philosophy and its dubious relation to the arts in general. At least in secret. Although the question of what truth could mean in post-truth times has meanwhile become a matter of public concern. Is truth a fiction? A myth? Something

---

32   German Original: "Über das Verhältniß der Kunst zur Wahrheit bin ich am frühesten ernst geworden: und noch jetzt stehe ich mit einem heiligen Entsetzen vor diesem Zwiespalt." (Nietzsche 1967-77, 500)

33   See Böhler 2019, 242.

34   On the relation between seriousness, laughter and irony with regard to philosophy and the arts see the articles by Avital Ronell and Susanne Valerie Granzer in this volume.

one should no longer treat seriously today but rather in an ironic, skeptical manner? A matter of art? A Phantasma? A good example of historically inherited fake news?

Reflecting on these concerns, it became definitely clear to me that I was not just facing a private but a cultural-historical problem which all people seemed to share, privately and institutionally, who are actually subjected to the intellectual history of Europe. A historical epoch that can, as Whitehead noted in a well-known remark, be best characterized as a series of footnotes to Plato; "the safest general characterization of the European philosophical tradition is that it consists in a series of footnotes to Plato." (Whitehead 1979, 91)

Due to Europe's colonial history and the academic institutionalization of the Platonic Episteme almost all over the globe, the socialization of our global elites in the academic world has meanwhile become the standard model of doing philosophy around the globe. When Spivak, for instance, demands a revision of aesthetic education in the era of globalization (Spivak 2013) to undo the hegemony of such an Eurocentric episteme, I would recommend to follow Nietzsche's deconstruction of the Platonic image-of-thought to fulfill this historical task.

Academic rituals... Plato is still haunting us from the past

Already as a student, while I was studying philosophy at the Department of Philosophy at the University of Vienna almost 40 years ago, I experienced the academic formats in which philosophy was bodily performed and presented as a performative self-contradiction. I was passionately fascinated by the texts we discussed, but the unquestioned academic rituals by which they were usually presented and performed—in the course of academic lectures which often took place in sterile rooms with bright white light, where coffee and cookies were served in a highly ascetic manner; in discussion groups which had to follow a strict schedule according to fixed academic rituals; at conferences where people presented their ready-made talks, came, talked and left again, most of them unpaid etc., etc., etc. The format of these academic rituals, I was convinced, did strongly contradict the content of the texts I was studying.[35] Mainly because they were missing the aesthetic awareness (taste) which would allow the texts to speak sensually; not just on an analytical, but also on an aesthetic level. As a rule, the light situation did not seem to matter, the voices were not tuned and trained, voice training seemed to be something for singers and actors but of no relevance for academic scholars. Frequently the talks did not address the audience, as actors and actresses would do, the dress-code seemed to be arbitrary and not relevant for the ideal content of their philosophical speech. Everything reminded me of a Protestant Church. non-sensible thinking, grounded in pure thinking without any lived-body.

Only after I had read Nietzsche it became convincingly clear for me that today's academic rituals are still haunted by the ascetic image-of-thought, without noticing. Socrates still shaped the way in which academic rituals are methodologically performed. Unquestioned, in secret. Even at Universities in Africa, in China, or in India. Even there... "This is the new antithesis: *the Dionysian and the Socratic*, and the work of art of Greek tragedy was destroyed by it."[36] (Translation A.B.)

The ascetic image of thinking still holds *our global academic culture* captive. In the very sense of Ludwig Wittgenstein's phrasing in his *Philosophical Investigations*: "An image held us captive. And we could not get out, for it lay in our language, and it only seemed to repeat it to us relentlessly." (Wittgenstein 2003, 82)

Could it be that Socrates was not only a spoiler of the youth but also of an arts-based concept of thought, in that he dissuaded the artist-philosopher Plato from conceiving philosophy as artistic research? Socrates accused the artists of thinking blindly, without reasoning. They seemed to be sensual, headless beings. Which is pre-

---

35 Schelling, Nietzsche, Heidegger, (Hegel, Kant, Husserl), later Derrida, Deleuze, Nancy, Ronell, Butler, Barad etc. My studies were always accompanied by the study of classical Indian Philosophies, Patañjali, Abhinavagupta, Aurobindo, Desikachar etc.

36 "Diess ist der neue Gegensatz: das Dionysische und das Sokratische, und das Kunstwerk der griechischen Tragoedie ging an ihm zu Grunde." (Nietzsche 1971)

cisely the reason why his Socratic method of thinking appears prior
to theirs.

> The true creative ability of the poet is mostly just treated iron-
> ically by *Plato*, because it is not conscious insight into the na-
> ture of things and regarded similar to the talents of soothsay-
> ers and augurs. The poet was not able to versify before he had
> become exalted and senseless, and reason no longer dwelled
> in him. (Nietzsche 1967-77, 543, English Translation A. B.)

The historical problem I shared with Nietzsche thus seemed to be at
least as old as Greek philosophy and the *antagonistic* turn of ancient
Greek philosophers *against* the poetic way of doing philosophy in
the mythological age which they actually still inhabited. Since then,
ancient Greek philosophers artificially constructed *a binary opposition* between mythological ways of narrating the world and argumentative ways of reasoning. From then on, continental philosophies
started to challenge, in a Socratic manner, the truth of handed down
myths and the arts by questioning the truth-value of their epic ways
of thinking.

> Plato confronts these 'unsagacious' artists with the image of
> the true artist, the philosophical one, and in no unclear terms
> tells us that he himself is the only one who has reached that
> ideal and whose dialogues may be read in his ideal state. (Ibid.,
> 543, Translation A. B.)

It therefore comes as no surprise that also Plato's own master student Aristotle, at the beginning of his Metaphysics, quoted the common dictum of his times that poets are said to be liars.[37] It is this historically induced struggle between mythos and logos, between the
tragic age of the pre-Socratic culture, when art and philosophy still
went hand in hand, and the end of tragedy, which Nietzsche identified with the arts of Euripides and the philosophy of Socrates, when

---

37   "poets tell many a lie" (Aristotle 1989, *Metaphysics*, 983a).

philosophy and the arts historically split apart, became rivals, opponents, if not even enemies, until today.

The Genesis of Pre-Socratic, Socratic and Post-Socratic times

I suggest reading each single contribution of this book as a unique response to this long intellectual history that *again* became questionable and problematic today. It seems *as-if* the pre-Socratic epoch and way of doing philosophy, an epoch which Karl Jaspers (1914) called the Axis Age (8ᵗʰ–3ʳᵈ BCE), is haunting us again. The archaic recurrence of pre-Socratic wisdom thinking, which was centered around Dionysus as its secret center and the Chorus as his mouthpiece, once again questions the Socratic victory over the pre-Socratic ways of thinking which were artistic in their style. I therefore would like to argue that it is the deconstruction, re-signification and re-evaluation of the Socratic image-of-thought for the sake of a post-Socratic, aesthetic image of thinking which is finally at stake in formats such as performance philosophy, arts-based-philosophy, artistic research, philosophy on stage and similar approaches.

When we respond to the question of what the emergence of performance philosophy and artistic research means for us, I would like to suggest reading the following articles as responses to the need for such a post-Socratic form of doing philosophy, in new alliances with artistic practices in which different styles of writing, thinking, reading and doing philosophy are actually in the making.[38]

Article by article synopsis...

In the first article "Poets of the Heart. Friedrich Nietzsche and Sri Aurobindo Ghose on the Heart of Philosophy and the Heart of the Arts" Arno Böhler argues that the cross-over of art and philosophy is actually a matter of the heart, because one's heart longs for a form of knowledge that goes hand in hand with one's 'bodily-felt-sense.' Lou Andreas-Salomé in her description of Nietzsche's works emphasized

---

38   On different reading experiences of philosophers see the contribution by Veronika Reichl in this volume.

that Nietzsche was incapable of thinking concepts without, simultaneously, tasting their sensual coherence. For artist-philosophers like him, tasting relational affairs seems to be not just a secondary matter but an aesthetic judgment, triggered parallel to any performance of perception. Böhler's article argues that the demand to balance one's concepts, ideas and judgments in accordance with one's bodily-felt-taste actually forced philosophers such as Nietzsche or Aurobindo to become artist-philosophers (sahṛdaya) and to align philosophical practices with artistic practices in order create concepts, ideas and judgments which are not merely logically but also aesthetically coherent. To tune one's thoughts, concepts and ideas with the voice of one's heart is precisely the new aesthetic image of thought which such artist-philosophers are calling into being by their poetic ways of doing philosophy. The article thus attempts to clarify: (1) The concept of the artist-philosopher (Kavi) and why such a concept is needed at all? (2) What it means that artist-philosophers taste the sensual appropriateness versus inappropriateness of a relational affair in a bodily-felt sense? (3) What role artistic-research plays in the stimulation of one's life-forces, as a mode of intoxication of the hidden chambers of one's heart. (4) And finally the article will address the question of a philosophy of the heart in which one's bodily-felt-sense assembles with the discursive mind into an assemblage which the poet-philosopher Sri Aurobindo Ghose called the (gnostic) Heart:-mind. A concept which ancient Vedic philosophies considered to be operative in the ancient sacred arts.

In the second article, Avital Ronell presents "A Melancholic's Survival Kit." The text suggests that philosophy can provide comfort and meaning in difficult times, even if not all philosophers are helpful or open-minded. To find the truly valuable ones, one must move past arrogant, rigid, or biased thinkers. The most significant philosophers engage with the arts—poetry, music, and literature—and accept the limits of human understanding. When philosophy is accompanied by imaginative, boundary-breaking forms of expression, it becomes a liberating and life-affirming force. Philosophy utters a call for artistic practice and its extreme insights. One thinks of Artaud's work on theater and the plague, where the staging of calamity—a social abscess—is linked to contagion. Philosophy hitches a ride on the death-drive, uniquely licensed out by aesthetic practice.

In the third article, Violetta L. Waibel is connecting "Hölderlin's 'Celebration of Peace' and Kant's Treaty 'Toward Perpetual Peace'". Hölderlin's song 'Celebration of Peace' ('Friedensfeier') was probably written on the occasion of the peace treaty of Lunéville of February 9th, 1801, during the author's stay in Switzerland. Immanuel Kant wrote his text 'Perpetual Peace. A Philosophical Sketch' ('Zum ewigen Frieden. Ein philosophischer Entwurf') most probably on the occasion of the Basel peace treaty of April 5th, 1795, between post-revolutionary France and Prussia. Hölderlin, who studied the philosophy of his times carefully and regularly incorporated philosophical thoughts into his poetry and artistic thinking most likely incorporated his reading of Kant's peace treaty in his song 'Celebration of Peace'. Despite their obvious differences—one is a philosophical treatise and the other is a poem—both works share the same subject and respond in a performative, self-referential manner to socio-political struggles around the French Revolution in close chronological and spiritual proximity. It has long been acknowledged in research that the style of writing Kant performs in his peace treaty follows the juridical form and structure of such treaties typical for his time. It is also well known that Hölderlin's peace celebration is not only a poem about peace but stages and celebrates peace itself by using a title without an article. It will be a major aim of Waibel's article to analyze the relationship between the two texts in order to provide an example of a historical cross-over of philosophical and poetical ways of writing and thinking in the name of a peace to come.

In article four, Soumyabrata Choudhury provides us with a text with the title "Thinking, Evaluating, Enjoying: On the Aesthetic Materiality of Thought". The article questions Heidegger's strong and profound thesis that poetry arrives at and occupies a place thought cannot reach; the poem tells what cannot be said or thought propositionally. Choudhury will not deny Heidegger's thesis but reorient it in the following way: He will accept that poetry, indeed, tells what is the arrival of the 'unthinkable' and in its saying opens up an experience inaccessible to a certain history of thought hitherto determining every subject-matter that can be thought. However, he will propose that the historicity of this poetic experience is the eventual condition for new thought which breaks the history of thought into two, between the hitherto place of the unthinkable and the new (non)-place of a thought—whose only support and promise is the poetic 'event' from where it emerges. As support, the poetic point of rupture is not to be received merely as an intuitively exceptional moment of inspiration or grace; it is to be grasped ontologically, as an aesthetic breach in the history of being. The poetic moment and the aesthetic event are always an unforeseen arrival of a singular, anonymous and common 'feeling' or 'experience'… an enjoyment hitherto blocked from any form of thought (or in Heidegger's view, according to which enjoyment and all forms of thought are separated). As promised, the aesthetic event and its poetic historicity are what every new thought must 'appreciate' and be true to. This subjective life of thought as 'evaluation' and 'enjoyment' is, then, also the aesthetic touchstone of every post-eventual life-to-come, that is to say, every true life.

In article five, "The Balloon Universe", Tanja Traxler & Reinhold A. Bertlmann test the relatedness of quantum-physics with the space of the arts. In their paper, conceptions of space will be investigated in a multidisciplinary perspective ranging from physics and philosophy to artistic research. In particular, the concept of the Balloon Universe will be examined as a model for the spatial expansion of the universe. As the paper is based on a lecture-performance by Tanja Traxler & Reinhold A. Bertlmann, this discussion of epistemological lessons of key phenomena in physics like black holes, gravitational waves and quantum vacuum will be completed by three written interventions in the tradition of a Platonic symposium. Additionally, a link to a video of the lecture-performance will be provided of which the authors hold the copyright. Space is a highly relevant research topic in contemporary physics, as it tackles the unification of general relativity and quantum theory.

In article six, "Nothing to Fix. Performative Strategies of Incompleteness and the Right to Bodily Integrity", Sandra Noeth investigates the relation of lived-bodies in relation to their (legal) grounds. The global experience of the pandemic, as well as recent events in a long record of institutional, racialized violence, are but two examples that bring to the fore the question of which bodies are worth protecting, and on which grounds. Incorporated in international humanitarian law and corresponding documents and action, the question of bodily integrity at stake here is even today closely tied to the idea of personhood: to the (notably western) idea of a subjectified, ableist, colonialist and bound body to be secured, saved and fixed. Against this backdrop, she argues that the unequal distribution of and access to legal and political protection and ethical recognition, however, is not only a matter of overarching and normative frameworks but also a matter of aesthetics: of how we imagine, represent, perceive, remember and perform bodies in the first place. In this essay she will examine strategies of incompleteness and repair that different artists develop in their performative work in an effort to counter universalist and individualist notions of the body and engage in an aesthetic economy of repair.

In article seven, "Along Each Other. On Shown and Told by Meg Stuart and Tim Etchells", Krassimira Kruschkova examines the relation between performance and philosophy and the aesthetic image-of-thought that actually pops up in such relations. Danced and spoken thoughts contaminate and comment on each other in the performance "Shown and Told" (2016) by and featuring choreographer Meg Stuart and writer and performance artist Tim Etchells. He improvises poetic-philosophical text fragments based on her improvised movement fragments and vice-versa. "Then she talks, and he moves... a bit." (ibid., 2016) They perform without either of them taking the lead, and we, the audience, cannot stop asking ourselves whether she is dancing what he is talking or whether he is talking what she is dancing. Meg Stuart's shown thoughts and Tim Etchells' told thoughts seem to escape showing as well as telling and thus become readable only in their mutual con-fusion. There is no easy going in this complex translation between accomplice languages, there is rather an uneasy going instead of anything goes. During this "structured improvisation" this "experiment in front of an audience", as Stuart and Etchells call their work, we are again and again apart from this artistic research situation and only thereby become part of it. In this situation, Meg Stuart and Tim Etchells abstain from any "shared methodology," as he says during an artistic talk (Decaesstecker 2016). "And thus: doing this performance together is a bit off territory with elements of it that are still mysterious to us." But where is this "a bit off territory" between showing and telling located, we might ask ourselves in order to think of artistic research as philosophy. "Are you there?" Etchells asks during the performance and Stuart replies: "Is that a serious or a philosophical question?" He says: "More of a political one."

In article eight, "The Feeling of Thinking – Stories on artists reading theory", Veronika Reichl is researching the reading experience of people who are reading philosophical texts. Reading is, for most people (and artists), the central activity of engaging with philosophy. For 4 years now Veronika Reichl has been working on a project in which she analyzed the experience of people who are reading philosophical texts. In the course of this project she developed (fictional) short stories based on confidential interviews with students, humanists, artists and other dedicated readers of philosophy. These interviews investigate the (emotionally charged) personal process of reading such texts and thereby explore the relationship between readers and texts/philosophers. Her article will propose a collection of 5 stories based on interviews with artists (fine arts) on their experience with readings of philosophy. The stories will deal with questions like: How can one relate to something so authoritarian as a magnum opus without approving of the authority? How does one's life and artistic practice change while indulging in reading Heidegger for many hours every day over a month? How can an artist refer to philosophical books which are some of the most perfect objects humans have ever created? Three such stories already exist in German versions. Some stories on the reading of students and academics from the field of humanities can be found in Reichl (2019).

In the last article, "Gay Troublemakers. None but Fools", Susanne Valerie [Granzer] reads Nietzsche's Gay Science (la gaya scienza) as the eponym to come to terms with the playful figure of the fool. For Nietzsche, the fool is a free spirit, a non-conformist, and also a provocateur. The first chapter of her article "Under cover..." considers the long tradition of the figure of the fool. One encounters the fool in the satyr play of antiquity, at the sovereign's court, by the jesters of the Middle Ages, at carnival, and again and again at the theater. Surprisingly, it can also be found in philosophy, e.g. in Diogenes in his barrel, or when Nietzsche praises the fool in his Dithyrambs of Dionysus: "'Suitor of truth – you?' [...] Only fool! Only poet!" In the second part of her text Granzer will analyze the special kind of wisdom which is operative with fools. Fools are strongly associated with the conceptual persona of the sage. Nevertheless, they are also clearly distinct from one another, as the fool Touchstone in Shakespeare highlights: "The fool doth think he is wise, but the wise man knows himself to be a fool." (Shakespeare [1862], As You Like It, Act 5, Scene 1) In the third chapter Granzer analyzes the fool Johnny as the alter ego of performer Barbara Kraus amidst the hurly-burly of contemporary performance art and performance philosophy. In improvised speech the 'couple' (Kraus and Johnny) discuss a foolish image of thinking. One that exemplifies a crossover of philosophical and artistic thoughts, giving back to philosophy the material conditions and driving forces of the body. Neither does this contemporary fool Johnny shy away from affects nor does s/he care about conventions. Even though the cross-over of art and philosophy seems to be a foolish endeavor for those who still defend the antagonistic relation between philosophy and the arts, the cross-over of both disciplines starts making sense for the new species of artist-philosophers that Nietzsche envisaged at the very beginning of his book Beyond Good and Evil. Prelude to a Philosophy of the Future.

Arno Böhler, Vienna, April 11, 2025.

Literature

Agamben, Giorgio. 1999. "Absolute Immanence." In Potentialities. Collected Essays in Philosophy, 220-243. Stanford University Press.

Aristotle. 1989. Aristotle in 23 Volumes, Vols.17, 18. Translated by Hugh Tredennick. Cambridge, MA, Harvard University Press; London, William Heinemann.

Aurobindo, Ghose. 1997. The Complete Works of Sri Aurobindo. Savitri, a Legend and a Symbol. Vol. 33 and 34. Pondicherry: Ashramverlag.

Aurobindo, Ghose. 1998. The Complete Works of Sri Aurobindo. The Secret of the Veda. Vol. 15. Pondicherry: Ashramverlag.

Aurobindo, Ghose. 1999. *The Complete Works of Sri Aurobindo. The Synthesis of Yoga*. Vol. 23, 24. Pondicherry: Ashramverlag.

Badura, Jens, Dubach, Selma, Haarmann, Anke, Mersch, Dieter, Rey, Anton, Schenker, Christoph and Germán Toro Pérez (eds.). 2014. *Künstlerische Forschung. Ein Handbuch*. Zürich: Diaphanes.

Banerji, Debashish. 2020. *Meditations on the Īśa-Upaniṣad. Tracing the philosophical vision of Sri Aurobindo Ghose*. Pink Integer Books: Concord, CA.

Barad, Karen. 2007. *Meeting the Universe Halfway*. Duke University Press: Durham and London.

Bäumer, Bettina. 1992. *Abhinavagupta. Wege ins Licht – Texte des tantrischen Shivaismus aus Kashmir*, Zürich: Benziger Verlag.

Böhler, Arno and Susanne Valerie Granzer (eds.). 2018. *Philosophy on Stage: Philosophie als künstlerische Forschung*. (Passagen forum). Wien: Passagen Verlag.

Böhler, Arno and Valerie Susanne Granzer. 2020. "Philosophy on Stage." In *The Routledge Companion to Performance Philosophy*, edited by Laura Cull Ó Maoilearca and Alice Lagaay, 387-394. London: Routledge. https://doi.org/10.4324/9781003035312. (Last access: 12.06.2025)

Böhler, Arno, Granzer, Susanne, Loughnane, A., and G. Parkes. 2016. "Kunst und Philosophie im Zwischen der Kulturen: ein E-Mail Gespräch." In *Polylog: Zeitschrift für interkulturelles Philosophieren* (35), 7-35.

Böhler, Arno, Schäfer, Elisabeth and Eva-Maria Aigner (eds.). 2017a. "Philosophy On Stage: Immanenz in zeitgenössischer Kunst und Philosophie." In *Performance Philosophy Journal*, (Vol. 3/2).

Böhler, Arno, Schäfer, Elisabeth and Eva-Maria Aigner (eds.). 2017b. "Philosophy On Stage: The Concept of Immanence in Contemporary Art and Philosophy." In *Performance Philosophy Journal*, (Vol. 3/3).

Böhler, Arno. 1996. *Das Gedächtnis der Zukunft*. Passagen Verlag: Wien.

Böhler, Arno. 2014. "Wissen wir, was ein Körper kann?" In *Wissen wir, was ein Körper vermag? Rhizomatische Körper in Religion, Kunst, Philosophie*, edited by Arno Böhler, Krassimira Kruschkova and Susanne Valerie Granzer, 233-252. Bielefeld: transcript.

Böhler, Arno. 2015. "Artist-Philosophers: Philosophy AS Arts-based-Research." In *Contemporary Code – Artistic Research. Documentation of an Exhibition Project by the University of Applied Arts*, edited by Bast, Gerald, Damianisch, Alexander and Romana Schuler, 12-13. The exhibition was part of the PEEK-Project (FWF): AR 275-G21 https://homepage.univie.ac.at/arno.boehler/php/?p=7913. (last accessed: 12 June 2025)

Böhler, Arno. 2016. "Post-Hermeneutik nach Derrida: erstaunliche Brüche." In *Narrative im Bruch: theoretische Positionen und Anwendungen*, edited by A. Babka. Göttingen: V&R unipress.

Böhler, Arno. 2017. "Immanence: A life... Friedrich Nietzsche." In *Performance Philosophy Journal* 3 (3): 580. https://doi.org/10.21476/PP.2017.33163. (last accessed: 12 June 2025)

Böhler, Arno. 2019a. "Becoming Worldwide: Transdisciplinary forms of Collaborations in Philosophy and the Arts – A case study." In *The Future of Education and Labor*, edited by G. Bast, E. G. Carayannis and D. Campbell, 203-225. Berlin: Springer.

Böhler, Arno. 2019b. "Philosophy as Artistic Research. Artist Philosophers." In *Artistic Research Charting a Field in Expansion*, edited by P. de Assis and L. D'Errico, 236-248. Lanham: Rowman & Littlefield.

Böhler, Arno. 2019c. "Philosophy AS artistic research: Philosophy On Stage." In *Journal for Artistic Research*, 17. Online: https://jar-online.net/en/philosophy-artistic-research-philosophy-stage. (last accessed: 12 June 2025)

Böhler, Arno. 2019d. "Denken des Gemüts: Spinoza, Nietzsche, Abhinavagupta." In *Liebe und Hass in Philosophie, Religion und Literatur: Gegen Manipulierbarkeit und für eine Orientierung in Fühlen, Denken, Urteilen.* Wiener Jahrbuch der Philosophie (Band 50). Wien: New Academic Press.

Böhler, Arno. 2025. "KHÔRA. Sensing Tasting Notating Reflecting Atmospheres." In *Contingent Agencies*, edited by Nikolaus Gansterer and Alex Arteaga. Berlin: De Gruyter.

Cull Ó Maoilearca, Laura and Alice Lagaay (eds.). 2020. *The Routledge Companion to Performance Philosophy*. London: Routledge. https://doi.org/10.4324/9781003035312. (last accessed: 12 June 2025)

De Assis, Paulo and Lucia D'Errico (eds.). 2019. *Artistic Research Charting a Field in Expansion*. Lanham: Rowman & Littlefield.

De Assis, Paulo and Paolo Giudici. 2017. *The Dark Precursor. Deleuze and Artistic Research*. Volume I and II. Orpheus Institute, Leuven: Leuven University Press.

De Man, Paul. 1979. *Allegories of Reading. Figural Language in Rousseau, Nietzsche, Rilke, and Proust*. New Haven/London: Yale University Press.

Decaesstecker, Eva. 2016. "For Me, Collaboration Is Being Out of Familiar Territory." Interview with Tim Etchells. November 2016. https://kaaitheater.be/fr/articles/me-collaboration-being-out-familiar-territory. (last accessed: 12 June 2025)

Deleuze, Gilles. 1994. *Difference and Repetition*. New York: Columbia University Press.

Derrida Jacques. 1989. *Mémories: for Paul de Man*. Revised edition. New York: Columbia University Press.

Derrida, Jacques. 1982. *Margins of Philosophy*. Translated, with Additional Notes by Alan Bass. Chicago: The University of Chicago Press.

Derrida, Jacques. 1992. *The Other Heading. Reflections on Today's Europe*. Translated by Pascale-Anne Brault and Michael B. Naas. Bloomington: Indiana University Press.

Derrida, Jacques. 1995. *As if I were Dead / Als ob ich tot wäre*. An Interview with Jacques Derrida by Ruth Robbins and Julian Wolfreys. Ed. by Karl-Josef Pazzini (engl./dt.). Vienna: Verlag Turia + Kant.

Derrida, Jacques. 2000. *Demeure. Fiction and Testimony*. Translated by Elisabeth Rottenberg. Stanford, California: Stanford University Press.

Deshpande, G. T. 1989. *Abhinavagupta*. New Delhi: Sahitya Akademi.

Desikachar, T.K.V. 1995. *The Heart of Yoga: Developing a Personal Practice*. Rochester: Inner Traditions International.

Dyczkowski, Mark (ed.). 1992b. *The Aphorisms of Śiva. The Śiva-Sūtra with Bhāskara's Commentary, the Vārttika SUNY Series in Tantric Studies*. New York: State University of New York Press.

Dyczkowski, Mark. 1992. *The Stanzas on Vibration*. New York: State University of New York Press.

Gansterer, Nikolaus. 2024. https://www.gansterer.org/, (last accessed: 12 June 2025).

Gnoli, Raniero. 1985. *The Aesthetic Experience according to Abhinavagupta*. Varanasi: Chowkhamba Sanskrit Series Office.

Gonda, Jan. 1977. *A History of Indian Literature*. Vol. 2, fasc. 1, *Medieval Religious Literature in Sanskrit*. Wiesbaden: Otto Harrassowitz.

Hamacher, Werner. 2015. *Minima Philologica*. Translated by Catharine Diehl and Jason Groves. New York: Fordham University Press.

Heidegger, Martin. 1996. *Nietzsche I (1936-1939)*. Martin Heidegger Gesamtausgabe 6.1. Edited by Brigitte Schillbach. Frankfurt a.M.: Vittorio Klostermann.

Hillman, James. 1981. *The Thought of the Heart. Eranos Lecture 2*. Michigan: Spring Publications.

Jayaraman, Dr. M. 2004. *Patañjali – Caritam The Legend of Sage Patañjali. Krishnamacharya Yoga Mandiram*. Chennai.

Kafka, Franz. 2009. *The Trial*. Oxford's World Classics, Oxford: Oxford University Press.

Lakshmanjoo: Kashmir Shaivism. 2015. *The Secret Supreme*. Lakshmanjoo Academy Book Series.

Larson, Gerald James. 2014. *Classical Sāṅkhya. An Interpretation of Its History and Meaning*. Motilal Banarsidass: Delhi.

Manning, Erin. 2004. *SenseLab*, http://erinmovement.com/about-senselab. (last accessed: 12 June 2025)

Muller-Ortega, Paul Eduardo. 1989. *The Triadic Heart of Siva. Kaula Tantricism of Abhinavagupta in the Non-Dual Shaivism of Kashmir*. New York: State University of New York Press.

Nancy, Jean-Luc. 2008. *Corpus*. Translated by Richard A. Rand. Fordham University Press: New York.

Nietzsche, Friedrich. 1967-1977. "Sokrates und die Tragödie." In Friedrich NIETZSCHE, *Nachgelassene Schriften 1870–1873*, (vol. 1 of the works in 15 volumes), edited by Giorgio COLLI, Mazzino MONTINARI. Berlin/New York: Walter de Gruyter.

Nietzsche, Friedrich. 1967–1977. *Nachgelassene Fragmente Ende 1870 – April 1871*, (vol. 7 of the works in 15 volumes), eds. Giorgio COLLI, Mazzino MONTINARI. Berlin/New York: Walter de Gruyter.

Nietzsche, Friedrich. 1967-77. *Nachgelassene Fragmente Herbst 1885 – Anfang Januar 1889*, (vol. 13 of the works in 15 volumes) edited by

Giorgio COLLI, Mazzino MONTINARI. Berlin/New York: Walter de Gruyter.

Nietzsche, Friedrich. 1989. *On the Genealogy of Morals.* Translated by Walter Kaufmann and RJ Hollingdale. Edited with Commentary, by Walter Kaufmann. New York: Vintage Books Edition/Random House.

Nietzsche, Friedrich. 2002. *Beyond Good and Evil. Prelude to a Philosophy of the Future,* edited by Rolf-Peter Horstmann and Judith Norman. Translation by Judith Norman. Cambridge Texts in the History of Philosophy. Cambridge: Cambridge University Press.

Nietzsche, Friedrich. 2003. "Brief an Paul Deussen." In *Sämtliche Briefe,* edited by Giorgio Colli and Mazzino Montinari, (vol. 8 of the works in 8 volumes). Berlin/New York: Walter de Gruyter.

Nietzsche, Friedrich: Sokrates und die griechische Tragödie. Basel 1971. Nietzschesource: http://www.nietzschesource.org/#eK-GWB/SGT (last accessed: 12 June 2025).

Reichl, Veronika. 2019. *The Feeling of Thinking: Stories and Animations on the Experience of Reading Theory.* Vol. 4, No. 2, Performance Philosophy. https://www.performancephilosophy.org/journal/article/view/229/338 (last accessed: 12 June 2025).

Shakespeare, William. [1862]. *As You Like It.* Vol. 2. London and Edinburgh: W. & R. Chambers.

Skora, Kerry Martin. 2007. "The Pulsating Heart and Its Divine Sense Energies: Body and Touch in Abhinavagupta's Trika." In *Numen,* Vol. 54, No. 4, Religion through the Senses. Leiden/Bosten: Brill.

Spivak, Gayatri Chakravorty. 2013. *An Aesthetic Education in the Era of Globalization.* Cambridge: Harvard University Press. https://doi.org/10.2307/j.ctv1n1bsfh.

White, David Gordon. 2014. *The Yoga Sutra of Patanjali: A Biography* (Lives of Great Religious Books, Band 43). Princeton: Princeton University Press.

Whitehead, Alfred North. 1979. *Process and Reality.* New York: Free Press.

Wittgenstein, Ludwig. 2003. *Philosophische Untersuchungen,* § 115. Frankfurt a.M.: Suhrkamp.

Poets of the Heart
Friedrich Nietzsche and Sri Aurobindo

Arno Böhler

Prelude...[1]

My article reads Friedrich Nietzsche and Sri Aurobindo Ghose as *artist-philosophers* and *poet-seers* who followed the great reason of their lived-bodies (Nietzsche 1985, 34). Taking the multiple planes and sheaths of their bodies seriously,[2] they were forced to invent a hybrid style of doing philosophy in which they constantly aligned the performance of thinking with their aesthetic sense (Böhler and Granzer 2019a; 2019b; 2021). Thinking philosophically thus became a sensible matter. A kind of arts-based-philosophy, in which thoughts are generated in a constant dialogue with emotions, which are stimulated, while one thinks: Does the production of a thought sound

---

1   This article is a revised and extended version of the research proposal "Art in Philosophy: Philosophy in the Arts. The Significance of the *Heart* in Artistic-Research (AR) and Performance Philosophy (PP)", sponsored by the Austrian Science Fund (FWF): Grant-Doi 10.55776/AR822. https://www.mdw.ac.at/the.heart/ (last accessed: 12 June 2025)

2   On an image of thought which thinks on a "thousand plateaus", see Deleuze and Guattari 1987. Later, in his book on Foucault, Deleuze clarified the concept of plateaus further, by interpreting the thousand plateaus of one's self as archeological layers which constitute the foundation of one's past. They are not just lying one above the other like slices, but they are also intra-connected by a thousand lines which run through them in a queer, criss-cross manner. Combining Guattari's concept of transversality (Guattari 2000, 43) with Foucault's concept of archeology, the lived-past thus becomes a dimension of the present. On the concept of transversality see Deleuze 1986; Deleuze 1994.

well? Does it feel coherent? Is the wording of a certain formulation well-tuned?

While one is performing arts-based-philosophy, one's aesthetic sense continuously tastes the coherence of thoughts in a logical, but also a sensible manner. Obviously, arts-based-philosophy is not just arguing with words but generates a sublime form of feeling that sensually informs us (*aisthesis*) about the coherence of a thought in a bodily-felt-sense (Skora 2007).

In the case of artist-philosophers, who are those to perform philosophy in such an aesthetic manner, the coherence of an assemblage of thoughts can therefore never simply be reduced to the question of its logical consistency. As-if thoughts would not be entangled at all with all the other planes of one's existence; with one's appetite, desires, feelings, visions, inspirations and intuitions, but also with external relations in which a lived-body finds itself right at the heart of its world in so many relational affairs with other human, non-human, and more-than-human beings. So many...!

Contrary to the image-of-thought, which considers thinking to be an entirely autonomous act, arts-based-philosophy experiences the creative performance of thinking as a sensitive form of mattering. It is no longer considered to be an immaterial event but has rather become an emergent matter in which thoughts emerge out of a sensible field of related thoughts, with which they are logically *and* sensibly connected. One's aesthetic sense constantly informs one in a bodily-felt sense whether a certain formation of thoughts *feels* coherent and tastes sound while one is thinking. The flashing of a thought has therefore not only a certain degree of logical coherence, but also a certain sensible quality. It could eventually be the case that a new thought appears in one's conceptual research which sounds coherent according to logic but feels unsound aesthetically. In this case, the mattering of a new thought within the relational field of related thoughts triggers a bodily-felt-resistance which gives a logically coherent thought a bitter, unsound taste.

Unthought thoughts...

This is even true for still unthought-thoughts which have not mattered yet but are about to matter—for thoughts in their making. Because once they emerge, they too are appearing in a relational field in sensitive connections with other thoughts, with which they are logically but also sensually entangled. As-if the flashing of a particular thought would send a subtle (electro-magnetic) impulse through the entire network of related thoughts with which it is physio-logically intra-connected in one's mind in a sensible manner. Whenever one thinks a particular thought, the entire network of related thoughts seems to be stimulated at once as the referential context which constitutes the referential meaning of a particular thought, where it starts to make sense.

This is true in particular if one is still *in search* of a yet unthought-thought. In such a case, the *researching* mind activates new combinations of thoughts in an *experimental* manner in order to probably find the yet unthought-thought one is searching for, through *playful variations* of already given sets-of-thoughts which are available in one's mind. It is this *free-associating* state of mind that is obviously trusted to eventually trigger the yet unthought-thought.

One could call the performance of such a kind of mindful research arts-based-thinking. Firstly, because it is an *experimental* mode of thinking *in search* of yet unthought-thoughts (mindful re-search), and secondly because it is an *aesthetic* mode of thinking, concerned with both, the logical *and* the sensible coherence of a certain set of thoughts. The performance of thinking thus becomes a creative act in-itself; it becomes arts-based-philosophy. That is, philosophy in search of new concepts (Deleuze 1994, p. 40).

Artist-philosophers...

Artist-philosophers are precisely those kinds of philosophers who in actu perform such an artistic-mode of thinking in their philosophical research. When they start thinking, they do not yet have the thought they are looking for but search for it in a sensible way. Being experimentally engaged in creative forms of mindful research, the playful mind-set of artist-philosophers is basically turned toward the *virtual* plane of their existence. Which is precisely that plane-of-being from which unthought-thoughts, unfelt-feelings, not-yet-staged modes of expressions *eventually emerge*: A non-place of a virtual 'future' which has not yet mattered but is about to matter. The conditions for the mattering of a particular thought are there, the searched for thought is currently about to matter, but it still has not yet been grasped fully so far.

In artistic research, the virtual future of something which has not yet mattered but is about to matter is evidently no distant, utopian matter. One does not search for a non-place in order to leave it at that. Artistic research is rather passionately interested in finding a way to let the non-place of the not-yet[3] *happen here-and-now*; right in the midst of one's artistic research; and induced by it. One is *currently* engaged with the *possible mattering* of a not yet *staged* thought, a not yet staged feeling, or other modes of yet unexpressed-expressions while one is performing artistic research. It is precisely this *eventuality* of a possible mattering here and now that one is currently concerned with.

One might even claim that artistic research is all about mattering: Mattering of thoughts, of feelings, of visions, of inspirations, of intuitions, of artefacts, of public demonstrations etc. etc. etc. It is not about matter as an already constituted thing or body of thoughts, feelings, artefacts which would already be ready at hand to be just used (natura naturata). Rather, artistic research is a process of mattering in which matter is actually about to matter in space and time. Toying with Karen Barad's new materialism, based on philosophy-physics, one might say that it is exactly the mattering of new forms of matter that matters most in artistic research and philosophy-physics (Barad 2007, 2012).

---

3   On the notion of locality and non-locality from the perspective of quantum-physics see the contribution by Tanja Traxler & Reinhold A. Bertlmann

The heart-mind...

The physiological sensibility of a thought, its special flavor, can never be entirely separated from the rhizomatic multitude (Böhler; Kruschkova; Granzer 2014; Deleuze; Guattari 1987) of all the sensible channels which run from one thought to another thought, but also from the plane of thoughts to the plane of feelings. Namely by traversing the mental and the vital planes of one's lived-body in a *transversal* manner.[4]

It has often been mentioned that in ancient Chinese philosophies the word *xin* was referring to the faculty of the heart with its capacity to feel as well as to the faculty of the mind with its capacity to think. Therefore, most Sinologists used to translate the word *xin* as *heart-mind*. Since one's heart-mind traverses different planes of one's existence at once in a queer, cross-chipping manner, it simultaneously belongs to the regime of the mind *and* the heart. From the perspective of one's heart-mind, finding a *sound* expression among thoughts, words, or other expressions in one's heart-mind is neither a matter of one's mind *nor* of one's heart but of both at once. One might therefore say that artist-philosophers who are performing arts-based-philosophy are in actu in search of a sound logical, but also of a sound aesthetic ratio in their heart-minds. A series of thoughts which pops up in their minds has to satisfy both faculties at once, their heart and their mind, and not just either one or the other; as-if one's heart and one's head would exist completely independent of each other in autonomous, entirely separated planes-of-being, without any *transversal line* that would be able to run through these planes in a queer, cross-chipping manner and thereby intra-connect one plane, the plane of thoughts, with the other, the plane of feelings. Questions such as: "How does a thought actually resonate in one's heart-mind?" "What does the mattering of a thought, its incarnation in a relational field, sound like?" "What is its flavor?" "How does it feel?" How does it taste?" "Does it actually satisfy the aesthetical sense operative in one's heart-mind?" Such questions are core for the

---

4   For transversal thinking as a queer cut through several separate planes, see also Guattari 2000, 43.

aesthetic mode of thinking, operative in one's heart-mind, because they take the alignment of mental thoughts in one's 'head' and their relatedness with a certain set of feelings in one's 'heart' seriously. Thoughts actually resonate with the feelings of one's 'heart' while one is thinking. As a consequence, they are in fact accompanied by a certain flavor and taste. Thinking-feeling / feeling-thinking. This is what one's heart-mind is in actu concerned with while one is thinking in an aesthetic manner.

If a performance of thinking tastes indeed unsound, one's aesthetic taste even starts to resist and intervene actively in the performance of thinking by *modulating and regulating* the given set of thoughts in accordance with one's aesthetic taste.[5] In such a case, the flavor of the entire cocktail of thoughts has been *corrected* by one's sense of taste in the course of a fine-tuning process that finally made the modulated set of thoughts sound also aesthetically coherent. Not just logically, but also in a bodily-felt-sense, that makes sense in a sensible manner.

Koinê aisthêsis...

This is true for all forms of artistic research, not just for the artistic mode of thinking. Either one is searching for a sound expression in painting, in music, in theater, in performances, film-making etc. What these modes of doing art have in common is precisely the fact that they are constitutively forms of *artistic research*. They all search, over and over again (re-search), for a sound expression that still lies in the air; unexpressed, unarticulated, unthought, unfelt, not-yet-staged. In Plato's *Tímaios*, Tímaios once called the element ether the most sublime form of air (Plato 2021, 58D). As-if artists would get in touch with the most etheric planes-of-being while they are doing artistic-research. As-if one could find the unthought-thoughts, the unfelt-feelings, the unexpressed-expressions precisely there, in the lofty, airy zones of a highly sublime etherical space that almost

---

5   On the laws operative in the association of thoughts and affects, see Spinoza *Ethics*, 1994.

resembles a non-place. A void, full of virtual possibilities (*vyoman*),[6] ready to matter once, as South-Asian-philosophies would probably call it.

In De Anima,[7] Aristotle therefore characterized the sense of taste as *koinê aisthêsis*. Taste is literally a *synesthetic* form of sensing, which gives us a bodily-sensed flavor of the overall taste of a certain sensorium of sensations. Even though Aristotle's term *koinê aisthêsis* has later been translated into the Latin language as *sensus communis* and in modern times even as *common sense* (Hagner 2008), originally it meant the place of an aesthetic experience in which a certain set of sensations comes together in one single impression (flavor) which reveals the overall coherence of a sensorium of substances, thoughts, feelings in the *taste* of the overall *flavor* of such compositions.

Artefacts of artist-philosophers…

Thus Spoke Zarathustra is probably one of the most striking examples in the genealogy of Continental Philosophies in modern times, in which the artist-philosopher Friedrich Nietzsche (1844-1900) was actually already realizing a crossover of art & philosophy, where words, concepts and thoughts started to dance; precisely due to their aesthetic soundness and coherence (Kimerer 2006; Tuncel 2020, 2021). Nietzsche himself considered the epic poem *Thus Spoke Zarathustra* to be primarily a musical composition (Parkes 2008, 11; Tuncel 2022). And Michel Foucault and Gilles Deleuze read Nietzsche's way of doing philosophy as a form of play-writing—longing for a stage to be performed (Foucault 1977; Deleuze 1994).

In the context of Indian philosophies, *Savitri. A Legend and a Symbol* (Aurobindo 1997), the poetic magnum opus by the *Kavi*[8] Sri

---

6   In South-Asian philosophies, the ether is an empty space, full of potentials. See Dyczkowski 1992, 55.

7   "tôn koinôn echomen aisthêsin koinên." (Aristoteles 1931, III, 2, 425, 15)

8   A Kavi is a spiritual poet. Aurobindo translates the word Kavi in the context of the Veda as poet-seers (Aurobindo 1998). It is an aim of this article to read Aurobindo as an artist-philosopher (Kavi), who has not only been nominated for the shortlist to get the Nobel Prize for literature in 1943, but who has written in many different artistic styles. See, for instance,

Aurobindo Ghose (1872-1950), is another striking example in modern times of a philosophical work that finally started to express its philosophy in the style of an epic poem rather than by sheer logical argumentation. Thereby, Aurobindo just reiterated a way of performing philosophy that was in fact the way in which one had been doing philosophy for centuries in India in ancient times, e.g. in the epic age (Gonda 1977; Banerji 2020). And the oldest of all Vedas, the *Ṛgveda*, was composed by poets (*Kavis*) in hymns, who expressed their insights into the cosmos-genesis of the world in poetic terms and public performances in which they chanted their hymns. Aurobindo's view in this regard was clear and unambiguous.

> In ancient times the Veda was revered as a sacred book of wisdom, a great mass of inspired poetry, the work of Rishis, seer and sages... The name given to these sages was Kavi, which afterwards came to mean any poet, but at the time had the sense of a seer of truth. (Aurobindo 1991, 1)

In Vedic times, the poets (*Kavi*) were considered to be holders of the truth-of-being (*satyam*).[9] They were obviously not considered liars, as they were regularly addressed in Hellenistic times by the philosophers of their time.[10] What gave them such a highly esteemed status in Vedic times was precisely their social reputation, that they were assumed to have envisioned the truth-of-being *themselves*. This was the reason why they were also called seers (*Ṛsi*). They had reached a certain stage of consciousness themselves, in which they could *intuitively see a truth* that appeared appealing. At the same time they

---

his collection of poems, the epic poem Savitri, his poetic masterpiece, and many reflections on art and poetry, in which he presents us an intellectual art theory.

9   *Satyam* is an adverb meaning "truly," "certainly," "necessarily." It derives from the Sanskrit term *sat*, which means "that which is true"; and yam, which means "to hold," or "to examine." It is often used as a synonym for the adjective *satya* ("true," "truthful" or "authentic").

10   Right at the beginning of his *Lectures on Metaphysics*, Aristotle quotes the widely used saying of his times that "poets tell many a lie" (Aristotle 1966, Metaphysics, 983a).

were also able to *translate* their visions and deep insights into sound words which finally found their well-tuned poetic expressions in the hymns of the Veda. Aurobindo therefore deliberately coined the word poet-seers[11] for them, to express this double character of their very nature. They were poets (*Kavis*), and at the same time they were seers (*Ṛṣi*), both at once.

In the context of the *Ṛg-Veda*, the term *satyam*, the truth-of-being, which they were supposed to hold (*sat-yam*), was often associated with two other attributes, namely the vast (*bṛhat*) and the upright (*ṛtam*).[12] The Kavis apparently experienced the realization of *satyam* in the course of their poetic research as an opening of their heart-minds. In their experience, envisioning the truth-of-being, *satyam*, was a mindful form of experience associated with a transformation of their hearts and their minds, which both became vast, bright, shiny (*bṛhat*), and, at the same, time honest, sincere, correct, right, upright (*ṛtaṁ*) in the course of this revealing event.

The other heading...[13]

If one compares this high estimation of the poets as seers-and-translators-of-the-truth-of-being in Vedic times with the widespread shaming of the poets by the philosophers of Hellenistic times, one can get a first taste of the differences between these two intellectual cultures concerning aesthetic matters. To mention just some telling examples.

Right at the beginning of his *Lectures on Metaphysics*, Aristotle quotes the widely used saying of his times that "poets tell many a lie." (Aristotle 1966, Metaphysics, 983a) Plato's ban of the poets from

---

11   Poiesis is the ancient Greek word for letting something appear in being, where poetry is the calling into being by words. The performative speech-act par excellence.

12   "satyam ṛtaṁ bṛhat (Satyam Ritam Brihat)..., the Truth, the Right, the Vast. [Atharva-veda 12.1.1]." Aurobindo 2001: https://incarnateword.in/dict/sans/satyam-rtam-brhat-satyam-ritam-brihat (last accessed: 12 June 2025) See also Aurobindo 1991, 17.

13   On the relation of caput, capitalism and the European heading see Derrida 1992.

his ideal state has become legendary in terms of the way in which the most respected philosophers of the Hellenistic period viewed the arts in the ancient Greek beginnings of Europe's intellectual history. Less well known is the rumor, handed down over centuries in ancient Greek and Latin cultures, that Socrates advised his master student Plato to burn his art-works before practicing the Socratic form of *epistémē* (Böhler 2019c).

One could easily extend the list by other examples from ancient Greek times, but also by numerous examples from the intellectual European history in modern times. For instance, the well-known claim by Hegel in his *Lectures on Aesthetics*, that the arts can no longer have the same privileged status for us which they once held in the ancient Greek culture. Or Schopenhauer's reduction of the function of art to a sedative, needed to calm down the souterrains of one's lived-body.[14] Or Kant's analysis of beauty as a kind of pleasure, rooted in a disinterested (non-pragmatic) form of intuition. For Kant, the primordial access to the arts actually takes place by contemplating them. He did not estimate the arts as a stimulating force, operative in artistic research, in which one's entire heart-mind is put in a Dionysian state of intoxication, as Nietzsche later holds. All these references, except the last one, show clearly one and the same tendency. Namely, that in the intellectual history of Europe the relation between art & philosophy has altered in favor of a philosophy of Science and not in favor of the arts.

This is true also, or even exemplarily true, in regard to our current times. In the so-called West and all the Westernized cultures, the arts are obviously no longer granted the privileged role of ancient Vedic times. Today, as a rule, people do not assume anymore that the arts could be capable of revealing the truth-of-being (*satyam*). Generally speaking, they do not hold such a privileged status anymore. And even the arts themselves are no longer claiming today to possess a vision of *satyam* that would inspire the public in such a way that their heart and mind would become bright and upright. As-if the truth-of-being (*satyam*), revealed in artistic research, would

---

14   See the introduction in this book.

quasi-necessarily go hand in hand with the feelings of beauty and delight (ānanda).

Who could believe such untimely myths today? In the midst of our contemporary societies? – – –. Indeed. One would have to become outmoded, uncontemporary and radically untimely if one shared such a Vedic belief today. But who is willing to confront herself with such untimely, foolish matters?[15]

The intellectual history of European modernity has shown in a striking manner that socio-political questions on the wellbeing of the human race should be the major concern of humanists in respect to the cosmo-genesis of nature within which humans find themselves.

Taking into consideration that the anthropomorphic socio-political point of view on the cosmo-genesis of nature became the core issue at stake in the wake of the intellectual history of European modernity, it is probably wise to mention that the de-evaluation of the arts in modern times in comparison to the Sciences is a historical process that in fact goes hand in hand with the rise of the colonial era of European Imperialism and the capitalization of the entire globe. A historical epoch in which the head (*caput*) first started to become the governing principle of our entire global Da-sein (Hagner 2008). At the very beginning of this epoch the leading thinkers of European Modernity started to imagine the faculty of thinking (*cogito*) to be an entirely autonomous one. As-if the act of thinking was a cōgitātiō which was able to act entirely independent of any empirical influence (*res extensa*) in a non-sensual, purely intelligible realm of freedom (*res cogitans*); autonomous, self-governing, entirely separated from the rest of the world, untouched by any worldly influences. In the course of this intellectual history, the kinglike status of the head (mind) was successively replacing the former government of the heart which in pre-modern times was considered by most cultures, and even by ancient philosophers such as Aristotle, to be the central organ and seat of cognition. As-if Western civilizations would have to

---

15   On the role of the fool in the context of artistic-research and performance philosophy see the contribution by Susanne Valerie [Granzer] in this anthology.

lose their hearts first in order to allow the history of colonial Imperialisms to emerge by subjecting everything, even one's feelings, under the government of the head (mental-mind) as the intellectual capital needed to capitalize Europe and finally the entire globe. Europe and the West thus became the head (*caput*) as well as the capital historical scene (*caput*) of this entire imperial-capitalist era (Derrida 1992).

Meanwhile, almost all academic cultures worldwide have been globalized in the sense of this intellectual history and its *epistémē*. Often without knowing anything about the historical genesis of the epochal rise of history, which lies behind the academic process of subjectivation that trains the academic elites all over the globe to more or less reproduce the academic image-of-thought developed in the course of the intellectual history of Europe and the so-called West. Viewed from the perspective of such a historical process of intellectual subjectivation—a process that usually takes place in secret, that is, unnoticed—the creation of academic agents of the European *epistémē* appears to be still in the making today. From this point of view, the so-called post-colonial times seemed to be less post-colonial than one usually imagines. If Whitehead is right, that the intellectual history of Europe can best be understood as a series of footnotes to Plato,[16] the Platonic *epistémē*, with its de-evaluation of the arts, has meanwhile reached a global scale. Would it not therefore be wise to begin the deconstruction of the hegemony of the Socratic *epistémē* with a reversal of Platonism, as suggested already by Nietzsche and Deleuze? (Deleuze 1994, Nietzsche 1967)

As a result of the genesis of this intellectual history, most academic departments of philosophy today are engaged in analytical philosophy as the hegemonic form of the Socratic way of thinking in contemporary times (Oßwald 2024). The *aesthetic taste*, operative in the heart-mind, has almost completely lost its reputation at such departments, in favor of logical analyses, formalized in mathematical terms. Hence, as a rule, the philosophers at today's philosophy departments are usually no longer artist-philosophers or poet-seers

---

16   "The safest general characterization of the European philosophical tradition is that it consists in a series of footnotes to Plato." (Whitehead 1979, 91)

(Kavi) who would perform arts-based-philosophy in the wake of an aesthetic image of thought, as the prelude to a philosophy of the future.[17] On the contrary. They appear as-if they had displaced the sensual, aesthetic layers operative in the souterrains of one's lived-body and even in the performance of thinking.

The day-break...

According to Aurobindo, the high estimation of the spiritual poets and the privileged status of the arts in general in Vedic times was grounded in the conviction of the people at that time that the arts were actually able to reveal a truth-of-being (*satyam*) that *originates from a plane-of-being* that is actually *beyond the mental plane-of-being* on which the human mind usually operates in its everydayness. These supra-mental planes—which are called supra-mental precisely because they operate literally beyond the reach of the mental plane—were assumed to be *virtually* there, but veiled, in secret, dormant, non-manifest (*avyakta*). They were *virtually real*, but since they currently rested in the background of the psycho-mental awareness of most people, they could not realize them themselves. As-if they would not be there at all.

Though these over-mental planes-of-being were said to *currently* sleep in the dormant chambers of nature (RV 10.129.1-5)—"*nature loves to hide*", said Heraclitus (Heraklit 2004, DK B 123),—they were considered to be accessible *in principle* (*tattvas*) for everybody in the wake of the further evolutionary developments of everyone's nature. It is a crucial doctrine of Aurobindo's philosophy and many other traditions of South-Asian philosophy that only some planes and principles-of-being (*tattvas*) are currently awake (*buddha*) in nature, while others are currently non-manifest (*avvakta*). And, as long as the non-manifest planes are sleeping, they are in fact not actively operative in nature-herself and in those beings which currently inhabit nature. For instance, human beings.

According to Aurobindo's reading of the ancient doctrine of the five sheaths of the body (*pañcakośa*) (Aurobindo 1990, 10-16)—a doc-

---

17 See the introduction to this book.

trine which one can find already in the *Taittirīya Upaniṣad* (~ 600 BCE)—the evolution of the human species has currently unfolded only three of five sheaths of the body. Namely the physical, the vital and the mental sheath. The third, the constitution of the mental sheath (*manomayakośa*) operative in the lived-body of humans, is characterizing the distinct nature of the human species in comparison to non-human forms of being. But even though only three sheaths are currently active in the lived-body of humans, there are two more sheaths sleeping in the background of the manifest nature of human beings. Currently they may be hidden, veiled, covered, occult, sleeping, latent, only virtually real for the human species. But according to Aurobindo, the mental human mind could *in principle* unfold these hidden planes of nature, namely by activating hidden chambers of one's intellect (*buddhi*), thereby developing supra-mental capacities of the intellect which so far have not yet been activated and therefore did rest in a non-manifest, veiled and inanimate manner in the background of the mental human mind, as-if dead.

This is exactly the reason why, according to Aurobindo, the psycho-mental awareness of most people is currently not aware of any supra-mental plane-of-being. The mental mind operative in humans has therefore a certain right to claim that supra-mental planes do not exist, because the mental mindset indeed lacks their experience. But this assumption fails once this anthropological view of the momentary condition of the human mental mindset and its own psycho-mental awareness stops to take itself to be the measure of all things. What, if nature herself would be capable of unfolding supra-mental capacities in *her* chronically recurrent unfolding? What if *her* evolutionary ascent and descent would be capable of producing such supra-mental beings sub specie aeternitatis?

While Aurobindo, in accordance with the Veda, assumes that the higher activations of the intellect (*buddhi*) are usually inactive in mental human beings (*manas*), he argues in alignment with the Veda that poetic-research can eventually awake some of the dormant chambers in one's *mental-mind* by virtue of the awakening of the intuitive mind and intuitive forms of reasoning (*pratibhā*) in the lived-body of a Kavi (Gnoli 1985; Saxena 2010; Desphande 1989). Such an intuitive form of mind is neither irrational nor entirely beyond the range of the human intellect (*buddhi*), but it is literarily supra-mental (*unmanā*) in the very sense that the poetic-mind operates on a plane-of-being that currently evolves *beyond-the-mental-mind* (*unmanā*) right next to the *mental-mind* (*manas*). While most people have activated the mental mind as part of their innate human nature, the intuitive mind (*pratibhā*) is momentarily activated only by some people, for instance in Kavis and other creative minds which in earlier societies were called geniuses. A word that has fallen into disrepute, as so many others in our times.[18]

Terminologically, Aurobindo called the successive break-through of one's mental mind into the supra-mental planes-of-being the realization of a *gnostic* plane-of-being (*vijñāna*) (Aurobindo 1999,11-18). Once it unfolds in a lived-body, it is said that the constitution of the gnostic knowledge triggers the mattering of a sublime gnostic sheath in a lived-body, which was traditionally referred to as *vijñānamayakośa*. Kośa means sheath, and *vijñānamayakośa* means a sublime sheath of the body that is composed (*maya*) in the course of the fabrication of gnostic knowledge (*vijñāna*). Jñāna literally means knowledge, and *vi-jñana* an intensified, intuitive form of knowledge in which the performance of the intellect speeds up and finally operates so quickly that it can intuit the unity of all principles of being (*tattvas*) at once in one single gaze (*trikāladṛṣṭi*).

Trikāladṛṣṭi; The Vision of The Threefold Temporality of Time...

While the human species, in the evolutionary course of its development, has usually activated only three of the five sheaths of the body (*pañcakośa*), namely the physical (*annamayakośa*), the vital (*prāṇamayakośa*) and the mental one (*manomayakośa*), the supra-mental planes-of-being, *vijñānamayakośa* and *ānandamayakośa*, are said to be usually inactive in them. They are virtually there in Nature, but not yet manifest and not yet awake in the mental-mind.

For Aurobindo, the historical unfolding of the higher, supra-mental faculties of the intellect (*buddhi*) will eventually take place in the

---

18   Almost nobody today seems to experience the discrimination of such words as a form of discrimination anymore.

evolutionary wake of a historical gnosification-process in the course of which the psycho-mental awareness of the ordinary human mental mind will become intuitive in its very nature and not just in some extraordinary human beings, as the Kavis were in ancient Vedic times. A historical process that is already in its making today, according to Aurobindo. But even though he considers our epoch to eventually jump beyond the mental sphere of being, by activating supra-mental forms of the intellect which have been sleeping in Nature for such a long time, only the full activation (prabuddha)[19] of the gnostic-plane-of-being, in which the gnostic sheath of a body is fabricated in a lived-body, will finally be able to grasp all principles-of-being (tattvas) at once by one single intuition. A state of gnostic awareness, which Aurobindo identified with trikāladṛṣṭi. The Sanskrit term denotes a sort of visionary seeing (draṣṭṛ) by which the threefold temporality (trikāla) of a particular past, present and future unites into one integral vision of all three dimensions of time in one single gaze.

For Aurobindo, trikāladṛṣṭi is therefore a state of awareness that does not treat objects as ready-made-things with a ready-made-sense but as forms of becoming (Banerji 2012) which themselves appear in the course of time as a particular unfolding of the three constitutive dimensions of time (kāla): the current unfolding of a past time, the current unfolding of a present time and the current unfolding of a future time that still rest in the background of nature as a hidden resource of future unfoldings and becomings. From the perspective of the gnostic vision of a threefold temporality (trikāladṛṣṭi), every single being appears in-itself to be in a state of statu nascendi;

---

19   The full activation (prabuddha) of the gnostic plane takes place in the trikāladṛṣṭi, the vision of the three dimensions of time at once (cf. Aurobindo 1999, 885-906). With the full-activation of the supra-mental planes of consciousness the three higher planes of the intellect, vijñāna-ānanda and saccidānanda, are activated. The concept of trikāladṛṣṭi shows striking similarities with Fichte's and Schelling's concept of Intellectual Intuition as well as with Spinoza's conception of a third kind of knowledge that unfolds in a scientia intuitiva which perceives all things sub specie aeternitatis (Fichte 2012; Schelling 2000; Spinoza 2007; Waibel et al. 2012; Böhler 2012). The tantric term unmanā literally means beyond the mental mind (Dyczkowski 1992, 23).

as a pregnant form of becoming and continuous sense-making that unfolds in time as its quasi-transcendental condition. Quasi, because the threefold temporality of time is not just a formal but also a material form in which the mattering of (everything) takes place: Transcendental Empiricism.[20]

> The progressive self-manifestation of Nature in man, termed in modern language his evolution, must necessarily depend upon three successive elements. There is that which is already evolved; there is that which, still imperfect, still partly fluid, is persistently in the stage of conscious evolution; and there is that which is to be evolved and may perhaps be already displayed, if not constantly, then occasionally or with some regularity of recurrence... (Aurobindo, 1999, 9-10)

The gnostic vision by which the Kavis envision the continuous unfoldings of the three-folds-of-time in one single stroke (*trikāladṛṣṭi*) is neither a determining nor a reflective form of judgment (Kant) but a *playful, experimental, associative, aesthetic* one, because it perceives all sorts of things as being in *statu nascendi* themselves. The things themselves evolve and thereby become what they are. And insofar as the unfolding of the threefold temporality constitutively implies a field of hidden potentials which are about to matter once, the current appearance of a thing is 'just' a prelude and a sign of further becomings.

In coherence with the vision of this threefold ground of time the Kavis had to compose their hymns in a way that corresponds with their gnostic vision of time. Their language could not just be logically stringent, which would have made the things, but also words, which they had in mind, determinate beings without future possibilities. Nor could their style of expression be entirely arbitrary, without any determinate nature which defines a thing from its inherent past. Perceiving everything to be in a state of statu nascendi, they had to express the apparent true state of beings in an experimental, play-

---

20   Rightly so, Deleuze characterized his own philosophy as transcendental empiricism (Deleuze, 1994).

ful, associative, aesthetic, necessarily vague manner. In short: They had to allow the letters, words, sentences of their hymns to dance in alignment with their heart-mind.[21]

Such a playful, freely-associating style of experimental thinking is a poetic form of artistic research that actually triggered a state of consciousness of heightened self-awareness in the heart and mind of the Kavis, which made their own heart-mind vast and upright. These blissful intoxications (*soma*) are obviously a core reason why so many artists are *passionately* longing for the eternal return of their artistic mode of existence. They usually *want* to be artists and *repeat* the intensive experiences they are going through in their artistic research. Precisely because the intensive state of awareness that pops up in artistic research tastes so desirous and appealing for those who consume it. Naturally, they want to loop it, make it return again, fullheartedly, passionately, chronically, in order to reveal more and more potentials which so far have been arrested in the dormant chambers of their heart-minds.

Presumably, it was the experience of this intensive state of intoxication (*soma*) in which hidden potentials of the human nature start to reveal what gave the ancient arts their sacred (and occult) character. They healed the heart-minds, who consumed them, from suffering. And if one recalls that the poet-seers of Vedic times were not just creating hymns for themselves but were *chanting* them in public rituals as "singers and priests of sacrifice" (Aurobindo 1991, 2), one starts to sense why the poetic truth-of-being has also been called a truth that was not just inspiring the eyes but also the ears of those people who were listening to and consuming their chants during public events,[22] which eventually made the audience upright and fast.

It is this intuitive, gnostic vision, and not the mental form of judgment and reasoning, which the ancient poet-seers in Vedic times were addressing by the word *satyam* (Gonda 1963; Aurobindo 1991, 1998). Through the acceleration of their intuitive, poetic minds (*prat-*

---

21   The German word "Stimmigkeit" literally refers to "voice" (Stimme), which runs through the entire multitude of feelings, measuring their common temper and grade of soundness.

22   On *satyaśrutaḥ* see also Aurobindo 1991, 16.

ibhā) they were finally able to stimulate a supra-mental plane of being (*sat*) and knowledge (*vijñāna*) that made them feel upright, vast and bright; *satyam, ṛtam, bṛhat*. In the wake of such an expansion of their own psycho-mental awareness they finally could see, but also intuitively hear (śruti) the sound coherence of the things they were cordially and mindfully in touch with by virtue of their fine aesthetic taste. Here lies the reason for Aurobindo why "the Veda itself describes them as *kavayaḥ satyaśrutaḥ*, 'seers who are hearers of the Truth'." (Aurobindo 1991, 1) The accelerated gnostic forms of thinking allowed the Kavis to see the truth-of-being (*satyam*), but also to hear the coherence and soundness of the statu nascendi of the things, they were mindfully in touch with themselves in their being-in-the-world.

The Dawn...

> Darkness hidden by darkness in the beginning was this all, an ocean without mental consciousness out of it the One was born by the greatness of Its energy. It first moved in it as desire which was the first seed of mind. The Masters of Wisdom [*Kavis*] found out in the non-existent that which builds up the existent; in the heart [*hṛdaya*] they found it by purposeful impulsion and by the thought-mind. ... Their ray was extended horizontally; there was something above, there was something below... Below is the dark sleep of the subconscient, above is the luminous secrecy of the superconscient. These are the upper and the lower ocean.[23]

---

23 RV 10.129.3-5. Translation Aurobindo 1998, 106-107. Cf. also ibid. 101-108, 111, 309. In *The Life Divine*, at the beginning of Chapter 25, Aurobindo gives a partially revised translation of this hymn. See Aurobindo 2005, 254. RV 10.129.1-5. It is said that Aurobindo meditated on the creation hymn regularly over several decades of his life, because he appreciated the extraordinary clarity and intensity of vision operative in this Sūkta. See: Sri Aurobindo Studies, The Integral Yoga, https://sriaurobindostudies.wordpress.com/2010/01/ (last accessed: 12 June 2025).

The *Nāsadīya Sūkta*, the famous hymn of creation which many schoolboys and schoolgirls still chant in India today, informs us that the *Kavis*, which in Vedic times were also addressed as masters of wisdom, actually bridged the utmost opposition one can imagine; namely the opposition between being (*sat*) and non-being (*asat*). They were able to traverse this opposition by virtue of their passionate and rigorous mindful research into their heart-mind. The *Nāsadīya Sūkta* explicitly highlights the fact that it was their research into the depth of the heart [*hṛdaya*] which actually opened their (gnostic) eyes and ears for a sound and coherent understanding[24] of the entire process of creation.[25]

In the first place, says the hymn, creation was operating on an unconscious layer in an ocean without mental consciousness. It became fully conscious only much later, namely in the wake of the rigorous and passionate mindful research [*pratīṣyā*] of the Kavis who, in the course of their artistic research, did dive into the very depth of the heart, in order to explore its abysses. Thereby they discovered, for the first time, the full architecture of the ocean of the heart (*hṛdyāt samudrāt*).

In the depth of the heart, at its very bottom, their researching souls encountered the lowest cardiac region, namely the ocean of the subconscient (*apraketaṁ salilam*). It was there from the very beginning, but in a dormant state; dark, unmoved, impassive. A darkness hidden by another darkness. As tantric philosophers will say later, this ocean without mental consciousness was located there "wrapping itself inwardly around the *Bindu* of the Heart it slumbers there in the form of a sleeping serpent and is aware of nothing at all.... like one affected by poison. O beloved, She is awakened by the resonance of supreme awareness..." (Dyczkowski 1992, 73) Since the heart was, in the first place, sleeping in the lower ocean of the sub-

---

24   Jean-Luc Nancy's text "A L'Ecoute" (Nancy 2002) provides a profound philosophical reflection on the connection of hearing and understanding.

25   In German, the word for togetherness is "Zusammengehörigkeit." It literally means hearing the togetherness of things. The focus is on listening to how things belong together.

conscient (*apraketaṁ salilam*), it has technically also been called "the emptiness of deep-sleep" (Dyczkowski 1992, 34 and 43-46) in several traditions of South-Asian-philosophies, in particular in tantric contexts.

From this dormant emptiness (*vyoman*) the rivers of clarity (*ghṛtasya dhārāḥ*), which are all off-springs of this lower heart-ocean (*hṛdyāt samudrāt*), actually do arise. Firstly, they appear as secret undercurrents within the ocean of the subconscient itself, but on their journey, in the course of which their streams expand, their currents are said to be successively purified, step by step, by the inner heart-mind (*antar hṛdā manasā pūyamānāḥ*) which is operative in Nature's evolutionary upraising. It constantly clarifies them, makes them more and more subtle, vibrant, vivid and knowledgeable. The lower ocean of the subconscious and all its off-springs are thus acquiring the form of vibrant matter (Bennett 2010), which culminates in the gnostic stream of awareness that awakes in the lived-body of the Kavis, triggered by their full-heartedly research into the depth of the heart. Precisely as-if the hymns of the poet-seers possessed the magic power to stimulate the ocean of the subconscient at the very bottom of their heart in such a manner that the dormant serpent, that so long had been arrested there in the emptiness of deep-sleep, suddenly woke up and erected a gnostic fountain of clarity and heightened awareness in the Kavis themselves.

With such a cardiology, the heart is evidently not considered to be just a human organ within a human organism, and also not only the seat of human emotions, but the very archetypical fabric of the cosmos itself, as Aurobindo highlights in the following passage.

The heart in Vedic psychology is not restricted to the seat of the emotions; it includes all that large tract of spontaneous mentality, nearest to the subconscient in us, out of which rise the [energetic streams of] sensations, emotions, instincts, impulses and all those [streams of] intuitions and inspirations that travel through these agencies before they arrive at form in the intelligence [as streams of consciousness]. This is the 'heart of Veda and Vedanta, hṛdaya, hṛd, or brahman. There in

> the present state of mankind the Purusha is supposed to be
> seated centrally. (Aurobindo 1998, 271f.)

The Kavis were passionately committed to dive into the ocean of the subconscious (*apraketaṁ salilam*) at the very bottom of their hearts, because their intuitive minds were said to reside nearest to the sub-conscious which allowed them to awake the rivers of clarity, which were sleeping there, to their full potential and expansion, by virtue of their profound and passionate research into the very cosmic architecture of the heart. Most ancient texts claim that the gnostic rivers of clarity can only erect in the psycho-mental awareness of the poet-seers once the rivers of clarity have been released from the obstacles (*kleśa*) which so far have blocked them from streaming upwards on serpentine roads, higher and higher, until they finally have acquired the capacity to touch the upper ocean of the heart, which Aurobindo identified with "the luminous secrecy of the supercon-scient." Only then the rivers of clarity are currently in touch with the truth-of-being (*satyam*), which opened the heart-mind of the Kavis horizontally and vertically. "Their ray was extended horizontally; there was something above, there was something below...", says the *Nāsadīya Sūkta*.

At the peak of their journey, the rivers of clarity, which have constantly been purified by the inner heart-mind (*antar hṛdā manasā pūyamānāḥ*) in their evolutionary upraising, opened the gnostic eyes and ears in the Kavis. Their psycho-mental awareness suddenly appeared to expand horizontally into a vast brightness (*bṛhat*) and vertically into an open, upright position (*ṛtaṁ*) that allowed them to transgress all archetypical regions of the heart at once in a transversal manner by descending and ascending all five planes of the body at once. The physical, vital, mental, but also the supra-mental regions of the heart, which now have started to become operative and active in the gnostified minds and the gnostic intellect of the poet-seers. Flooded by the gnostic river of clarity (*ghṛtasya dhārāḥ*), which runs through themselves from the very bottom of the heart-ocean, the psycho-mental streams of consciousness operative in the Kavis finally reached that gnostic quality of awareness that provided their arts with a sacred, healing character.

Above, they found the cardiac region of the upper ocean of the superconscient, and below, at the very bottom of their hearts, they found the lower ocean of the subconscient. They both marked the lowest and the highest cardiac region of their Vedic heart-mind. In-between them all the rivers of clarity streamed from the lower to the upper ocean and from there back again into the lower ocean. This is the triple world of Vedic times, according to Aurobindo. The flame of inspiration,[26] which drives and feeds the intuitive mind of the poets, now allowed them to constantly ascend and descend between these two cardiac regions of the heart-mind and to express the gnostic streams of consciousness by the hymns and chants they were performing for the public in public performances.

The poetic truth of creation...

What their mindful and passionate research into the depths of their hearts finally revealed to the poets themselves was the profound truth that lies at the basis of every creation: Namely that being (*sat*) is grounded in non-being (*asat*). Being (*sat*) appears to follow non-being (*asat*), because everything that is, in the first place, came into being and finally returns into non-being after it has been. It is this astonishing fact which seemingly made the poetic-heart of the *Kavis* wonder (*camatkāra*). Things obviously have not been before they started to be. But what do we mean by this *asat*, non-being, from where everything comes into being and into which everything seems to fade away again? Does it not imply that the existence of finite beings has been granted to them by others who actually did let them come into being? But in this case, non-being is not just something that comes before or after something comes into being or vanishes from being. In this context, *asat* rather appears in the middle of those who are already and who seem to be able to bring something into being in

---

26   The flame arises from *Agni*, the god of fire, who is the first of all Gods addressed in the Veda. This flame of aspiration is operative in the Kavis as their seer-will (*kavikratu*) which resides in the middle of their hearts (*kratur hṛdi*). "Agni is a seer-will, *kavikratu*, he is the 'will in the heart', *kratur hṛdi*" (Aurobindo 1991, 16).

the middle of their own Da-sein (being-there). As-if non-being was a dimension of beings who are alive. As-if creative beings had access to non-being right in the middle of their lives.

And this is not only true for physical beings which bodily appear in time and space. It is also true for the mattering of thoughts, feelings and psychological matters in general. They all arise out of non-being. They originate, appear, show up and fade away again. Before they were thought, or felt, or expressed, they actually did not exist (*asat*) but rather had to be fabricated in a creative way.

It is this *access of beings to non-being* that is effective in every creation, which one could call, with Deleuze, the *virtual* plane of one's existence. It is an inherent dimension of all creative beings in which the eventuality of events is at stake. Something that so far has not mattered and so far has played no role is about to matter and play a role. Once beings *access* the virtual plane of their existence, they actually enter a plane of possibilities (posse esse), ready to matter once.

The creative minds of the poet-seers, by virtue of their passionate and rigorous artistic research into their hearts, allowed them to finally realize the overall architecture of the Vedic heart. It is this revelation which they themselves brought into being as creative wanderers between *sat* (being) and *asat* (non-being) in the course of their artistic research.

The quasi-transcendental map of the heart...

For Aurobindo, the creation hymn thus draws a quasi-transcendental map of the overall architecture of the Vedic experience of the gnostic heart. At the very bottom of the heart-ocean (*hṛdyāt samudrāt*) one finds the lower ocean of the subconscient (*apraketaṁ salilam*), void of any mental activity. The researching mind of the poets is perceived to be the place nearest to the subconscient (Aurobindo 1998, 271-272) which is the lowest cardiac region of one's heart-mind. Queering[27] the utmost binarities of being & non being by virtue of

---

27   Crossing binaries in a chiastic, fleshly manner (Merleau-Ponty 1964) is definitely one of the typical functions of the Heart in many traditions of ancient Indian philosophies (cf. Dyczkowski 1992, 211-212).

their wholehearted research (*pratīṣyā*) into the heart, in the wake of their profound research the poet-seers found the truth that lies on the basis of all creation. Namely, that all forms of being (*sat*) are fundamentally grounded in non-being (*asat*). Realizing this truth (*satyam*) as the quasi-transcendental horizon under which all becoming is appearing, will appear and has been appearing, the poet-seers became capable of releasing the (gnostic) waters of clarity (*ghṛtasya dhārāḥ*) which up to then had been veiled in the ocean of the subconscient at the bottom of the heart. Their passionate artistic research woke them up, so that the purified rivers of clarity could finally unfold their full potential. Full-heartedly following the offspring of these waters of clarity, which were constantly purified by the *Inner-Heart-Mind (antar hṛdā manasā pūyamānāḥ)* in the course of their evolutionary upraising in nature, the Vedic poets finally became capable of arriving at the upper ocean of the heart, the ocean of the superconscient, which was the peak and destiny of their entire journey. This upper cardiac region of the heart-ocean was said to be the home of Agni, the truth-consciousness, into which the passionate flame of the seer-will awakes, once the gnostic-rivers-of-clarity have released the dormant serpent that has been arrested in the emptiness of a deep-sleep in "the secret heart-cave, *hṛdaye guhāyām*, as the Upanishads put it" (Aurobindo 1999, 149-150). Being currently in touch with this (supra-mental) upper region of the heart, the Vedic poets became capable of realizing the gnostic dimension of the heart behind the vital heart that had been veiled in the secret heart-cave of the lower heart-ocean from the very beginning of time. By entering the realm of a gnostic truth-consciousness (*vijñāna*), which is the abode of the seer-will operative within the Kavis, the gnostic sheath finally unfolds within the lived-body of the Kavis themselves, as a sublime bodily layer of their (own) lived-bodies (Aurobindo 1999, 703-704; Muller-Ortega 1989, 68; Dyczkowski 1992, 43).

While the mattering of the gnostic heart necessarily appears to be trans-human for those who identify themselves with the vital heart—the gnostic heart was actually the virtual object the Vedic poets were aspiring for in their heart-minds (Banerji 2020; Beldio 2015; Böhler 1996, 2022, 2023; Maharaj 2018; Mascha und Seubert

2022; Wolfers 2017). And since for Aurobindo the vital heart-mind, in its everydayness, is actually an *amalgam* of both hearts—of the vital heart in the foreground, and of the gnostic heart in the background (Aurobindo 1999, 72, 181, 203, 231),[28] Faust's legendary words, "two souls are dwelling, alas!, in my breast,"[29] appears to be indeed a perfectly proper description of the *cardiac amalgam* pulsating in the human breast in two different modes, tempers and rhythms in a hybrid manner.

Transimmanence...

For Aurobindo, as well as for Indian philosophies in general, the not yet manifest sheaths that have not yet been activated in a lived-body are actually *virtual* possibilities of nature. Virtual possibilities have not yet been actualized but eventually could matter in a future to come. Considered from the perspective of eternity, they are *substantial* possibilities *of nature* herself in the very sense in which Spinoza defined the words 'substance' and 'nature' in his *Ethics* (Curley 1994). Virtual possibilities are considered from a *substantial* point of view, precisely when one views nature *sub specie aeternitatis*, that is, under the gaze of eternity. Can *she*, in her *eternal* (evolutionary) unfolding, *once* matter the possibility one has in mind? Questioning nature in such a manner, sub specie aeternitatis, is precisely that *third-kind-of-knowledge* which Spinoza called *scientia intuitiva* (Curley 1994; Waibel 2012; Böhler 2012). On the other hand, substantial possibilities of nature are precisely virtual, insofar as they are potentials of nature herself, which have not yet been actualized so far in the evolutionary upraising of nature herself (*natura naturata*) but could matter once in a future to come (*natura naturans*). Insofar as virtual possibilities have *not yet* been *actualized* in nature, they are indeed *virtually real*, in the very sense in which Deleuze defined the virtual plane of being in *Difference and Repetition*. "*The virtual is not actual, but it is fully real in so far as it is virtual.*" (Deleuze 1994, 208)

---

28   On the notion amalgam see also Latour 2004; Debaise 2017.
29   Original German: "zwei Seelen wohnen, ach!, in meiner Brust" (Goethe 1949, Vers 1112).

Virtually real possibilities are eventually real. They are about to matter. And the event of their mattering is precisely the decisive moment in which they are actualizing their virtual reality.

To claim that possibilities have the ontological status of being virtual-real implies that eternal possibilities are finally self-existent entities (*svayambhū*) which rest *beyond our manifest nature* (natura naturata) but *not necessarily beyond the substantial regime of Nature*. That is, nature considered from an integral perspective sub specie aeternitatis (Böhler 2022). The virtual plane of nature therefore possesses, in a strict sense, a *transimmanent character* (Agamben 1999; Steinweg 2012). Virtual possibilities *currently transcend* the constitution of one's *manifest* nature (*vyakta*), but they are nevertheless *immanent* possibilities of one's not-yet-manifest (*avyakta*) nature which eventually matters in a future to come (*Para-nature*). From the perspective of eternity; that is, from a substantial, integral point of view, the not-yet-manifest part of one's nature is always already an integral part of one's nature. What Spinoza once called *amor dei intellectualis*, the intellectual love of God, in which the scientia intuitiva unfolds a third kind of knowledge which intuits everything sub specie aeternitatis, apparently comes very close to Aurobindo's Vedic vision of the overall architecture of the gnostic heart which culminates in the three-fold-vision-of-time, *trikāladṛṣṭi*.

Nietzsche's Day-break...

The ontological dilemma of the trans-immanent nature of the virtual has been brought to a striking point on the cover-page of Nietzsche's book *The Daybreak* (1997), where he placed the overall motto of his book by quoting the following sentence from the *Ṛgveda*. "There will have been given so many daybreaks which have not yet gleamed. Rigveda." (English translation A. B.)[30]

What is core for us concerning this quote is the *materialism-of-the-dangerous-perhaps* that Nietzsche's citation from the *Ṛgveda* implies. When Nietzsche, in *Beyond Good and Evil*, charac-

---

30   German Original: "Es gibt so viele Morgenröthen, die noch nicht geleuchtet haben. Rigveda" (Nietzsche 1997, coverpage).

terized the new species of philosophers of the future to be philosophers of a "*dangerous perhaps*" (Nietzsche 2002, 6), he was actually
highlighting the fact that philosophers of the future will aspire the
mattering of *contingent events* that per-haps happen (Derrida 1997).
The aspirations which arose in the wake of this new species of philosophers of the future from the bottom of their hearts are obviously drawn toward a virtual future. But the *mattering* of the virtual
future, which they currently approach in their heart-minds, is still
a matter of eventuality. *Event-ually* it will have taken place, once.
Event-ually not.

It is therefore no coincidence that Nietzsche, with his fine taste
for words, in the German original starts the quote literally with the
words "Es gibt Morgenröthen...": "Day breaks are given..." They are
given when the virtual cloud of possibilities is *in fact* collapsing, to
borrow a formulation from quantum physics (Barad 2007, 280; Traxler 2017).[31]

Contrary to many traditional *darśanas* in the history of Indian
philosophies and fully in agreement with Nietzsche's attempt to
overcome "The ascetic Ideal" (Nietzsche 1967, 97-163; Böhler 2017),
Aurobindo does not call on the plane of the virtual to finally reach
merely a peaceful state of mind, as classical Patañjali-Yoga would
hold.[32] On the contrary. Aurobindo's Integral-Yoga rather demands
a *Sādhak* (Yoga-Practitioner) to enter the silence and calmness of a
virtual void that rests beyond (para) one's *manifest* Nature with the
trans-immanent aspiration of one's heart to actually mobilize, in-
flame and induce virtual possibilities to matter. In this very sense
one might claim that the poetic heart, in its deepest depths, cares
for the mattering of events that so far have not yet flashed by virtue
of burning and inflaming what Aristotle called first matter: The first
and most sublime form of yet unformed matter, *prote-hyle* (πρώτη

---

31   In their contribution in this volume, Tanja Traxler & Reinhold A. Bertlmann give us a view on this matter from the perspective of quantum-physics.

32   The classical definition of yoga in Patañjali's Yoga-Sūtra considers yoga
"yogaś citta-vṛtti nirodaḥ". Yoga is the calming down (*nirodaḥ*) of turbu-
lent movements (*vṛtti*) operative in one's mind (*citta*). (Translation A.B.).

ὕλη), in which matter is 'present' in a virtual state of matter—materia-in-potentia. South-Asian philosophies have addressed this root-matter as *mūla-prakṛti*. It is a virtual, shapeless form of matter; not an empty void (*śūnyatā*), but a space full of potentiality, where the particularization of physical particles (*annamayakośa*) actually originates (Böhler 2024; Jung 1996, 18, 20).

The Virtual,...

Insofar as the epic poems *Savitri* and *Thus spoke Zarathustra* are no narratives of the world as one finds it completed (*natura naturata*), but rather of the world *in its making* (*natura naturans*), they both aspire to a future that, at first, has to be addressed *poetically*, precisely because it had to be called into being first in the constitution of a poetic language. Referring to something that *event-ually* takes place—perhaps it will happen, perhaps not—both artist-philosophers had to hold in advance the speculative belief and confidence (*śraddhā*) that Nature herself will be capable of realizing the future they are striving for, at least *sub specie aeternitatis* (Nietzsche 2002; Derrida 1997; Waibel 2012).

Nietzsche, the other artist-philosopher...

According to Lou Andreas Salomé's description of Friedrich Nietzsche's works (Salomé 1894), Nietzsche himself must be considered a precursor (Paulo De Assis and Lucia D'Errico 2019; Böhler and Granzer 2017, 193-213) of the new species of philosophers to come which he envisioned in *Beyond Good and Evil*. Precisely because he followed already the *aesthetic image of thought*[33] (Deleuze 1994, 129-167) he had described as the typical feature of the new species of the philosophers of the future he saw arriving. Whenever Nietzsche performed thinking, writes Salomé (1894, 70), he actually did *taste* simultaneously the flavor (*rasa*) of the thing he was addressing in a mindful manner. Regardless whether the object was physical, psychic, mental or supra-mental. His sense of taste and artistic temperament appar-

---

33 See the introduction in this book.

ently forced him to continuously produce a *"bodily-felt-sense"* (Skora 2007, 421) toward anything that crossed his mind—quasi-automatically, in passive synthesis,[34] that is to say, machine-like: How does the atmosphere among people taste? Which bodily-felt-sense does a thought trigger? Does a particular idea taste sound or contrecœur? How does an artefact move us—sensually, bodily, aesthetically, cordially? Does a word or artefact reach one's heart at all? And if so, which registers and regions of the heart? Or does it stimulate no feeling at all?

Even the most abstract logical ideas, says Lou A. Salomé, triggered an emotive response in Nietzsche's heart. Which apparently proves that he himself was an artist-philosopher who already possessed this new, contrary taste to that of most ancient philosophers who still followed the ascetic ideal (Böhler 2017, 2019d; Sommer 2019). In other words, Nietzsche was no longer thinking *against* the sense of taste in his heart but in co-operation with it. Thereby he literally became an aesthete in the very sense of the Sanskrit term *sahṛdaya*, which literally means "somebody with a (sublime, sensitive, purified, well-formed) heart-mind".

Educating one's taste...

In her book Actors and the Art of Performance: Under Exposure (2016), Valerie [Granzer] has shown how actors and actresses develop an extremely fine taste of the environmental circumstances they are actually exposed to on stage: The light- and soundscapes they are physically embedded in while acting on stage. The requisites, costumes, and the stage design, which they experience as non-human co-actors on stage. And of course, actors and actresses possess a very fine taste for the social relations with the other performers and the audience while acting. It is a sublimation of one's sense of taste that actually takes place in the art of acting.

At the same time, their artistic awareness is not just sensitively aware of external relations but also of the animation of their souls, which goes hand in hand with the art of acting on stage. The intox-

---

34   On "passive synthesis" see Husserl 2001; Deleuze 1994; Böhler 2005.

ication of the performers actually catapults them out of their familiarity with themselves, into a dimension which can frighten them,
precisely because it de-subjectivates them by virtue of opening an
uncanny dimension of themselves within themselves (Valerie [Gran-
zer] 2016, 5-15).

But even offstage, in one's everydayness, people taste the flavor of
the relational affairs they find themselves environmentally, socially
and mentally (Guattari 2000) ex-posed[4] to and actively engaged with.
For instance, what it tastes like when much-needed water is missing. Or what a shitstorm tastes like that circulates on the Internet.
Or what it tastes like when one suddenly loses one's job in a certain
situation. Or what it tastes like when one gets a new job after having
been unemployed for a long time. Or what it tastes like when one falls
in love, writes a book, grasps a new thought etc. A lived-body actually
feels the *worldwide* circumstances it is environmentally, socially and
mentally embedded in and actively engaged with in its heart, while it
finds itself atmospherically tuned in to a certain situated mood and
manner.[35]

According to ancient Indian philosophies, the *relational affair*
with the rays of the sun, for instance, does actually trigger a special
feeling within a lived-body, insofar as it milks (Aurobindo 1998, 125,
126, 217, 236) the rays of the sun under its skin (White 2009). The *experienced* temperature of the sunlight might actually taste hot, cold,
warm, bright, or even too hot, too cold, too warm, too bright for the
lived-body that has been affected by the rays of the sun on its bodily
surface (Folkers 2022). But what a lived-body is currently experienc-
ing in a bodily-felt-sense under such a condition is neither the sun as
an 'object' at a certain distance that would exist entirely separated
from the sensing 'subject,' nor the lived-body as a so-called 'subject'
that would exist entirely separated from the affecting sun, but the
relational affair among them. It is no wordless subject that currently
feels too hot, too cold, quite warm etc. but an environmental, rela-

---

35 The German word for mood, Stimmung, still echoes the waving nature
of atmospheric bodies. Cf. Böhler 2024; Ingold 2016; https://contingent-
agencies.net/contingent-agencies symposium/ (last accessed: 12 June
2025).

tional subjectivity (Guattari 2000; Manning and Massumi 2014) which finds itself in a relation to the sun. Only after an environmental contact with the sunrays has 'objectively' been established, a lived-body is actually capable of 'subjectively' measuring, sensing, tasting and feeling its specific relation toward the sunlight in a bodily-felt-sense of the temperature that currently shows up in the relation of the affecting sun *and* the affected body. It is still the sun that makes us feel hot while we 'milk' its rays and finally taste the quality of our bodily relation toward it (Ingold 2016; Derrida 2005).

We therefore consider taste not to be just a subjective, secondary quality (Locke 1997) or even simply a private affair within an individual that would take place merely inside a body but a primary quality of an intimate relational affair that actually takes place among more than one body in an environmental manner (Debaise 2017; Stengers 2011; Deleuze 1988; Bösel and Wiemer 2020; Hörl and Burton 2017; Böhme 1995; Angerer, Bösel and Ott 2014; Massumi 2010; Folkers 2022).

A *sahṛdaya*, that is somebody thinking mindfully in companionship with one's heart, can even emphatically feel in the place of many others. Somebody else may experience a shitstorm on the Internet, but nevertheless one can compassionately (Nancy 2008, 39, 149) feel what it tastes like in place of the other. A *sahṛdaya* from the rank of Fyodor Dostoevsky was even capable of emphatically and compassionately feeling like a multitude of characters at once in his writings. For example, how bitter it tastes when one lives in the midst of a milieu that finds pleasure in torturing others.

It is important to emphasize that the concept of *sahṛdaya* in Indian philosophy and aesthetics has also a strong social-political value; hence it is written, for instance in the Śiva-Sūtra, that once a mind enters into the emptiness of the heart, "(all sense of being) a brahmin, Ksatriya or (even) a murderer [ceases]" (Dyczkowski 1992, 42). Cast and gender distinctions have long been relevant for the social sphere, but they are left behind as being insignificant once somebody enters the aesthetical sphere of a *sahṛdaya*; of somebody in touch with the heart (Lakshmanjoo 2000, 105).

As Martin K. Skora (2007, 424) has convincingly shown in the context of Kashmir Shaivism, touching a thing or an idea in a self-reflexive manner (*vimarśa*, from the root *mr̥ś*, to touch) should not be considered to be merely a *cognitive* sort of abstract knowledge in the context of ancient Indian philosophies in general and in the philosophies of Kashmir Shaivism in particular but rather the *aesthetic experience of a bodily felt-sense* (Skora 2007, 432, 444; Muller-Ortega 1989).

Epilogue...

I would like to conclude my article with some aphorisms by which I practice a style of thinking that attempts to grasp the mattering of a thought in actu. Thinking thus becomes an experimental laboratory of thoughts in their making. A kind of thought-image (German: Denkbild).

*****

In the laboratory of thought, where matters unthought-of so far are made thinkable, one is thinkingly confronted with the driving forces of thought. Here, thoughts no longer blaze their trail independent of one's instincts, of one's desires, of one's desiring-production, of one's dreams, but in communion with them. Thinking consults its own desires when thinking while thinking. In this case one thinks with one's heart and one's mind.

*****

On his long peregrinations in the forbidden, Nietzsche eventually realized that "most conscious thinking of a philosopher ... is secretly guided by his instincts and forced into certain channels" (Nietzsche 2002, 7).

*****

For Nietzsche, as for Spinoza, thinking is not opposed to the affects; rather, it writes them out in full. Articulates them. Lets them, the affects, have a say and thus get a voice. By challenging–wholly in the sense of Sigmund Freud–the independence of cogito from the souterrains of our corporeality he has installed a new concept of thought that even includes a corporeal foundation of logic.

*****

"Even behind all logic and its autocratic posturings stand valuations or, stated more clearly, physiological requirements for the preservation of a particular type of life." (Nietzsche 2002, 7) For Nietzsche, even logical considerations do not take place in dissociation from the conatus of those who execute these considerations. Does this aphorism not bear clear witness to Nietzsche's Spinozism?

*****

But what is meant by a lived-body striving to remain in being? Spinoza strongly insists that being is not identical with existence. To strive to remain in being? Is this probably supposed to mean to strive to chronically remain within the loop of the eternal unfolding of Nature herself?

*****

"I will not stop emphasizing a tiny little fact that these superstitious men are loath to admit: that a thought comes when 'it' wants, and not when 'I' want. It is, therefore, a falsification of the facts to say that the subject 'I' is the condition of the predicate 'think.' It thinks: but to say the 'it' is just that famous old 'I' – well that is just an assumption or opinion, to put it mildly, and by no means an 'immediate certainty.'" (Nietzsche 2002, 17)

*****

"Is intuition not acknowledged as a legitimate argument in decision processes in many situations in life?" (Böhler 2019, 243)

*****

Should artistic research in this case be nearer to our life-world than 'purely' scientific research methods which downgrade intuition to a private feeling, *as-if* by feeling one did not quote a historically generated heritage we share with others wherever someone feels something within one's lived-body from the perspective of a given cultural background? (Cf. Böhler 2019, 243).

*****

Is not intoxication just that condition of the lived-body when it experiences this being-outside-itself within its own lived-body? Is this not confusing?

*****

The orgiastic: one is outside oneself, wholly in touch with others. One feels the other, within one's own lived-body. It is confusing indeed... (Cf. Böhler 2019, 244).

*****

Nietzsche thinks intoxication as the mind's most primordial experience in which one is entirely in touch 'with-oneself' only, because it allows for the organism's 'getting out of itself.' Intoxication is an intimate form of ec-stasis. It opens up the organism, makes it ec-static. In a state of intoxication, a lived-body opens up to its own surrounding. It becomes world-wide, open to the world, porous, flesh; part of a world intimately shared with others. "As soon as one gets outside oneself, one senses the world in a Dionysian, that is to say, artistic manner." (Böhler 2019, 244)

*****

"All seeing is essentially perspective, and so is all knowing. The more emotions we allow to speak in a given matter, the more different eyes we can put on in order to view a given spectacle, the more complete will be our conception of it, the greater our 'objectivity'. But to eliminate our will entirely, once and for all to unhinge our affects, be it that we were able to do so: how? Would that not mean castrating our instinct?..." (Nietzsche 1967, 119)

*****

In *Beyond Good and Evil* Nietzsche gets to the point regarding his new, arts-based concept of thought that understands itself as and antipode and counter-ideal to the ascetic ideal of a thinking becoming fleshless–he writes: "I have kept a close eye on the philosophers and read between their lines for long enough to say to myself: the greatest part of conscious thought must still be attributed to instinctive activity, and this is even the case for philosophical thought." (Nietzsche 2002, 6-7)

*****

"In this passage Nietzsche challenges the possibility of entirely isolating and separating the sphere of thought from the plane of our corporeal being-in-the-world. Because, for him, thinking is too intimately entangled with the driving forces of our corporeality and guided into certain directions by them–in secret." (Böhler 2019, 243)

*****

This is exactly what to me seems to be a decisive feature of a philosophy about to ascertain itself as artistic research. It is no longer enough to keep the research problems away from one's own lived-body in the 'good' old ascetic manner, as if one were not corporeally affected and touched by the game of asking questions in which one is involved, seeking, researching, thinking, enquiring, investigating, reflecting, analyzing, sorting, musing, feeling ...

*****

"In that case, is it not the development of the history of ideas to which 'my' idea of thinking philosophy as artistic research is indebted to? One *captures* a thought when one thinks it *oneself.*" But one is also part "of a conceptual field in which one thinks, *with* which one thinks, when one is thinking." (Böhler 2019, 241)

*****

"When one researches artistically, one cogitates, sorts, reflects, analyses problems *rationally*, but one also follows one's own intuition, and now and then one even obeys one's instincts if one thinks and researches *artistically*. Is not this moment of research commonly suppressed methodically when one thinks *about* research *scientifically*?" (Böhler 2019, 243-244)

*****

Arts-based research obviously demands a double reading by which one engages rationally as well as affectively in the research one is dealing with. On the one hand, one is required—as Deleuze writes in *Spinoza. Practical Philosophy*—to set out soberly on the "search for the idea of the whole and the unity of the parts" of the research one dedicates oneself to; on the other hand, in parallel one is likewise required to get involved with an affective reading, "without an idea of the whole". A reading "into which one is dragged or put", because it puts one's lived-body "into motion or at rest, moves intensely or calms down, according to the speed of this or that part." (Deleuze 1988, 167f.)

*****

It was not only Spinoza and the doctrines of affection and the need for a scientia intuitiva which he developed in the third and fifth book of his *Ethics*. Of course, it was also the philosophy of Friedrich Nietzsche which became more and more crucial for the question that struck my mind and finally the depth of my heart.

*****

Artistic research is a playful, associative, experimental form of re-search, on the wait of something ready to matter. Is this not exactly what Deleuze meant when in his Bacon book he wrote that painting and music are not about the "reproduction or invention of forms, but about the capturing of forces" (Deleuze 2003, 56)

*****

I am still brooding over my research proposal and asking myself whether research on the heart should not be negotiated in public space? The research festivals Philosophy On Stage at Brut Wien and Adishakti (Tamil Nadu), which we plan to realize in the framework of our current research project, was supposed to tackle precisely this aspect: philosophy, as artistic research, should not always take place behind closed doors. Its research is public. The public itself has to be taken seriously as a core moment of the research performance itself.

*****

"For the sensitive observer or listener who commands an aesthetic sense, there is a very beautiful term in Sanskrit: *sahṛdaya*. *Sahṛdaya* literally means as much as 'one who has a heart' ... One who has a heart also is capable of taking up the prevailing mood of a work of art." (Bäumer 2016, 92, translated by AB) Well then, heart, take your leave and be well!

Literature

Agamben, Giorgio. 1999. *Potentialities. Collected Essays. In Philoso-phy.* Stanford: Stanford University Press.

Angerer, Marie-Luise, Bernd Bösel and Michaela Ott, eds. 2014. *Timing of Affect. Epistemologies, Aesthetics, Politics.* Zürich: Di-aphanes.

Aristoteles. 1931. *De anima*. Oxford: Clarendon Press.

Aristotle. 1966. *Metaphysics*. Bloomington: Indiana University Press.

Aurobindo, Ghose. 1991. *Complete Works of Sri Aurobindo. Hymns of the Mystic Fire*. Pondicherry: Ashramverlag.

Aurobindo, Ghose. 1997. *The Complete Works of Sri Aurobindo. Savitri, a Legend and a Symbol*. Vol. 33 and 34. Pondicherry: Ashramverlag.

Aurobindo, Ghose. 1998. *The Complete Works of Sri Aurobindo. The Secret of the Veda*. Vol. 15. Pondicherry: Ashramverlag.

Aurobindo, Ghose. 2001. *The Complete Works of Sri Aurobindo. The Records of Yoga*. Vol. 10,11. Pondicherry: Ashramverlag.

Aurobindo, Ghose. 2005. *The Complete Works of Sri Aurobindo. The Life Divine*. Vol. 21,22. Pondicherry: Ashramverlag.

Aurobindo, Ghose. 1999. *The Complete Works of Sri Aurobindo. The Synthesis of Yoga*. Vol. 23, 24. Pondicherry: Ashramverlag.

Banerji, Debashish. 2012. *Seven Quartets of Becoming*. Los Angeles: Nalanda International.

Banerji, Debashish. 2020. *Meditations on the Īśa-Upaniṣad. Tracing the philosophical vision of Sri Aurobindo Ghose*. Pink Integer Books: Concord, CA.

Barad, Karen. 2007. *Meeting the Universe Halfway – Quantum Physics and the Entanglement of Matter and Meaning*. Durham & London: Duke University Press.

Beldio, Patrick. 2015. "The Androgynous Visual Piety of the Mother and Sri Aurobindo and St. Clare and St. Francis." In *Journal of Hindu-Christian Studies*: Vol. 28, Article 4. https://doi.org/10.7825/2164-6279.1603.

Bäumer, Bettina. 2016. "Die flüssige Natur ästhetischer Erfahrung." In *Polylog*, 35, 89–95.

Bennett, Jane. 2010. *Vibrant Matter. A Political Ecology of Things*. Durham/London: Duke University Press.

Böhler, Arno. 2005. *Singularitäten. Vom zu-reichenden Grund der Zeit. Vorspiel einer Philosophie der Freundschaft*. Wien: Passagen.

Böhler, Arno, Kruschkova, Krassimira and Susanne Valerie Granzer (eds.). 2014. *Wissen wir, was ein Körper kann? Rhizomatische Körper in Religion, Kunst, Philosophie*. Bielefeld: transcript.

Böhler, Arno and Susanne Valerie [Granzer]. 2017. "Corpus Delicti #2 // Untimely Precursors." In *The Dark Precursor: Deleuze and*

Artistic- Research, edited by P. de Assis and P. Giudici. Vol. 1., 193-213. Leuven: Leuven University Press. https://doi.org/10.2307/j.ctt21c4rxx.19.

Böhler, Arno and Valerie S. Granzer. 2021. "In Love with Art & Philosophy. Zwischen Kunst & Philosophie." In *Knowing in Performing. Artistic Research in Music and the Performing Arts*, edited by Huber et al., 161-184. Bielefeld: transcript. https://doi.org/10.14361/9783839452875-013.

Böhler, Arno. 2012. "Deleuze in Spinoza – Spinoza in Deleuze. Wissen wir, was das Medium Körper kann?" In *Affektenlehre und amor Dei intellectualis: die Rezeption Spinozas im Deutschen Idealismus, in der Frühromantik und in der Gegenwart*, edited by Violetta L. Waibel et al., 167-186. Hamburg: Meiner.

Böhler, Arno. 2017. "Immanence: A Life... Friedrich Nietzsche." In *Performance Philosophy*, 3 (3), 576-603. https://doi.org/10.21476/PP.2017.33163.

Böhler, Arno. 2019a. "Becoming Worldwide: Transdisciplinary forms of Collaborations in Philosophy and the Arts – A case study." In *The Future of Education and Labor*, edited by G. Bast, E. G. Carayannis and D. Campbell, 203-225. Berlin: Springer. https://doi.org/10.1007/978-3-030-26068-2_12.

Böhler, Arno. 2019b. "Philosophy as Artistic Research. Artist Philosophers." In *Artistic Research: Charting a Field in Expansion*, edited by Paulo de Assis, and Lucia D'Errico, 236-248. London New York: Rowman & Littlefield International.

Böhler, Arno. 2019c. "Philosophy AS artistic research: Philosophy On Stage." In *Journal for Artistic Research*, 17. https://doi.org/10.22501/jarnet.0014. (last accessed: 12 June 2025)

Böhler, Arno. 2019d. "Denken des Gemüts: Spinoza, Nietzsche, Abhinavagupta." In *Liebe und Hass in Philosophie, Religion und Literatur*. Wiener Jahrbuch der Philosophie (Band 50), 79-98. Wien: New Academic Press. http://dx.doi.org/10.15496/publikation-78072.

Böhler, Arno. 2022. "Sri Aurobindo Ghose – Vom Herz des integralen Yoga." In *Integrale Anthropologie*, edited by Andreas Mascha and Hubert Seubert, Band 1: Grundlagen, 57-88. München: Verlag Andreas Mascha.

Böhler, Arno. 2025. "KHÔRA. Sensing Tasting Notating Reflecting Atmospheres." In *Contingent Agencies*, edited by Nikolaus Gansterer and Alex Arteaga. Berlin: De Gruyter.

Böhme, Gernot. 1995. *Atmosphäre*. Suhrkamp, Frankfurt a.M.

Bösel, Bernd, and Serjoscha Wiemer (eds.). 2020. *Affective Transformations. Politics – Algorithms – Media*. Lüneburg: Meson Press. https://doi.org/10.14619/1655.

Curley, Edwin. 1994. *A Spinoza Reader. The Ethics and other works*. Princeton: Princeton University Press.

De Assis, Paulo and Lucia D'Errico. 2019. *Artistic Research: Charting a Field in Expansion*. London New York: Rowman & Littlefield International.

Debaise, Didier. 2017. *Nature as Event. The Lure of the Possible*. Durham: Duke University Press. https://doi.org/10.2307/j.ct v116898h.

Deleuze, Gilles. 1986. *Foucault*. Minnesota: University of Minnesota Press.

Deleuze, Gilles and Félix Guattari. 1994. *What is Philosophy?* Translated by Hugh Tomlinson and Graham Burchell. New York: Columbia University Press.

Deleuze, Gilles and Félix Guattari. 1987. *A Thousand Plateaus. Capitalism and Schizophrenia*. London: Continuum.

Deleuze, Gilles. 1988. *Spinoza: Practical Philosophy*. Translated by R. Hurley. San Francisco: City Lights Books.

Deleuze, Gilles. 1994. *Difference and Repetition*. New York: Columbia University Press.

Deleuze, Gilles. 2003. *Francis Bacon. The logic of sensation*. Translated by Daniel W. Smith, London/New York: continuum.

Derrida, Jacques. 1992. *The Other Heading. Reflexions on Today's Europe*. Bloomington: Indiana University Press.

Derrida, Jacques. 1997. *Politics of Friendship*. London/New York: Verso.

Derrida, Jacques. 2005. *On Touching–Jean-Luc Nancy*. Translated by Christine Irizarry. Stanford: Stanford University Press.

Deshpande, Ganesh Tryambak. 1989. *Abhinavagupta*. New Delhi: Sahitya Akademi.

Dyczkowski, Mark (ed.). 1992. *The Aphorisms of Śiva. The Śiva-Sūtra with Bhāskara's Commentary, the Vārttika SUNY Series in Tantric Studies*. New York: State University of New York Press.

Fichte, J. G. 2012. *Gesamtausgabe der Bayrischen Akademie der Wissenschaften*. Band 1,4: Werke. Frommann Holzboog.

Folkers, Andreas. 2022. "Das Soziale als Gefüge. Der Deleuze-Effekt in der Soziologie." In *Soziale Denkweisen aus Frankreich*, edited by H. Delitz. Wiesbaden: Springer Fachmedien. https://doi.org/10.1007/978-3-658-36949-1_14.

Foucault, Michel. 1977. "Theatrum philosophicum." In *Der Faden ist gerissen*, 21–58. Berlin: Merve.

Goethe, J. W. 1949. "Faust. Eine Tragödie." In *Goethes Werke. Hamburger Ausgabe in 14 Bänden*, Bd. 3: Dramatische Dichtungen, Bd. 1. Hamburg: Christian Wegner Verlag.

Gnoli, Raniero. 1985. *The Aesthetic Experience according to Abhinavagupta*. Varanasi: Chowkhamba Sanskrit Series Office.

Gonda, Jan. 1963. *The Vision of the Vedic Poets*. The Hague: Mouton & Co.

Gonda, Jan. 1977. *A History of Indian Literature*. Vol. 2, fasc. 1, *Medieval Religious Literature in Sanskrit*. Wiesbaden: Otto Harrassowitz.

Granzer, Susanne Valerie. 2016. *Actors and the Art of Performance: Under Exposure*. Bielefeld: transcript. https://doi.org/10.1057/9781137596345.

Guattari, Félix. 2000. *The Three Ecologies*. Translated by I. Pindar and P. Sutton. London: Continuum.

Hagner, Michael. 2008. *Homo Cerebralis. Der Wandel vom Seelenorgan zum Gehirn*. Frankfurt a.M.: Suhrkamp Verlag.

Heraklit. 2004. *Die Fragmente der Vorsokratiker*. Greek and German by Hermann Diels, edited by Walther Kranz. 17th ed. Berlin: Weidmannsche Verlagsbuchhandlung, 1922, Vol. 1, 77-102.

Hörl, Erich and Edward Burton (eds.). 2017. *General Ecology: The New Ecological Paradigm*. London New York: Bloomsbury Academic.

Husserl, Edmund. 2001. *Analyses Concerning Passive and Active Synthesis: Lectures on Transcendental Logic* (Husserliana: Edmund Husserl – Collected Works, 9). Dordrecht: Springer Science + Business Media.

Ingold, Tim. 2016. "Lighting up the Atmosphere." In *Elements of architecture: Assembling archaeology, atmosphere and the performance of building spaces*, edited by Mikkel Bille and Tim Flohr Sørensen, 163-176. Abington: Routledge. https://doi.org/10.5840/chiasmi20121410.

Jung, Carl Gustav. 1996. *The Psychology of Kundalini Yoga. Notes of the Seminar Given in 1932 by C. G. Jung*, edited by Sonu Shamdasani. Bollingen Series XCIX. Princeton: Princeton University Press.

Kimerer, L. LaMothe. 2006. *Nietzsche's Dancers. Isadora Duncan, Martha Graham, and the Revaluation of Christian Values*. New York: Palgrave Macmillan. https://doi.org/10.1057/9781403977267.

Lakshmanjoo, Swami. 2000. *Kashmir Shaivism: The Secret Supreme*. Lakshmanjoo Academy.

Latour, Bruno. 2004. *Politics of Nature: How to Bring the Sciences into Democracy*. Translated by Catherine Porter. Cambridge: Harvard University Press.

Locke, John. 1997. *An Essay concerning Human Understanding*. London: Penguin Books.

Manning, Erin, and Brian Massumi. 2014. *Thought in the Act: Passages in the Ecology of Experience*. Minnesota: University of Minnesota Press. https://doi.org/10.5749/minnesota/9780816679669.001.0001.

Maharaj, Ayon. 2018. *Infinite Paths to Infinite Reality*. Oxford: Oxford University Press.

Mascha, Andreas and Harald Seubert (eds.). 2022. *Integrale Anthropologie. Band 1. Grundlagen*. München: Verlag Andreas Mascha.

Massumi, Brian. 2010. *Ontomacht. Kunst, Affekt und das Ereignis des Politischen*. Berlin: Merve Verlag.

Merleau-Ponty, Maurice. 1964. *Le Visible et l'invisible, suivi de notes de travail*, edited by Claude Lefort. Paris: Gallimard. Muller-Ortega, Paul Eduardo. 1989. *The Triadic Heart of Siva. Kaula Tantricism of Abhinavagupta in the Non-Dual Shaivism of Kashmir*. New York: State University of New York Press.

Nancy, Jean-Luc. 2002. A L'Ecoute. Paris: Édition Galilée.

Nancy, Jean-Luc. 2008. *Corpus*. New York: Fordham University Press.

Nietzsche, Friedrich. 1985. *Nietzsche. Thus Spoke Zarathustra.* Translated and with a Preface by Walter Kaufmann. New York: Penguin Book.

Nietzsche, Friedrich. 1967. *On the Genealogy of Morals,* edited by Walter Kaufmann. New York: Vintage Books.

Nietzsche, Friedrich. 1997. *Daybreak. Thoughts on the Prejudices of Morality.* Cambridge: Cambridge University Press.

Nietzsche, Friedrich. 2002. *Beyond Good and Evil,* edited by Rolf-Peter Horstmann and Judith Norman. New York: Cambridge University Press.

Oßwald, Jonas. 2024. "Normalize and Control: Philosophy in Neoliberalism." In *Pli: The Warwick Journal of Philosophy,* 35, 17–45.

Parkes, Graham. 2009. "The Symphonic Structure of Thus Spoke Zarathustra." In *Nietzsche's Thus Spoke Zarathustra Before Sunrise,* edited by James Luchte. New York/London: Bloomsbury Publishing. https://doi.org/10.5040/9781472547187.ch-001.

Plato. 2021. 58D. *Plato, Plato's Timaeus.* Translated by David Horan. https://cdn.platonicfoundation.org/2021/04/platos-timaeus-english-translation-by-david-horan.pdf (last accessed: 12 June 2025)

Salomé, Lou Andreas. 1894. *Friedrich Nietzsche in seinen Werken.* Wien: Verlag von Carl Konegen.

Saxena, Sushil Kumar. 2010. *Aesthetics. Approaches, Concepts and Problems.* New Delhi: Sangeet Natak Akademi.

Schelling, F. W. J. 2000. *Gesamtausgabe der Bayrischen Akademie der Wissenschaften.* Band 1,5: Werke. Frommonn-holzboog.

Skora, Kerry Martin. 2007. "The Pulsating Heart and Its Divine Sense Energies: Body and Touch in Abhinavagupta's Trika." In *Numen,* 54(4), 420–458. https://doi.org/10.1163/156852707X244298.

Sommer and Heidelberger Akademie der Wissenschaften. 2019. *Historischer und kritischer Kommentar zu Friedrich Nietzsches Werken. Band 5.2, Kommentar zu Nietzsches "Zur Genealogie der Moral".* Berlin/Boston: De Gruyter.

Spinoza, Baruch de. 1994. "Ethics, Third Book." In *A Spinoza Reader: The Ethics and Other Works,* edited by E. Curley, 152–197. Princeton, NJ: Princeton University Press.

Spinoza, Baruch de. 2007. *Ethik in geometrischer Ordnung dargestellt.* Latin-German edition, translated and edited by Wolfgang Bartuschat. Hamburg: Felix Meiner Verlag.

Steinweg, Marcus. 2012. *Art between Immanence and Transcendence.* URL: http://www.flashartonline.com/interno.php?pagina=onweb_det&id_art=808&det=ok&titolo=art between-Immanence-and-Transcendence – Download 15.12.2022. (last accessed: 12 June 2025)

Stengers, Isabelle. 2011. *Thinking with Whitehead.* Cambridge MA: Harvard University Press.

Traxler, Tanja. 2017. "Immanence in Physics." In *Performance Philosophy Journal* (Vol 3). https://doi.org/10.21476/PP.2017.33146.

Tuncel, Yunus. 2020. "Diogenes." In *The Routledge Companion to Performance Philosophy,* edited by Alice Lagaay and Laura Cull, 322–325. London/New York: Routledge. https://doi.org/10.1386/jdsp_00067_5.

Tuncel, Yunus. 2021. *Nietzsche on Human Emotions.* Basel/Berlin: Schwabe. https://doi.org/10.24894/978-3-7965-4365-4.

Tuncel, Yunus, Durakoglu, Aysegul and Michael Steinmann (eds.). 2022. *Nietzsche and Music. Philosophical Thoughts and Musical Experience.* Newcastle upon Tyne: Cambridge Scholars Publishing.

Waibel, Violetta L. et al. 2012. *Affektenlehre und amor Dei intellectualis: die Rezeption Spinozas im Deutschen Idealismus, in der Frühromantik und in der Gegenwart.* Hamburg: Meiner.

White, David Gordon. 2009. "Yogic Rays: The Self-Externalization of the Yogi in Ritual, Narrative and Philosophy." In *Paragrana,* 18(1), 64–77. Available at: https://doi.org/10.1524/para.2009.0005.

Whitehead, Alfred North. 1979. *Process and Reality.* New York: Free Press.

Wolfers, Alex. 2017. "The Making of an Avatar: Reading Sri Aurobindo Ghose (1872–1950)." In *Religions of South Asia,* 11(2-3), 274-341. https://doi.org/10.1558/rosa.37030.

A Melancholic's Survival Kit

Avital Ronell

Against all odds, I am, it seems, still in the ring, pressed by an inexorable rope-a-dope technique of quasi-defeat. I depend on my coaches—those who keep me awake enough to have me take the hits—to get back on the ropes. As a survival technique, landing punches in this back-and-forth of borrowed stamina can be wearing, clocking out, on a theoretical plane, with the exhaustion of Metaphysics. Slapped around and Wiped out, I have my complaints to air. For instance, I am chronically annoyed that philosophy has wasted so much of our time on the pursuit of Truth, when the drawn-out matter of its status and overreach indicates the least of our necessities in the face of the outrageous repertoire of human <u>cruelty</u>—an unrelenting combination of dispositions that pummels us without end.

This philosophical obsession with truth-hunting, a stubborn orientation that separates it from literature and art in the widest sense, may require another perspective, however, if we are to get a handle on the complications that face us henceforth. In one of the earlier rounds of his thought, Jean-Luc Nancy pinpointed, by means of Hegel's "restless negative," our need for truth nowadays according to a specific slant, and against the temptation to seek consolation in philosophy (Nancy 2002). I would like to concede the point, for it is undeniable that we tend to seek refuge in edifying discourses offering solace, a habit that serves only to increase the misery of the world's predicament. Prompted by the Hegelian appropriation of the negative, Nancy's articulation pivots on a certain kind of courage that exposes the core of an inescapable ordeal—unsheltered, "we," in our singular-plurality, are thrown into the restless slams of Being. Philosophy should not be used as a "self-help" manual or sedative, a means of forgetting the violence delivered historically and accorded by its own stealth form of compliance. In this regard, the rhetorical contrivance of a "survival kit" needs to deal with the shattering collapse of our vocabu laries, their pretense of assuring groundedness, sovereignty, and subject, while bracing an obsolescing concept of the "world" and its corresponding globalizations. I have in mind a survival kit that somehow answers the impossible call of the negative without succumbing to the deluded exuberance of an accomplished rescue or the triumphalism of forgetting. Understanding that Hegel handed art its death certificate, and Nietzsche upped the ante with a notion of scientificity that more or less surpasses art, we enter a field of ongoing clashes that Heidegger would eventually complicate in his own way, rethinking the premises of an eviction notice served by Plato & co.

Ach! There are so many misgivings and serious deterrents constraining thought. Let me go on anyway, prompted by an aporetic suspension of doubt and an aptitude for shadow-boxing. Maybe I can pull up an attitude of grateful world-boundedness, if only as an enabling fiction, which is what a survival kit promises, even as it is skeptically cast.

*****

To the extent that I exist in my spareness as a being, I remain on the gratitude side of "Envy and Gratitude," tending to oversaturate others with thankfulness. This renders me suspicious, no doubt, for what could be concealed in the overload of thanking? What kinds of debts are pending symbolic payoff? Who, barring Heidegger, links thanking to thinking, and look at him ... What does the "gratitude pose" cover or repress, and how does philosophy—which doesn't quite pass any breathalyzer test, but is often drunk on the excess it can give—offer some sort of solace, or its shadow?

In an epoch pockmarked by extermination, one is grateful for the scrap of existence that has been thrown to the bizarre clump of life-clinging vitality that you are. I'm not saying it's easy or suicide-free to kick with life, or that one isn't strained by sheer anguish. One carries an overpopulated and frazzled community of those who didn't make it, still screaming in your invisible headphones.

If it's one's destiny, as my friend, Lacoue, asserts, to be abandoned and live out one's abandonment with no recourse, then the worst of it is that your unique package of persecution is not even addressed to you. You may sign for it at some reception desk of Being, knowing you are not a destination. And certainly not a destiny. You are no Wagner, and your persecutor is no Nietzsche, saying while shelving you that you are a destiny. You suffocate in your own corner, puffing along. How can I convey the tone here? I do not feel the supplement of jouissance that comes with pity for our predicament, suffocating and portentous. Part of me is over the pity parties the world throws for itself and celebrates on particularly grim occasions. A related part, the unaddressed and unWe part, doesn't really see a point of entry, doesn't feel the right to bloat into a story or sustained reflection. Yet I am trained to scour the unconscious of disaster areas, prodded by a sense of obligation, no matter how thin a subject imposes itself at this time, cutting a path for us. Such a prod, the Stoß, is part of our philosophical heritage, a traumatic punch delivered by an "aesthetic Erziehung." No one has asked philosophy to go on a rescue mission, even when it conspires with theology and nurtures a relation to art. But let us consider, if as a mere thought experiment, where it still proves capable of placing a call or sounding an alert.

Fragments from my survival kit

****

Ever on the alert, philosophy offers some emergency supplies of meaning when one feels especially exposed and vulnerable (cf. Ronell 2013). Very often, when the chips are down, philosophers can be a welcoming crew – well, not all of them. One has to sift and sort, find the byways, pass the arrogant know-it-all types, overtake the misogynists, manage the analytic philosophers, and leave in the dust those who claim to have a firm hold on truth. Not many are left standing, but they are the worthy ones. They stay close to poetry and music, and let themselves be instructed by literature's astonishing agility off the cognitive grid. There are things that we simply cannot know or understand, events that refuse representation. Literature lives with that sublime stall, and fires off extravagant hypotheses, basking in transgression and feats of rhetorical frontier-crossing. When philosophy becomes accomplice to such stretches of imagination and frees itself up from a certain number of constraints, it can turn in exhilarating and life-affirming performances. It can deliver even when you are seriously in the dumps, ready to call it a wrap. Then philosophical language, as if roused by frequencies of acute pain, vigorously invents a mesh of enabling fictions that helps you cope with incomprehensibilities. There is no getting around the fact of one's helplessness, the way we are faced in so many ways with strains of cruelty on the prowl and someone's killer instinct unleashed. Philosophy is especially good at not making sense, but of cutting through to our core survival issues, which never meant to stand on sense-making ceremony and, despite it all, manage to sideline an historical obsession with Truth, while calling for its uncompromising rigor. Other lines of urgency and unavoidable stalemate push through. Matters of *Sinn* and *Bedeutung* are still trailing a question mark, latecomers to the table. Plato invented hell and the perks of authority, part of a mostly symbolic intervention giving a weakened philosopher the upper hand, while other philosophers set up and took down the strictures of theodicy.[1] Nietzsche, harried by Spinoza, drove us beyond good and evil, throwing the whole onto-theological engine in reverse, creating a pileup that Heidegger & co. had to deal with. Some people may not consider such hard-hitting inquiries a reliable source of bracing, but I am making a point about the theoretical conditions for survival in the double sense that Benjamin gave to it, in terms both of *fortleben* and *überleben*. Derrida picked up the relay to give us a thinking of *sur-vie* and what straddles "*la vie la mort.*" When he switched over from sign to *trace*, Derrida's thought made our relation to language a matter of sur-vie, neither entirely ruled by the domains of life or death and yet inevitably inflected by their relation and fragile boundaries. On a different scale, upon reviewing my own dossier of reflections, I notice that I'm very concerned with the survival of the *misfittest*, those beings who barely scrape through.

---

1   I have addressed some of the finer points of these statements in *Loser Sons: Politics and Authority* (2012) with a view to Alexandre Kojève and Hannah Arendt's concerns about vanishing "authority," the tragic erosion of a strong philosophical invention.

Of course, many people tend to assume that the study itself of philosophy can bring one down, keeping one mired in dusty philology and speculative overreach – a charge that cannot be altogether denied. Yet, I have to hope it's the other way round: With all its faults, exhausting retakes and dreadful itinerary of assertion, I consider the philosophical attitude a basic component in my survival kit, pushing back on tyrannical dogma and moralistic overkill (cf. Ronell 2013). Even where it becomes despotic in some of its contentions, philosophy, in any case, has done the groundwork that takes to task any easy resolution of problems it faces. I don't see the philosophical attitude putting to rest incessant dilemma, especially when driven by Nietzsche's imperative to test things out and Husserl's sense of crisis.[2] This means that some trial balloons will burst, hypotheses will falter and, like technical tryouts, thought will have to retract its provisional certitude when tested to failure. Nietzsche makes it a point to secure the insecure nature of the experimental disposition that shares the domain of art and its philosophical training partner.

At times the philosophical probe comes face to face with a basic repertory of distress and our existential impoverishment.[3] It does not hesitate to get a close-up of forlornness, the shakes, and other signs of world-weary discomfort (cf. Ronell 2013). These themes arise whether philosophy ascribes or removes predicates of interiority to the so-called human subject. The problem is that we have become *beyond weary* in our exposition, on our last legs and legacy, and have no solid claims on reconstituting the world. Acts of philosophical promise in tandem with Earth herself, have been exhausted, over-dominated, made susceptible to distortion and misstep, steered by human forms of hubris and suicidal frivolity in the sense of Hölderlin's understanding of trespass. Still, there is reason – or unreason – to orient oneself toward the obsessive questioning of a questioning for which philosophy still stands, tormented by a re-

---

2   I have given more latitude to the disruption in and of philosophical thought due to testing and experimental structures in *The Test Drive* (2005).

3   *La détresse* would be a prominent facet of Philippe Lacoue-Labarthe's approach to impoverishment as a philosophical urgency, giving focus to Heidegger's later thoughts on *Armut* in Being.

lentless drive that remains excessive and very likely necessary, even where we are stomping on the continual splintering rumble of *Holzwege*. Maybe I am kidding myself, and questioning has lost its edge. It can be the case that no one cares anymore about the philosophical adventure, nor should they. What a congregation of masculinist exploits, pompous and unrelenting! But something locks me in, cleaves me to its preposterous craving for knowledge in an age that devalues and expropriates such claims. And, despite all disclaimers, I can't rule out the danger indicated by a call that still sirens up.

As a type of calling structure the philosophical attitude teaches us to accept and decline certain calls to inclination or action, to call up strength where none seems available. In some sectors, the philosophical attitude jumps off the page to take language into the streets, managing, together with inscriptions of street art, to re-circuit the dropped call of decency, a remnant of *care*, community and their social morphs. Poetry infiltrates social media on rare but poignant occasions to call out or reveal its concealment, lament a predicament of unbelonging. Philosophy maintains a mostly muted repertoire of calls that invite an exertion no longer necessarily part of its job description, though philosophers cannot seem to shake the temptation to heal and clear pathways, offer regimes and recipes for human nourishment and just governance, adjusted with the upgrades or offramps of contemporary refurbishment. Some of this language is admittedly jarring, for it holds witness to our paleonymic strictures, the way we are limited by an obsolescing vocabulary of claims. One cannot say with a theoretical straight face that we can rerun "imagination," "decency," "subject," etc., without adjustment or programmed blowout. For sheerly didactic purposes one still hitches a ride with obsolesced idioms and throwaway concepts, if only to dispense with them when they fall apart. But one cannot simply dispense with a store of inherited signifiers and infratextual relays. They stick to you and are part of the faltering body that we carry and care for. Besides, mere conceptual erosion does not deter philosophy, nor is it significantly fazed by the signs of its own "irrelevance" and philological hurdles. On the contrary.

Not always, and not consistently, not openly stated in the style of cards-on-the-table – but there's usually a *will-to-power element* pushing philosophical arrangements beyond any ostensible deadline, whether supported or not by a cognitive threshold. When tendencies of inherent *Selbstbehauptung* reach destinal proportions, philosophical intervention can prove calamitous, belonging to a habit of positing edging on prophesy, an often arrogant propensity of the philosophical attitude. One can see why some philosophical tribes take recourse to *mathèmes* and non-representational, objectivist formulae to get their thinking done, in some measure pushing past stubborn metaphysical barriers. I take all these disturbances, licenses, and puzzles into account, limiting the scope of what can be hoped for, putting the brakes on exhortations that can still be made as promises tendered. The very problem of survival qua survival barely can be said to survive today.

Like so many other "exscriptions" (Nancy), including formations such as art and music, philosophy carries a wide-ranging passport. To the extent that it folds in a state of compromised shortfall, often self-acknowledged, philosophy can be found *anywhere* – on the streets, in institutions of higher learning, under a car, on a subway sign, in a breakout room, in discussion with children, or in libraries housed by our penitentiary subculture. From the start, before Socrates walked the walk, philosophy has been easily displaced and rerouted. Set nowadays to travel according to stealth itineraries as well as overt proclamation, it shows up in the plumber's preference for the pre-Socratics or in a stylist's makeup kit as a thinking of rhetorical masking. In America, especially, I suppose, everyone "has" a philosophy or wants to have one, likes to bulk up on its aporetic difficulty/clarity. The people come equipped with a personalized version of *Lebensphilosophie*. I cannot explain why the most unschooled stances are still hospitable to philosophically-pitched statement, how it has come about that the type of inquiry associated with philosophy is vulnerable to widespread libidinal cathexes, particularly in a culture impatient for answers, primed on the shutdown of hesitation, calibrated on "moving on," known for being fast on the trigger, and being "over it." Unless the very desirability such inquiry excites takes us back time and again to the origins of philosophical thought as sheer astonishment – assuring not much more than a persistent vertigo of not-knowing. Perhaps, moreover, the connections it maintains with alien forms of being, the various modalities of estrangement that philosophy emphasizes, draws a seeker to unprobed borders, welcoming the unrecognizable encounter, the angel, the freak. Or perhaps the philosophical urge to clarify (or mystify), to explain while acknowledging the limits of knowing, the resolve to leave Gd alone while depending on the theological insistence – the way it stumbles into sacred peripheries of thought – keeps one captivated by the exultation of aporia.

Scrambling for its sovereignty, philosophy does not stand alone, having logged in a history of important if ambivalent alliances. Philosophy puts out a call to artistic practice, aesthetic valuation, and the reciprocal bounce of an extreme insight. Today more than ever. In the throes of the pandemic, we contend with a new cocktail of unintelligibilities mixed with ancient fears and forms of contamination, documents of intrusive violence. Along with theoretical comorbidities and the multifactorial collapses therein inscribed, one is invited to think of Artaud's work on theater and the plague, where the staging of calamity – a social abscess – is linked to contagion. It is no wonder that, when world plunges into its nothingness (Bataille's RIEN), philosophy hitches a ride on the death-drive, uniquely licensed out by aesthetic practice.

Whatever is left in something like philosophy faces its own annulment and the disappearance of notions associated with the "world' – a vexed entity that cannot be recomposed by fiat. In many ways the world, left behind, persists by the strength of what has been bequeathed to us as the philosophical. One cannot make claims in good faith about a "Weltanschauung" to the extent that neither *Welt* nor *Anschauung* survives finitude or seriously proposes to restabilize as viable expositions of Being.

*****

Ach! It is easy to lose one's bearings or any sense of safety. At times, the relation to loss is sprawling and does not stop with a recognizable person or object. Nearly every philosophy that we know has built a sanctuary, however remote and uncharted, for the experience of mourning. Sometimes a philosopher furtively mentions the pull of loss, even when trying, like Nietzsche, to affirm life's tragic edges and the necessity of mourning a lost friendship or the destructive operations (and operas) of love (cf. Ronell 2013). French philosopher Jean-Luc Nancy writes compellingly of shattered love and the loss of ground. He also admonishes, and I have oft repeated, that philosophy is never where you expect to find it. Similar to earth's coastlines, philosophy recedes from appointed places, finding different hideouts and morphologies, erodes as it dissipates, weakening its hold and boundaries before it bounds back differently. This recession of philosophy is accompanied by a type of leakage and untrackable dissemination, a mutation that distributes philosophical thought to other districts of Being that cannot as yet be seen, not even by means of existential night goggles or sci-fi timers. While philosophy appears to lose ground, art strengthens on its nothingness, having no remaining illusions about itself that would except the rule of illusion.

Yet the nature of their encounter is still vibrant, spiced with feisty dissent. Where content and meaning structures are voided, the *encounter itself*, and what this interrupts, holds our fascination. The co-intrication of art and the philosophical attitude should not be split into opposing forces or a logic of clashing inscription, even though philosophy gives art fluctuating ratings when trying to dominate a given scene. Some philosophies fuel up on "weakness," allowing for unexpected flares of self-alienation and otherness, as passages from Rousseau to Levinas and Blanchot attest, bracing extremes of self-relinquishment in the thought of passivity and the attenuation of the subject. Still, there's a roster of differences to be accounted for in terms of basic *Einstellungen*, attitudes and attunement, that each modality of Saying carries. I will not even go into the polydependencies that constitute their tentative pairing, the way art and philosophy call to, need and *use* each other and their various offspring, as if remembering a shared ground of reflection. Let us simply retain at this point the way Greek tragedy turned into Greek philosophy, handing representations over to this other mode of ringing the death knell. Nancy asks us to listen for the vanishing traces of Greek tragedy in the surging self-assertion of Greek philosophy, the spark of fateful drama still coiled in all types of philosophical *Darstellungen* and a hidden theatrical lexicon, mostly evicted from the premises of philosophical demonstration. We know of Plato's aversion to poetic squatting when he cleared the poets out of the *Republic*, hoping to secure a home for Truth without the intrusive trauma of fiction hanging around, disrupting the presentation of a reliable scheme for just governance. But even when Heidegger, the latecomer, calls on poetry with a friendly enough demeanor, there is the impingement of implicit hierarchies and distortion at work, a massive kidnapping of something like poetic intention.

There are many appropriations of art and poesy in the adventure of philosophical thought – many defining seductions and acts, conversely, that repel the artistic intrusion. The reining in of art by philosophy recalls a familiar story of repressed origins in which the philosophical takeover has a part. Still, a preliminary standoff between the two mega-domains cannot be avoided if we are to be honest about the way the stakes fall and what kind of forces are in play. Their bequeathed values may seem provisional, at points exchangeable, yet remain instructive in a first cut of codified difference. Art has never promised to nail meaning, prescribe grammars, trim behaviors still called "human" – or to point political entities, such as emerging or established states, in ethical directions. Nor, despite its calling, has art proclaimed any reason to establish its own kingdom and apportion a reliable dosage of justice. Often kicked to the sidelines of historical action, art in modernity has fed on its own insubstantiality and allegorical push off points. It may have bowed in submission to myths of representation and mimetic recuperation, yet it has consistently refused to bend like a court stenographer taking it all down, word by containable word. When not signifying its apartness, a condition anointed or appointed by the exigency of self-transcendence, art breaks itself down ruthlessly, at times resembling the portrait of a drunken bystander offering barely a broken syntax of beings and Being, hardly a testimony, close to the sort of unfiltered offering and slice of self-estrangement vaunted by Hölderlin.

Wait. For the record, I do not like such generalities about "art and philosophy," exhibiting a falsifiable frenzy of meddling in their secret correspondence while fast-tracking dense histories that often bear contradiction and annulment of their principles, grammatical turnarounds and sneaky self-sabotage. Even type A signifiers such as "art" and "philosophy" are all wrong, part of a shaky inheritance, nor do they account for specific movements and schools, or subversions of accepted labels. So why do it, indulge generalities, why go there? I suppose the uses of not-so-disposable language lay down some parameters for us to go by. At this point of my own history as a reader, I have taken out a permit that lets me condense and squeeze out the essence of voluminous materials, moving the argument along. *Maybe the permit should be revoked, I tell myself.* Maybe it will soon expire anyway, letting painstakingly minute disquisitions on aporia and troubled positing return to these pages. Something in me hopes that I will indeed be asked to back up each of one these fast-paced assertions, a pedagogical indulgence that I relinquish for now. Nothing would please me more than to dive into passages that handle these matters with acuity, so that it becomes possible again to recruit artworks and poetic enunciation that push us along – or *stop* pushing, precisely, in order to halt us in our rhetorical tracks, allowing things to fall apart. A contemporary impulse to suspend philological slow-pacing has gotten me to quicken the rhythm of theoretical demonstration. Ok. Enough of the self-inflicted lament, neither entirely philosophical nor sufficiently poetic. Let us return to Hölderlin's example, with the understanding that this name provides more than a mere example, remaining, after Heidegger, problematically exemplary yet, in my view, unavoidable.

*****

Resubmitted to thought by Benjamin, Hölderlin's "Dichtermut" – together with "Blödigkeit," the double and voiding of poetic courage – leans into the aporia of heroic delivery (repurposed by Heidegger). The pair of poems features a poetic attitude that stares down the certitudes of philosophical positing in a match of sacrificial exposures. Both philosophers and poets have taken their hits, having been hounded historically by state hostility and, according to different decrees, put to death by political override. Poets and philosophers are dead Daseins walking, unless they have in some ways secured the status of *Staatsphilosophen* or court poets, which can leave them in precarity, like the supreme poet, Torquato Tasso.

Headed for seclusion, Hölderlin focuses on an inner death drive to which the poet succumbs. The rendering of the poetic word emerges in a condition of sheer stupor, whether inspired and intoxicated or more onto-theologically appointed (or both). "Dichtermut," in league with "Blödigkeit," teaches us that feeblemindedness (Blödigkeit) fuels the temptation of poetic Saying, peeling away to a core of stupidity. Under the sway of an unshakable stupor, poetry struggles with its own inhibition, a level of diffidence and ground rule prohibition that leaves poetic insight at the altar, radically unmoored. At this point philosophy, with few standout exceptions and Spinoza, scrams.

As Deleuze saw it, philosophy was too arrogant to accept the gift left at its doorstep by literature. That was the gift of bêtise, which philosophers thought they could bypass, retaining the bonus of sovereignty and a run of legislative powers. Philosophy, according to Deleuze, thought it could move ahead without confronting barriers posed by fundamental stupidity. Big mistake, calamitous oversight: Philosophy's arrogant presumption about its superpowers left it vulnerable to internal attack and a shaky premise for self-understanding. There were of course exceptions here and there, such as Schelling seeing the stupid and chaotic origins of the world (an assertion that pissed off Hegel to no end). There were other power failures of cognition and material framing noted as well, because philosophy is too smart and *too parricidal* to snuff out without marking the hideouts of stupidity and instances of non-knowledge in the yields of predecessors. The maneuvers around bêtise hinge on a power grab and political presumption, the capacity philosophy exercises for crafting transcendental principles, keeping them under the control of theoretical mechanisms of surveillance. Art operates differently, if it *operates* at all, for it relates to groundlessness and sacred effusions differently, and must befriend the nether world of illusion when reaching for the blueness of the sky. I don't want to get this wrong by risking the loss of nuance and necessary complication that beset the philosophical inquiry and artistic-poetic delivery – the inevitable return-to-sender notice. Given the leakage and disseminative overflow of these domains they cannot merely be pitted against each other, even where they flee each other or regularly issue eviction notices from their premises, as if these clashes of transcendence could be regulated.

A hybrid being in this regard, Nietzsche injected himself with art in order to secure a kind of suicide-prevention center. At some points along his journey he wanted to position a buffer against the stark positing prowess of science, or at least to bring the self-explication of *Wissenschaft* around to create new openings for the scientific drive, and attach it to "new galaxies of joy."[4] Understanding the bait of rhetoric, its artifice and place in the will to scientific assumption, Nietzsche would not clear science of illusory bolsters, but looked at the way fiction was incorporated and spit out. Nietzsche was the philosopher who reversed dialectics by spitting things out. At the same time, he was no enemy of artifice, urging us to think more seriously about unavowed cultures of intoxication and our *Rausch*-rushes in philological and scientific areas of thought, the various degrees of artificial paradise on which we count.

Theoretical habits that push *Rausch* can go far, as Nietzsche understood. It's all a matter of dosage, he claimed in regard to history and its oppressive weightiness. Dionysian meltdowns, by nature uncontrolled, induce a frenzy of de-individuation in the contrasting climes of Apollonian dreaming. Such boundaries cannot be drawn with absolute conviction. Left unpatrolled, a thirdness happens in this encounter, something neither entirely philosophical nor of art. Still, philosophy tries to hold its own when approaching art. The way philosophy reaches for art and poesy at crucial junctures – or consorts with theological scruples about Being – betrays a strong ambivalence toward its manifold alterities.

*****

At times a movement of repulsion overtakes states of dependency. Modern philosophical relatedness involves domination, if not *need*, when it comes to other discursivities, an adherence to spacing that lends stability when establishing quasi-worlds in the rubble of a pass-

---

4   I analyze the scientificity of science – the tragic drive and joyous runs of Nietzschean programs – in *The Test Drive* (2005).

ing world. It may be, in Heidegger's phrasing, that somehow *die Welt weltet*, but this does not mean that we bask in a presence – that we have clear access to a remnant of world, or know where to locate the "in" of being-in-the world. Nancy has named our recently shared time here the epoch of haunting. We are swarmed by ancestral roamers who come through, crackling in unanticipated ways. Yet, according to Heidegger & Rilke, due largely to technological gridwork, our ghostly predecessors, especially in North America, have little room to spread transcendence; they are housed in the vacancy of inhospitable spaces, unwelcoming and sterile, repugning for the most part the approach of ghostly intruders.

Goethe, the great undead, opened up for me the ethics of haunting. What I try to convey by means of his life-and-works can be understood in terms of the inducements, mostly unfathomable, in response to which we subject ourselves to phenomena that exceed us, often evaluated as "great" – freedom, work, or love, a version of Gd. Following the logic of Nancy's questioning, I wonder, What is it that holds sway over us like an unconditional prescription? (Cf. Ronell 2006.) What commands us to obey some hidden yet imperative force that may make sense, at least provisionally, or that may be discoverable outside of us, or on some inner limit still beyond our grasp, ahead of us, or in the past? Without being able to measure it out, there is a distance between us and what commands our moves – or what fixes our immobility. It is a distance that varies, closing in at times, announcing a proximity closer than any intimacy or familiarity we have ever known. At times it speaks to you, guiding you without manifesting itself as an identifiable or subjectivable someone. Yet, you subject yourself to this remote force that disables significant agency, is prior to self-constitution and works according to an ungraspable yet invasive pull. "It could be something that has been lost, obscured and forgotten, leaving you to be haunted by a sense of loss without substance. Nonetheless, what haunts is also a haunt – something that doubles for a place, a familiar place."[5] Haunting belongs to the family

---

5   Nancy (1983, 10–11). See my *Dictations: On Haunted Writing* (2006, updated [1986], xviii), for a close-up of Goethe's impending and still-scary haunts.

of *Heim*; in fact it has never been properly released from the home, Nancy reminds us. The proximity of a command or imperative doubles for the *Unheimlichkeit* that haunts our thinking because, in its remoteness, something very close incessantly pings and impinges, disquieting only to the extent that it burrows thisclose. The most lucid moments are beholden to the haunting foreboding stamped by the apotropaic sign of "home sweet home" – the foreboding abode.

As abode, whatever is to be called home, a familiar dwelling, is related to ethos. The question of hauntings by which we have been invaded thematically and eerily is not merely a strange fixation of filmmakers and obsessional neurotics. The relation to the past is never behind us. Restless and insistent, invisible sticking points of the past obsess, hound, overwhelm, and call up to us, disclosing frenzied effects associated with the force of law. The obsession with what remains unaddressed and yet to be resolved – be this made up of acts of cruelty or the primal scene – involves nothing less than an ethics. The ethical slant has little to do with the Ethics found in philosophy books or contained in works of science or the precepts of an institutional authority or discipline. Nor will it appear as moral sentiment or prescriptive rejoinder. Nonetheless, this epochal sense of impingement can be grasped as an ethics of the haunted. *Haunted*: What this means is that thought is not thinking beyond its time but *in its time*. Pinched by the pangs of melancholic review, the writing of hauntedness writes on this limit, which is that of our time – a time that dissipates, abandons, exposes, marks, approaches and continually throws us. Thinking, Nancy writes, means "exposing oneself to that which comes with time, in this time. In the time of being-haunted, there can and should not be any other thought or ethics – if that's what it is – other than that of haunting" (ibid.).

Nancy has commented upon the excessive nature of the categorical imperative, a force that holds sway over a subject that in the first place is a subjected singular-plural – haunted, hearing, heeding, adhering to commands. In this spirit, I follow the remote control effects of Goethe's name (on Benjamin and Kafka – and on so many others: Nietzsche, Freud, Arendt), pursuing effects of literary hauntings that have little to do with a thematizable occurrence, and even less with presence. Something about "Goethe," oppressive and close, has inundated the dreams and writing of these thinkers, disclosing an unconscious program that jumps barriers and also has played its part in the *imaginaire* of nation-building. Goethe's haunting has long remained in these works and state monuments a point of rare cult vitality, establishing unconscious authority in the different morphs of his immense oeuvre. The name's survival also operates as a menace that seeks a home base, whether infrapsychic or collectively apportioned.

*****

The imposition of "Goethe" and expositions ascribable to Nancy teach us that what haunts our existence now, in our time, is linked to the "domestic" dimension that can never be domesticated – the definition of being-haunted. Whether we are speaking of the categorical imperative or of Goethean command systems, this effect does not belong to the economy which it haunts. Hauntedness allows for visitations without making itself at home (cf. Ronell 2006). Not everyone or every place is ripe for the nearly auratic devastation of the experience of a haunting. According to Heidegger & Rilke, who saw America as an "absolute void," the American household, suffused with technological sterilizers, has vacated the phantomal reception center. This extreme instance of unhousing, much different from Celan's untrackable *unWo*, is no doubt a strange projection launched across the Atlantic. Yet, one sees their point, and the necessity they must have sought of establishing a failed experience of hauntedness, with a fleet of ghosts barred from arranging their American comfort zone around New World domesticity. Still, one has to wonder. Don't Rilke and Heidegger have a lot of nerve opting for a place (or *Erörterung*) of "proper" hauntedness? But the point is well taken. Maybe we no longer have homes in some geo-cognitive areas to cushion our ghosts of the past and glimmers of futurity.

In our day, honestly, I'm not convinced of anything that would assure friendly relations with unappeased ghosts, as if the ghosts hadn't been shooed away from genocidal Europe.

*****

My teacher, Jacques Derrida, considered various forms of mourning disorder – the difficulty we have in letting go of a beloved object or libidinal position.[6] Without seeking analysis, he consulted psychoanalysis. Freud says that we go into mourning over lost ideals or figures, which includes persons or even your country when it lets you down. Loss that cannot be assimilated or dealt with creates pockets of obdurate remainders in the psyche, maybe a crypt-formation or false presence. One may incorporate a phantom other, keeping the other both alive and dead; or, one may fall into states of melancholy, unable to move on, trapped in the energies of an ever-shrinking world. Things become little or belittling. Many of the key themes in films give expression to failed mourning, part of a key lexicon, a relation to death that invents the population of the undead – vampires, zombies, trolls, real housewives of Beverly Hills or wherever in America (a popular television series). In Anglo-American districts, we are often encouraged to "let go," "move on," "get over it," even to "get a life," locutions that indicate a national intolerance for prolonged states of mourning, discouraging mourners from sitting with loss for extended periods. Yet the quickened pace of letting go may well mean that we have *not* let go, that we are haunted and hounded by unmetabolized aspects of loss while hitting the accelerator. In Freud's work, the timer is set for two years of appropriate mourning. When Hamlet tries to extend that deadline, the whole house threatens to fall apart, and he is admonished by Claudius to get over himself, to man up. The inability to mourn or let go is sometimes called melancholy. Many of us have slipped into states of melancholic depression for one reason or another, for one unreason or another – one cannot always nail the object that has been lost or causes pain, though Pandemic, weather, and other shutdowns supply plenty of materials for melancholic brooding.

For Derrida, melancholy hosts an ethical stance, a relation to loss inviting vigilance and constant re-attunement. One does not have to know or understand the meaning of a loss and the full range of its disruptive consequences, but one somehow dwells with it, leaning

---

6   The following section contains passages that were previously published by the author in Ronell 2013 and Ronell 2022.

into a depleting emptiness. It takes courage to resist the temptation to bail or distract oneself from unhinging loss. (In the most recent U.S. election, one chose between a candidate who *deplored* and one who *embraced* mourning: Joe Biden's first act was to hold a ceremony to mark the casualties of the aggressively disavowed virus. His public demeanor has been built on the loss of his son, offering a political portraiture of a leader in mourning. The other candidate, Trump, has mourned no one; he may be too shallow even to house a crypt-formation or relocate suppressed loss. Countries can be profiled according to the way they mourn or refuse to mourn, measuring their capacity to acknowledge loss.) One is largely dissuaded by institutions from surrendering to the exigencies of mourning. Entire industries stand ready to distract the inconsolable mourner, without exception, including during the times of COVID-19. I see no off-switch to the effects of the pandemic, which prompts a new set of focused responses to neighboring areas of thought and artistic practice, taking cues from Montaigne and other seers of contamination.

As for me, I have lost so many friends and essential interlocutors in the recent past. My first attempt to put together a survival kit involved a close friend with whom the book version of an installation was planned. Anne Dufourmantelle and I went far into the question of what an exhausted philosophical corpus could still do for us in impossibly dark times. I abandoned the project immediately after her tragic disappearance. A part of our intention returned in fragments, shuttled into podcasts I delivered for Philomonaco's *Rencontres philosophiques* during the first year of confinement in Monaco and Paris, in 2020. This was a series labeled "Survival Kit for the Anguished," emerging from various theories of *angoisse*, *Angst*, *Furcht*, and psychic effects of viral aggression. Despite discontinuities and unbridgeable caesurae, the idea of a *kit*, together with other emergency supplies packed into philosophical and poetic Saying, offered a subtle viability for thinking the aporias of *überleben*. Poetry has known shipwreck from the starting block, lives by celebrating the departed, inventing new names and addresses of mourning. Philosophy has a long history of handling – or bracketing – the experience of distressed states. Poetry signals from its solitary base, pulsing with anticipatory bereavement. Poetic utterance retrieves loss in the very turn to the stutter of language, a kind of *stutterance*. Philosophy has a history of calming that stutter, perhaps only until Nietzsche picks it up again by way of philosophizing with a stammer. But philosophy sticks close to pain, too, and knows cruelty. Yet both modalities have stayed close to the edges of non-recuperable suffering, a suffering without returns or rewards in a mystified Elsewhere – without, in some cases, a Christian savings or rollover account. They covered up what they knew with the non-starter of dogmatic truth. Still, there was plenty of room for fissuring and rhetorical indication of another philosophical urge throughout its history that could not simply be blinkered.

*****

(I fast-track the credits.)
Thus the Ancients were concerned with stand-out types of psychic debilitation; Descartes, Kant, and Nietzsche probed, each in his own way, into the dark side of mood and temperament; Kierkegaard passed the mic to fear and trembling; Heidegger based his existential analyses on *Sorge*; and Sartre drilled down on sheer nothingness. From day one, philosophers wondered whether it was possible to feel at-home in the world, given our basic homelessness – a predicament that many of them came to see as the uprooted nature of our dwelling on this earth. Many of us counted on these abyss-gazers to land us safely, without much illusion, and somehow to keep us going, even if the trek was bound to be mournful (cf. Ronell 2013). Lately we've been traveling the edges of acute unreliability in language and reference, contending with crashing worlds and the imponderables of disgraced Being in a Schillerian sense that will have to be explored elsewhere, in another survival kit based on Schiller's thinking of "Anmut und Würde," in and despite shattered worlds. Philosophy is built to handle downgrades linked to the unreliability of language's positing stints, the steady humbling of Being. But we, or some facet of what remains of the children of finitude: We are not built to last or to push back incessantly on programmed slap downs (cf. Ronell 2022).

*****

In some ways, what art and philosophy have struggled with since their bursts of documented emergence seems to be slipping away. One feels massively betrayed, abandoned to a hollow in existence. People and institutions, crude bureaucracies, seem to get away with murder, but I have to wonder whether anyone really gets away from the effects of tireless serves of insult, the jouissance of malevolence or misconstrual.

Acts of misconstrual, as Shakespeare has shown in his drama on honor and betrayal, can lead to suicide. According to Nietzsche's literary appraisal, *Julius Caesar* was Shakespeare's favorite play among the great works that were produced under that name. The true hero was Brutus (according to Nietzsche), for he had to bear the brunt of betrayal and has initiated for philosophy the thought of the "noble traitor"—how much it takes to go up against a beloved power, a friend, a mentor. I am not sure that those who continue openly to denounce the world-remnant as it forms and deforms, disarticulates, make the grade of "noble traitors," or can be credited with a strategic renunciation of self-interest as in the worlds that Shakespeare commands. In his play those marked as most vulnerable to group psychology remain "unshaken" as the earth shakes and the climate bounds senselessly, striking down randomly, unleashing corpses from their graves—the hits are organized around Shakespeare's name and the registers of Shakes-peare. The ghosts glide past one another, earth convulses. I can't say that this weather report accords with our roster of calamities, but the ground has *shakenspeare'd* beneath our feet and the general climatology portends ill as updated forms of tyranny sully the earth and deregulate *Sorge* on all scales. Nowadays all this seems cast hyperbolically, a minor spinoff of *Caesar*, a cut and caesura of historical moment, truly a tale told by an idiot ...

Literature

Nancy, Jean-Luc. 1983. "Le Katègorien de l'excès." In *L'Impératif catégorique*, 5–32. Paris: Flammarion.
Nancy, Jean-Luc. 2002. *Hegel. The Restlessness of the Negative.* Translated by Jason Smith and Steven Miller. Minneapolis: University of Minnesota Press.

Ronell, Avital. 2005. *The Test Drive*. Urbana and Chicago: University of Illinois Press.

Ronell, Avital. 2006 [1986]. *Dictations. On Haunted Writing*. Urbana and Chicago: University of Illinois Press.

Ronell, Avital. 2012. *Loser Sons. Politics and Authority*. Urbana and Chicago: University of Illinois Press.

Ronell, Avital. 2013. "Stormy Weather: Blues in Winter." In *New York Times*, February 2. https://archive.nytimes.com/opinionator.blogs.nytimes.com/2013/02/02/stormy-weather-blues-in-winter/ (last accessed: 14 June 2025).

Ronell, Avital. 2022. "Vexed and Vaxxed: What Now?" In *Philosophy World Democracy*. https://www.philosophy-world-democracy.org/articles-1/vexed-and-vaxxed-what-now (last accessed: 14 June 2025).

Hölderlin's 'Celebration of Peace' and Kant's Treaty 'Toward Perpetual Peace' Performative Types of Writing in Poetry and Philosophy[1]

Violetta L. Waibel

---

1   This piece was written in German for the lecture series "Kunst, Kultur, Gesellschaft" ("Art, Culture, Society") on the topic "1770 – *ein starker Jahrgang. Beethoven, Hölderlin und Hegel im Jahr ihres 250. Geburtstags*" ("1770 – *A Strong Vintage. Beethoven, Hölderlin and Hegel in the Year of their 250*[th] *Birthdays*"), and due to the pandemic was shown as a video film with the title "Seit ein Gespräch wir sind ... bald sind wir aber Gesang. Hölderlin und die 'Friedensfeier'" ("Since we have been a discourse... but soon we shall be song." Hölderlin and the 'Celebration of Peace') ONLINE on July 21, 2020, at the Centre for Courses for Senior Citizens in Munich. The video film was once more presented at the conference at the University of Zadar, which took place from October 1 to 3, 2020 on the topic of *Urteilskraft und Demokratie – Huldigung des Rechts? (Judgment and Democracy – Homage to the Law?)* under the direction of Jure Zovko. This is the first English translation of the German text. In the case of references to classics such as Friedrich Hölderlin, Immanuel Kant or Theodor W. Adorno, the years of first publication or creation are given in order to make it easier for readers to find the textual references who do not have the relevant English translation at hand or who wish to read the German text. Many thanks to David Hellbrück and Andreas Wintersperger for their careful revision of this contribution. Reuse of this content in OA publications is permitted provided the original title is cited. This article is licensed by Springer Nature Customer Service GmbH and is not part of the primary OA/Creative Commons license.

Friedensfeier[2]

Friedrich Hölderlin

Ich bitte dieses Blatt nur gutmüthig zu lesen. So wird es sicher nicht unfaßlich, noch weniger anstößig seyn. Sollten aber dennoch einige eine solche Sprache zu wenig konventionell finden, so muß ich ihnen gestehen: ich kann nicht anders. An einem schönen Tage läßt sich ja fast jede Sangart hören, und die Natur, wovon es her ist, nimmts auch wieder.

Der Verfasser gedenkt dem Publikum eine ganze Sammlung von dergleichen Blättern vorzulegen, und dieses soll irgend eine Probe seyn davon.

1

1. Der himmlischen, still wiederklingenden,
2. Der ruhigwandelnden Töne voll,
3. Und gelüftet ist der altgebaute,
4. Seeliggewohnte Saal; um grüne Teppiche duftet
5. Die Freudenwolk' und weithinglänzend stehn,
6. Gereiftester Früchte voll und goldbekränzter Kelche,
7. Wohlangeordnet, eine prächtige Reihe,
8. Zur Seite da und dort aufsteigend über dem
9. Geebneten Boden die Tische.
10. Denn ferne kommend haben
11. Hieher, zur Abendstunde,
12. Sich liebende Gäste beschieden.

---

2   Friedrich Hölderlin, "Friedensfeier", in *Sämtliche Werke und Briefe* (MA), vol. 1, ed. Michael Knaupp (Darmstadt: Wissenschaftliche Buchgesellschaft, 1998), 361–366.

Celebration of Peace[3]

Friedrich Hölderlin

All I ask is that the reader be kindly disposed towards these pages. In that case he will certainly not find them incomprehensible, far less objectionable. But if, nonetheless, some should think such a language too unconventional, I must confess to them: I cannot help it. On a fine day – they should consider – almost every mode of song makes itself heard; and Nature, whence it originates, also receives it again.

The author intends to offer the public an entire collection of such pieces, and this one should be regarded as a kind of sample.

1

1. With heavenly, quietly echoing,
2. With calmly modulating music filled,
3. And aired is the anciently built,
4. The sweetly familiar hall; upon green carpets wafts
5. The fragrant cloud of joy and, casting their brightness far,
6. Full of most mellow fruit and chalices wreathed with gold,
7. Arranged in seemly order, a splendid row,
8. Erected here and there on either side above
9. The levelled floor, stand the tables.
10. For, come from distant places,
11. Here, at the evening hour,
12. Loving guests have forgathered.

---

3   Friedrich Hölderlin, "Celebration of Peace", in *Selected Poems and Fragments*, trans. Michael Hamburger, ed. Jeremy Adler (London: Penguin Books, 1998), 208–216.

2

13. Und dämmernden Auges denk' ich schon,
14. Vom ernsten Tagwerk lächelnd,
15. Ihn selbst zu sehn, den Fürsten des Fests.
16. Doch wenn du schon dein Ausland gern verläugnest,
17. Und als vom langen Heldenzuge müd,
18. Dein Auge senkst, vergessen, leichtbeschattet,
19. Und Freundesgestalt annimmst, du Allbekannter, doch
20. Beugt fast die Knie das Hohe. Nichts vor dir,
21. Nur Eines weiß ich, Sterbliches bist du nicht.
22. Ein Weiser mag mir manches erhellen; wo aber
23. Ein Gott noch auch erscheint,
24. Da ist doch andere Klarheit.

3

25. Von heute aber nicht, nicht unverkündet ist er;
26. Und einer, der nicht Fluth noch Flamme gescheuet,
27. Erstaunet, da es stille worden, umsonst nicht, jezt,
28. Da Herrschaft nirgend ist zu sehn bei Geistern und Menschen.
29. Das ist, sie hören das Werk,
30. Längst vorbereitend, von Morgen nach Abend, jezt erst,
31. Denn unermeßlich braußt, in der Tiefe verhallend,
32. Des Donnerers Echo, das tausendjährige Wetter,
33. Zu schlafen, übertönt von Friedenslauten, hinunter.
34. Ihr aber, theuergewordne, o ihr Tage der Unschuld,
35. Ihr bringt auch heute das Fest, ihr Lieben! und es blüht
36. Rings abendlich der Geist in dieser Stille;
37. Und rathen muß ich, und wäre silbergrau
38. Die Loke, o ihr Freunde!
39. Für Kränze zu sorgen und Mahl, jezt ewigen Jünglingen ähnlich.

4

40. Und manchen möcht' ich laden, aber o du,
41. Der freundlichernst den Menschen zugethan,

2

13. And already with eyes dusk-dim,
14. With solemn day-labour smiling,
15. I think that I see him in person, the prince of the feast-day.
16. But though you like to disavow your foreign land,
17. And weary, it seems, with long heroic war,
18. Cast down your eyes, oblivious, lightly shaded,
19. Assuming the shape of a friend, you known to all men, yet
20. Almost it bends our knees, such loftiness. Nothing in
21. Your presence I know; but one thing: mortal you are not.
22. A wise man could elucidate much for me; but where
23. A God as well appears,
24. A different clarity shines.

3

25. Yet not sprung up today, nor unproclaimed he comes
26. And one who did not balk at either flood or flame
27. Not without reason astonishes us, now that all is quiet,
28. Dominion nowhere to be seen among spirits or mortals.
29. That is, only now do they hear
30. The work that long has prepared them, from Orient to Occident,
31. For now immeasurably, fading away in the deeps,
32. The Thunderer's echo, the millennial storm
33. Rolls down to sleep, intermingled with peaceful music.
34. But you, grown dear to us, O days of innocence,
35. It's you, beloved, that bring this feast-day too, and round us
36. The spirit flowers, vespertine in this quiet;
37. And, friends, I must advise you, though
38. Our hair had turned silver-grey,
39. To see the garlands and banquet, now like men immortally young.

4

40. And many there are I would invite, but you,
41. O you that benignly, gravely disposed to men

42. Dort unter syrischer Palme,

43. Wo nahe lag die Stadt, am Brunnen gerne war;

44. Das Kornfeld rauschte rings, still athmete die Kühlung

45. Vom Schatten des geweiheten Gebirges,

46. Und die lieben Freunde, das treue Gewölk,

47. Umschatteten dich auch, damit der heiligkühne

48. Durch Wildniß mild dein Stral zu Menschen kam, o Jüngling!

49. Ach! aber dunkler umschattete, mitten im Wort, dich

50. Furchtbarentscheidend ein tödlich Verhängniß. So ist schnell

51. Vergänglich alles Himmlische; aber umsonst nicht;

5

52. Denn schonend rührt des Maases allzeit kundig

53. Nur einen Augenblik die Wohnungen der Menschen

54. Ein Gott an, unversehn, und keiner weiß es, wenn?

55. Auch darf alsdann das Freche drüber gehn,

56. Und kommen muß zum heiligen Ort das Wilde

57. Von Enden fern, übt rauhbetastend den Wahn,

58. Und trift daran ein Schiksaal, aber Dank,

59. Nie folgt der gleich hernach dem gottgegebnen Geschenke;

60. Tiefprüfend ist es zu fassen.

61. Auch wär' uns, sparte der Gebende nicht

62. Schon längst vom Seegen des Heerds

63. Uns Gipfel und Boden entzündet.

6

64. Des Göttlichen aber empfiengen wir

65. Doch viel. Es ward die Flamm' uns

66. In die Hände gegeben, und Ufer und Meersfluth.

67. Viel mehr, denn menschlicher Weise

68. Sind jene mit uns, die fremden Kräfte, vertrauet.

69. Und es lehret Gestirn dich, das

70. Vor Augen dir ist, doch nimmer kannst du ihm gleichen.

71. Vom Alllebendigen aber, von dem

72. Viel Freuden sind und Gesänge,

42. Down there beneath the Syrian palm-tree, where
43. The town lay near, by the well were glad to be;
44. Round you the cornfield rustled, quietly coolness breathed
45. From shadows of the hallowed mountainsides,
46. And your dear friends, the faithful clouds
47. Cast shade upon you too, so that holy, the bold,
48. The beam through wilderness gently should fall on men, O youth.
49. But oh, more darkly, even as you spoke,
50. And dreadfully determining a deadly doom overshadowed you there. So all
51. That's heavenly fleets on; but not for nothing;

5

52. For sparingly, at all times knowing the measure,
53. A God for a moment only will touch the dwellings
54. Of men, by none foreseen, and no one knows when.
55. And over it then all insolence may pass,
56. And to the holy place must come the savage
57. From ends remote, and roughly fingering works out his
58. Delusion, so fulfilling a fate, but thanks
59. Will never follow at once upon the godsent gift;
60. Probed deeply, this can be grasped.
61. And were not the giver sparing
62. The wealth of our hearth long ago would
63. Have fired both the roof and the floor.

6

64. Yet much that's divine nonetheless we
65. Received. The flame was entrusted
66. To us, and shore and ocean flood.
67. Much more than humanly only
68. Are these, the alien powers, familiar with us.
69. And you are taught by the stars
70. In front of your eyes, but never you can be like them.
71. Yet to the All-Living from whom
72. Many joys and songs have sprung

73. Ist einer ein Sohn, ein Ruhigmächtiger ist er,
74. Und nun erkennen wir ihn,
75. Nun, da wir kennen den Vater
76. Und Feiertage zu halten
77. Der hohe, der Geist
78. Der Welt sich zu Menschen geneigt hat.

7

79. Denn längst war der zum Herrn der Zeit zu groß
80. Und weit aus reichte sein Feld, wann hats ihn aber erschöpfet?
81. Einmal mag aber ein Gott auch Tagewerk erwählen,
82. Gleich Sterblichen und theilen alles Schiksaal.
83. Schiksaalgesez ist diß, daß Alle sich erfahren,
84. Daß, wenn die Stille kehrt, auch eine Sprache sei.
85. Wo aber wirkt der Geist, sind wir auch mit, und streiten,
86. Was wohl das Beste sei. So dünkt mir jezt das Beste,
87. Wenn nun vollendet sein Bild und fertig ist der Meister,
88. Und selbst verklärt davon aus seiner Werkstatt tritt,
89. Der stille Gott der Zeit und nur der Liebe Gesez,
90. Das schönausgleichende gilt von hier an bis zum Himmel.

8

91. Viel hat von Morgen an,
92. Seit ein Gespräch wir sind und hören voneinander,
93. Erfahren der Mensch; bald sind wir aber Gesang.
94. Und das Zeitbild, das der große Geist entfaltet,
95. Ein Zeichen liegts vor uns, daß zwischen ihm und andern
96. Ein Bündnis zwischen ihm und andern Mächten ist.
97. Nicht er allein, die Unerzeugten, Ew'gen
98. Sind kennbar alle daran, gleichwie auch an den Pflanzen
99. Die Mutter Erde sich und Licht und Luft sich kennet.
100. Zulezt ist aber doch, ihr heiligen Mächte, für euch
101. Das Liebeszeichen, das Zeugniß
102. Daß ihrs noch seiet, der Festtag,

73. There's one who is a son, and quietly powerful is he,
74. And now we recognize him,
75. Now that we know the Father
76. And to keep holidays
77. The exalted, the Spirit of
78. The World has inclined towards men.

7

79. For long now he had been too great to rule
80. As Lord of Time, and wide his field extended, but when did it exhaust him?
81. For once, however, even a God may choose
82. Mere daily tasks, like mortals, and share all manner of fate.
83. This is a law of fate, that each shall know all others,
84. That when the silence returns there shall be a language too.
85. Yet where the Spirit is active, we too will stir and debate
86. What course might be the best. So now it seems best to me
87. If now the Master completes his image and, finished,
88. Himself transfigured by it, steps out of his workshop,
89. The quiet God of Time, and only the law of love,
90. That gently resolves all difference, prevails from here up to Heaven.

8

91. Much, from the morning onwards,
92. Since we have been a discourse and have heard from one another,
93. Has human kind learnt; but soon we shall be song.
94. That temporal image too, which the great Spirit reveals,
95. As a token lies before us that between him and others,
96. Himself and other powers, there is a pact of peace.
97. Not he alone, the Unconceived, Eternal
98. Can all be known by this, as likewise by the plants
99. Our Mother Earth and light and air are known.
100. Yet ultimately, you holy powers, our token
101. Of love for you, and the proof
102. That still you are holy to us, is the feast-day.

9

103. Der Allversammelnde, wo Himmlische nicht
104. Im Wunder offenbar, noch ungesehn im Wetter,
105. Wo aber bei Gesang gastfreundlich untereinander
106. In Chören gegenwärtig, eine heilige Zahl
107. Die Seeligen in jeglicher Weise
108. Beisammen sind, und ihr Geliebtestes auch,
109. An dem sie hängen, nicht fehlt; denn darum rief ich
110. Zum Gastmahl, das bereitet ist,
111. Dich, Unvergeßlicher, dich, zum Abend der Zeit,
112. O Jüngling, dich zum Fürsten des Festes; und eher legt
113. Sich schlafen unser Geschlecht nicht,
114. Bis ihr Verheißenen all,
115. All ihr Unsterblichen, uns
116. Von eurem Himmel zu sagen,
117. Da seid in unserem Haußе.

10

118. Leichtathmende Lüfte
119. Verkünden euch schon,
120. Euch kündet das rauchende Thal
121. Und der Boden, der vom Wetter noch dröhnet,
122. Doch Hoffnung röthet die Wangen,
123. Und vor der Thüre des Haußes
124. Sizt Mutter und Kind,
125. Und schauet den Frieden
126. Und wenige scheinen zu sterben
127. Es hält ein Ahnen die Seele,
128. Vom goldnen Lichte gesendet,
129. Hält ein Versprechen die Ältesten auf.

9

103. The all-assembling, where heavenly beings are
104. Not manifest in miracles, nor unseen in thunderstorms,
105. But where in hymns hospitably conjoined
106. And present in choirs, a holy number,
107. The blessèd in every way
108. Meet and forgather, and their best-beloved,
109. To whom they are attached, is not missing; for that is why
110. You to the banquet now prepared I called,
111. The unforgettable, you, at the Evening of Time,
112. O youth, called you to the prince of the feast-day; nor shall
113. Our nation ever lie down to sleep until
114. All you that were prophesied,
115. Every one of you Immortals,
116. To tell us about your Heaven
117. Are here with us in our house.

10

118. Winds lightly breathing
119. Already announce you,
120. The vapour that drifts from the valley
121. And the ground still resounding with thunder,
122. But hope now flushes our cheeks,
123. In front of the door of their house
124. Sit mother and child,
125. And look upon peace,
126. And few now seem to be dying;
127. The souls of the oldest even
128. Held back by a hint, a promise
129. Conveyed by the golden light.

11

130. Wohl sind die Würze des Lebens,
131. Von oben bereitet und auch
132. Hinausgeführet, die Mühen.
133. Denn Alles gefällt jezt,
134. Einfältiges aber
135. Am meisten, denn die langgesuchte,
136. Die goldne Frucht,
137. Uraltem Stamm
138. In schütternden Stürmen entfallen,
139. Dann aber, als liebstes Gut, vom heiligen Schiksaal selbst,
140. Mit zärtlichen Waffen umschüzt,
141. Die Gestalt der Himmlischen ist es.

12

142. Wie die Löwin, hast du geklagt,
143. O Mutter, da du sie,
144. Natur, die Kinder verloren.
145. Denn es stahl sie, Allzuliebende, dir
146. Dein Feind, da du ihn fast
147. Wie die eigenen Söhne genommen,
148. Und Satyren die Götter gesellt hast.
149. So hast du manches gebaut,
150. Und manches begraben,
151. Denn es haßt dich, was
152. Du, vor der Zeit
153. Allkräftige, zum Lichte gezogen.
154. Nun kennest, nun lässest du diß;
155. Denn gerne fühllos ruht,
156. Bis daß es reift, furchtsamgeschäfftiges drunten.

11

130. Indeed it is travails, designed from
131. Above and there carried out,
132. That are the spice of life.
133. For now all things are pleasing
134. But most of all the
135. Ingenuous, because the long sought,
136. The golden fruit,
137. In shattering gales fallen down from
138. An age-old bough
139. But then, as the dearest possession, by Fate herself
140. Protected with tender weapons,
141. The shape of Heavenly it is.

12

142. Like the lioness you lamented,
143. O Mother, when you lost
144. Your children, Nature,
145. For they were stolen from you, the all too loving, by
146. Your enemy, when almost
147. Like your own sons you had nursed him
148. And with satyrs made gods consort.
149. So there is much you built
150. And much you buried,
151. For you are hated by
152. That which too soon
153. All-powerful, you raised to the light.
154. Now you know the fault, and desist,
155. For, till grown ripe, unfeeling
156. What's timidly busy likes to rest down below.

Kant's and Hölderlin's Self-Referential Instantiations of Peace

It is believed that Friedrich Hölderlin began the poem, the hymn, *Celebration of Peace* on the occasion of the peace treaty of Lunéville on February 9, 1801, during his stay in Hauptwil, Switzerland. Two letters from Hölderlin to his sister Heinrike and to his friend Christian Landauer have survived, in which Hölderlin reports with emphasis on the peace agreement. To his sister he writes on February 23, 1801:

> I am writing to you and the rest of the dear family on the day when among us here all is full of the news of the negotiated peace, and knowing me as you do I do not need to tell you what my feelings are. [...] I think all will now be well in the world. Whether I consider the recent or the distant past, everything seems to be leading up to an exceptional period, days of beautiful humanity, days of certain, fearless goodness and ways of thinking that are lucid and holy and exalted and simple all at once. (Hölderlin to Heinrike Breunlin, February 23, 1801, Hölderlin 2009a, 193)

Remarkably, Hölderlin adds "all that is good and sacred must be celebrated" (Hölderlin to Heinrike Breunlin, February 23, 1801, Hölderlin 2009a, 194). In February 1801, he wrote to Christian Landauer:

> I would of course have begun by speaking of the peace but the first pages of this letter were written I think a fortnight ago. What pleases me most about it is that with it the over-important role political alliances and misalliances have played is over and a good beginning has been made towards the simplicity that is proper to them. [...] It is everywhere a necessary evil to have compulsory laws and their executors. With the end of war and revolution I think that inner Boreas, the spirit of envy, will also cease, and let us hope a lovelier form of sociability than the merely solid and bourgeois will unfold! (Hölderlin to Christian Landauer, February, 1801, Hölderlin 2009a, 196)

Hölderlin is evidently moved by the signing of the peace treaty, and this in turn is how he perceives his immediate surroundings. He anticipates a better time, "the days of beautiful humanity", looks to days long past just as he looks ahead to the future; and he will do the same in his hymn *Celebration of Peace.*

Broadly speaking, the peace treaty of Lunéville represents a peace in the wake of the turmoil following the French Revolution of 1789, a political event with far-reaching consequences that was of profound importance to the poets and thinkers of the late 18th and early 19th centuries. Jean-Pierre Lefebvre argues that the poem was finished under the impression of the peace treaty of Amiens in 1802 (see Hölderlin-Jahrbuch 1957 and Lefebvre 2011). The political and historical ramifications are not something I want to go into here, as it is of secondary importance to Hölderlin (for details see article "France" 2005, 87–89).

Immanuel Kant penned an essay named *Toward Perpetual Peace* on the occasion of the Basel Peace Treaty of April 5, 1795, signed between post-revolutionary France and Prussia. The title of Kant's piece, which appeared in 1795 and was read across a wide audience at the time, is *Toward Perpetual Peace: A Philosophical Project (Zum ewigen Frieden. Ein philosophischer Entwurf)*. It has long been recognized among academics that Kant's peace text follows the form and structure of peace treaties of the time (Höffe 2011, 2; Patzig 1996, 17). Kant's peace essay includes six Preliminary Articles and three Definitive Articles. This is followed by two supplements, "On the Guarantee of Perpetual Peace" and one about a "secret article for perpetual peace". Two appendices come after this. The first is called "On the disagreement between morals and politics with a view to perpetual peace", the second is "On the agreement of politics with morals in accord with the transcendental concept of public right".

The self-referential aspect of this peace treaty that Kant concludes with humanity provides a format that can also be found in Hölderlin's *Celebration of Peace.* Those who write and publish normally want to be heard and to convince readers of their ideas and thoughts. Those who write want to share their thoughts with others. Enlightenment thinking aimed in a special way to spread the light of reason, which male and a few female authors saw themselves as having, among the reading public. In this respect, it cannot be surprising that with his essay on *Perpetual Peace* Kant sought to publicise the idea of peace in the deepest sense of the word in a forceful way that recommends itself to the thinking of the other. Giving the philosophical thoughts on peace the form of a treaty turns the readers into contracting parties. Admittedly, this is a treaty that the author, Kant, hands over to the public without receiving any guarantee that the treaty will also be legally signed and honoured on the part of the readers. It is all the more important that the reason and power of judgement of the target audience are addressed through good argumentation, but also that the need emerges to be and become part of the determination to reject the inhumanity of war, as intended in particular by the Preliminary Articles, and to participate in the peace project, as outlined in the Definitive Articles. In this way, the peace treaty invites every individual to consider the proposals of the author Immanuel Kant and to join the peace project in the spirit of humanity. The road to achieving this is the call for the establishment of republics, the idea that corresponds to modern, liberal democracies at their core.

Hölderlin read Immanuel Kant's three Critiques with a great intensity and incorporated numerous ideas. There is no direct evidence that he studied the peace treaty, but there is indirect evidence, which I will discuss briefly. Some ideas from Kant's writing on *Toward Perpetual Peace* might have been authoritative for Hölderlin, which is why it seems appropriate to me to refer to the most important ideas of the essay here.

The three Definitive Articles of Kant's *Peace Essay* develop the actual ideas for securing a lasting peace. According to the first definitive article, this consists in the establishment of a republican state, the only form of state, which, as Kant writes, is, "first on principles of the *freedom* of the members of a society (as individuals), second on principles of the *dependence* of all upon a single common legislation (as subjects), and third on the law of their *equality* (*as citizens of a state*) – the sole constitution that issues from the idea of the original contract, on which all rightful legislation of people must be based – is a *republican* constitution." (Kant 1999a [1795], AA VIII, 349/350) According to Kant, the republican state constitution is the best form of founding a state, the one that is most in line with reason, but also the one that is the most difficult to implement. What is fundamental to it is the principle of representation of citizens by representatives of the state. Kant is critical of what he calls democracy, namely direct rule by the people that dispenses with representation. Furthermore, in his Republic he already envisages a separation of powers of the legislative, judicial and executive branches, as is realised in modern democracies, which largely correspond to Kant's idea of a republic (see Kant 1999a [1795], AA VIII, 351–353).

International law is dealt with in the Second Definitive Article and requires a similar order at the level of peoples. Kant considers the ideal international legal order to be a federation of free states. However, he warns against the development of a single superstate uniting all peoples, a monocracy, which could very easily turn into a dictatorship. The core idea of federalism is that the confederation of states should "not look to acquiring any power of a state but only to preserving and securing the *freedom* of a state itself and of other states in league with it" (Kant 1999a [1795], AA VIII, 356). The primary and principal task of the confederation is to secure peace and to do everything possible to avoid future wars.

Kant envisages all this,

> yet reason, from the throne of the highest morally legislative power, delivers an absolute condemnation of war as a procedure for determining rights and, on the contrary, makes a condition of peace, which cannot be instituted or assured without a pact of nations among themselves, a direct duty; so there must be a league of a special kind, which can be called a *pacific league (foedus pacificum)*, and what would distinguish it from a *peace pact (pactum pacis)* is that the latter seeks to end only *one* war whereas the former seeks to end *all war* forever. (Kant 1999a [1795], AA VIII, 356)

For Kant, in any case, it is certain:

> This league does not look to acquiring any power of a state but only to preserving and securing the *freedom* of a state itself and of other states in league with it, but without there being any need for them to subject themselves to public laws and coercion under them (as people in a state of nature must do). (Kant 1999a [1795], AA VIII, 356)

The republican idea unfolds best, Kant hoped,

> if good fortune should ordain that a powerful and enlightened people can form itself into a republic (which by its nature must be inclined to perpetual peace), this would provide a focal point of federative union for other states, to attach themselves to it and so to secure a condition of freedom of states conformably with the idea of the rights of nations; and by further alliances of this kind, it would gradually extend further and further. (Kant 1999a [1795], AA VIII, 356)

According to Kant, the idea of republicanism of individual states serves as the seedbeds of a transnational legal and peace order, which gradually replaces the natural state of war – a constant risk – in favour of a legal order (see Kersting 1996, esp. 172–186).

In the Third Definitive Article, Kant asserts that the cosmopolitan right "shall be limited to conditions of universal *hospitality*" (Kant 1999a [1795], AA VIII, 357). Kant explicitly emphasises that he is not talking about philanthropy, a gift by grace or inclination, so to speak, but about a right. A right, however, is something to which everyone is entitled, to which one can lay claim. The fact that Kant, like many others of his time and those before, indeed like many to this day, speak of universal rights and yet then advocate exclusive rights in favour of White Men, is regrettably demonstrated by Kant's attitude to women on the one hand in his *Metaphysical First Principles of the Doctrine of Right*, the first part of the *Metaphysics of Morals*, and in *Anthropology*, as well as in his devaluation of people of some nations, as can be read in his *Anthropologie in pragmatischer Hinsicht* (Anthropology from a Pragmatic Point of View) of 1798 (Kant 1999a [1797], AA VI, 313–315 and Kant 2006 [1798], AA VII, 303–321 and elsewhere; see also Kleingeld 2019 for a very good discussion on the topic).

What one must be able to assert in general is not the right to be a guest, but a right to visit, which enables one to go where one wants as a visitor. From a cosmopolitan perspective, this right cannot be prevented from being violated in certain states.

> Here, as in the preceding articles, it is not a question of philanthropy but of *right*, so that *hospitality* (hospitableness) means the right of a foreigner not to be treated with hostility because he has arrived on the land of another. The other can turn him away, if this can be done without destroying him, but as long as he behaves peaceably where he is, he cannot be treated with hostility. (Kant 1999a [1795], AA VIII, 357/358)

On the other hand, if one wants to grant a right of hospitality, as the current problem of large migratory movements makes necessary, then, as Kant laconically adds, without going into detail, "a special beneficent pact would be required", to regulate the domestic community (Kant 1999a [1795], AA VIII, 358):

> What he can claim is not the *right to be a guest* (for this a special beneficent pact would be required, making him a member of the household for a certain time), but the *right to visit*; this right to present oneself for society, belongs to all human beings by virtue of the right possession in common of the earth's surface on which, as a sphere, they cannot disperse infinitely but must finally put up with being near one another; but originally no one had more right than another to be on a place on the earth. (Kant 1999a [1795], AA VIII, 358)

Kant limits world citizenship to the right of visitation because he is most concerned with arguing against the horrors of colonisation and with it the displacement or restriction of those who have settled in an area:

> If one compares with this the *inhospitable* behavior of civilized, especially commercial, states in our part of the world, the injustice they show in *visiting* foreign lands and peoples (which with them is tantamount to *conquering* them) goes to horrifying lengths. When America, the negro countries, the Spice Islands, the Cape, and so on and so forth were discovered, they were, to them, countries belonging to no one, since they counted the inhabitants as nothing. (Kant 1999a [1795], AA VIII, 358; see also Brandt 2011)

These reflections by Kant are still frighteningly relevant today, considering the inconceivable injustice that has occurred over a long period of colonisation in various parts of the world.

Similar to Kant, who, in the face of injustice and recurring wars with all their devastation, used the occasion of the Peace of Basel on April 5, 1795 to formulate a peace treaty with all mankind in his essay *Toward Perpetual Peace*, and in doing so expresses a self-referential, performative moment of his political philosophy, Friedrich Hölderlin, on the occasion of the Peace of Lunéville on February 9, 1801, creates a celebration of peace that is not merely a statement, nor a poetic statement about peace, but performatively stages a celebration of peace.

The moment of performativity, the moment of self-fulfilment is already articulated in the title. It reads: *Celebration of Peace*. Unlike many of Hölderlin's other poems, the title is set without an article. It is not called 'The Celebration of Peace', which would start a poetic narrative, but rather, laconically, *Celebration of Peace (Friedensfeier;* see MA 3, 206). It is a "mode of song" ("Sangart") as the introductory words note, a singing of peace.

The self-referential character of the poem as a celebration and as a celebration of peace can be seen in several instances and contexts. Not only is the poem, according to Hölderlin's understanding, a song to begin with. Not only Hölderlin's poetry and especially his later poetry, but also his Bildungsroman *Hyperion or The Hermit in Greece* as well as his Sophocles-oriented tragedy *The Death of Empedocles* are linguistic testimonies to a highly musical, language-sensitive, tonally well-formed and rhythmic way of speaking.

The performative aspect of Hölderlin's *Celebration of Peace* emerges in the way

- that a festive space is created in the minds of the reader and listener;
- that a sonic composition with a rich, almost modern sounding landscape is set up and composed for our inner ear, which goes far beyond the composition of poetic speech and song (Gesang);
- that it is in fact composed to a high degree at all;
- that the prince of the celebration is sung about in a present-absent manner, his identity changing through various contexts of the poem *Celebration of Peace*;
- that the present / future / past (beautiful) humanity is invited and includes the readers and listeners throughout the ages;
- that the time formed in the poem and the time of the addressed readers are therefore created in a highly virtuosic manner

The poem consists of 12 stanzas that vary in number of verses and a total of 156 lines. Three stanzas each form a closer thematic unit. These four units of three stanzas each count 39 verses, subdivided into 12, 12 and 15 verses. The thematic structure of the four strophic triplets can be summarised as follows:

- Stanzas 1–3 introduce the banquet hall, the guests, the prince of the feast, the occasion of the feast
- Stanzas 4–6 widen the view into the depths of time, evoking the Gospel of John, the dying of Jesus with hope for a better world; reflecting on the long time, the length of time it takes people to comprehend God-given gifts
- Stanzas 7–9 join the beginning at the end and can essentially be understood as philosophical reflections that identify the celebration of peace not merely as a momentary event, but as a new presence of the divine

- The stanzas 10–12 broaden the concrete time of the celebration of peace into a perspective of the peace of the future, but also remind us of the fragility of peace. The linguistic style is clearly different here with the shorter verses, which makes the joy of peace perceptible with lighter, faster movement, but also the breathless concern of not being able to preserve the fragile treasure of peace

The Evocation of the Banquet Hall, the Arrival of the Guests, the Prince of the Feast

The first stanza conjures up a banquet hall that Hölderlin discovers in the blueprint of nature, various interiors within it and visible to our inner eye. It is a landscape in which the narrator sees festively set tables, mountains of tables, or so it seems. The boundary of the hall may be thought of as mountain ranges, the sky above is the roof. The space is furnished with "green carpets", "sweetly familiar" is what Hölderlin calls the room, in a phrase that is typical for him, making a blissful dwelling apparent, but also bringing a good, positively charged familiarity into play. The phrase "The sweetly familiar hall" ("Seeliggewohnte[r] Saal", verse 4) creates a feeling of security, almost embraces the reader and takes him into this hall, where the culinary delights are provided for, "Full of most mellow fruit and chalices wreathed with gold" ("Gereiftester Früchte voll und goldbekränzter Kelche", verse 6); one might imagine fruit trees on the hillsides. The hall is an "anciently built" one because, after all, it is mountains that form the tables and walls. If the solid old walls of the mountains provide strength, we are also granted a sense of well-being, for: "And aired is the anciently built, / The sweetly familiar hall" (verses 3–4).

Moreover, Hölderlin already evokes a festive mood with the first and following verse, which creates a world of sound as well as atmosphere and specifically appeals to the senses: "With heavenly, quietly echoing, / With calmly modulating music filled" ("Der himmlischen, still widerklingenden, / Der ruhigwandelnden Töne voll", verses 1 and 2). There is a sacred, solemn mood for and in the performance through carried "calmly modulating music" tones and sounds, one's breath is free and open in the "aired" hall, despite its venerable age, for it is "anciently built" and "sweetly familiar", as mentioned earlier. The German phrase "Seeliggewohnt[]" – that Michael Hamburger translated as "sweetly familiar" – implies at least two different meanings; in the sense of 'blissfully dwelt' it awakens the idea of a good, joyful, pleasant dwelling in this hall of nature, which is both nature and shelter, being a hall. But the second part of the phrase, "[] gewohnt", reminds us of 'Gewohnheit' and therefore also implies a habit, a sense of orientation and being at home.

Now it can also be said that nature, the outdoors, is the place where wars are waged, where lives are threatened, unprotected, where people die in great numbers. Hölderlin does not speak of it, at least not directly. Admittedly, peace as a theme makes war present in a passive way, in its absence. The declaration of peace, the celebration of peace turns the inhospitable place into a blissful, festive, dwelling place. What a glorious image to place before the eye of the imagination.

In his poetic works, Hölderlin artfully interweaves the most diverse levels of the senses, in other words of seeing, hearing, breathing, feeling in general, with levels of thought. What emerges in the verses of the first stanza presented here is not only the description and presence of the banquet hall, but a banquet hall for seeing, hearing, feeling, the perception of mood, forming and arranging itself before the inner senses. This hall, now ready, is prepared for the reception of the guests at the evening hour: "For, come from distant places, / Here, at the evening hour, / Loving guests have forgathered." ("Denn ferne kommend haben / Hieher, zur Abendstunde, / Sich liebende Gäste beschieden.", verses 1/10–12) Long distances have been travelled, the guests have arrived, the feast can begin. But who are the guests?

Throughout the poem, there are only a few individuals who emerge from the anonymous group of "Loving guests" with a tangible identity. I will return to these later on. There is much to suggest that the reader belongs to the large anonymous group of guests. At the end of the third stanza, the implicit I appears as host, and lets – all of us – know: "But you, grown dear to us, O days of innocence, /

It's you, beloved, that brings this feast-day too, and round us / The spirit flowers, vespertine in this quiet; / And, friends, I must advise you, though / Our hair had turned silver-grey, / To see to garlands and banquet, now like men immortally young." (Verses 3/34–39)

These verses indicate that all are invited who count themselves among the beloved guests. On the one hand, guests have come, as the end of the first stanza states, and on the other hand, the host advises people of all generations to provide wreaths and food: "And, friends, I must advise you, though / Our hair had turned silver-grey, / To see to garlands and banquet, now like men immortally young".

The lyrical narrator also states: "And many there are I would invite" ("Und manchen möcht' ich laden", verse 4/40). *Celebration of Peace*, I argue, has a here and now just as much as it embraces places and times virtually. Thus it also addresses the future of any reader.

If one tries to make the host of this feast, this celebration of peace, tangible, one should be careful not to identify the frequently appearing narrator-I throughout the poem with Friedrich Hölderlin. The sometimes implicit, sometimes explicit lyrical I is a singer and poet (Sänger), as becomes clear in some passages; he, the host, is a person of knowledge who embraces the depths of time just as he embraces a style of singing that, as Hölderlin wrote in one of the letters mentioned earlier, who "consider[s] the recent or the distant past"; he goes on to say, "everything seems to be leading up to an exceptional period, days of beautiful humanity, days of certain, fearless goodness and ways of thinking that are lucid and holy and exalted and simple all at once" (Hölderlin to Heinrike Breunlin, 23.2.1801, Hölderlin 2009a, 193). The poet Hölderlin most certainly projected some of his convictions into the implicit singer in his poetry. However, the two should be kept clearly separate.

One important figure is missing in our evening gathering, in the presence of the guests – the prince of the feast-day. "And already with eyes dusk-dim, / With solemn day-labour smiling, / I think that I see him in person, the prince of the feast-day." ("Und dämmernden Auges denk' ich schon, / Vom ernsten Tagwerk lächelnd, / Ihn selbst zu sehn, den Fürsten des Fests.", verses 2/13–15) On the one hand, guests have arrived, on the other hand, further guests, who are apparently still to come, are advised to provide wreaths and food. But one person in particular is also emphasised, namely the "prince of the feast", Michael Hamburger translates twice, "the prince of the feast-day", "Fürst des Festes", who is first explicitly addressed as prince in stanza 2 verse 2/15 and then again in stanza 9 verse 112. He is expected in stanza 2, "I think that I see him in person" ("denk ich schon [...] Ihn selbst zu sehn", verses, English 2/15, German 2/13 und 15). The context in stanza 9 is: "To whom they are attached, is not missing; for that is why / You to the banquet now prepared I called, / The unforgettable, you, at the Evening of Time, / O youth, called you to the prince of the feast-day;" ("denn darum rief ich / Zum Gastmahl, das bereitet ist, / Dich, Unvergeßlicher, dich, zum Abend der Zeit, / O Jüngling, dich zum Fürsten des Festes", verses 9/109–112). He was sent for, but he did not explicitly come. It is open, whether he will come or not. He is present in the expectation. The question is: is it the prince of the feast – a youth, who is called to the feast by the lyrical protagonist, the host – or is a youth called to come to the prince of the feast. Grammatically, this cannot be clearly ascertained here in the German text of the poem. The translation decided to make a difference between the youth and the prince of the feast. However, the overall context rather suggests that it is the prince of the feast, a youth, who is invited here. The prince of the feast, who is he, what is his role? The prince, the one who is first, why is he not the one inviting to the feast? Why is he invited?

In literary circles, there are various interpretations for the identity of the Prince of the Feast. He, addressed as a youth in particular, could be Napoleon Bonaparte, whom not only Hölderlin revered for a long time as the messenger of a post-revolutionary new and better time. In the second stanza, it is said of the prince of the feast that he "like[s] to disavow [his] your foreign land", that he is "weary, it seems, with long heroic war", that he takes on the "shape of a friend", and that he is addressed as someone "known to all men", that is, in German, an "Allbekannter". The verses in question are found here:

But though you like to disavow your foreign land,
And weary, it seems, with long heroic war,
Cast down your eyes, oblivious, lightly shaded,
Assuming the shape of a friend, you known to all men, yet

> Almost it bends our knees, such loftiness. Nothing in
> Your presence I know; but one thing: mortal you are not.
> A wise man could elucidate much for me; but where
> A God as well appears,
> A different clarity shines. (Verses 2/16–24)

Identifying Napoleon, as the saviour of the European post-revolutionary world, as one candidate of the prince of the feast here in the poem is plausible. The storming of the Bastille on July 14, 1789 is considered the magical date of origin of the French Revolution, which stands for the disempowerment of the aristocracy and the establishment of the new civil rights of liberty, equality, fraternity (in other words, peace, I might add). As is well known, these new freedoms and political hopes were initially deeply disappointed when events were derailed by the Terreur, the guillotine, radical democracy; this later gave Napoleon the role of saviour of the new bourgeois ideals in the eyes of many, including Hölderlin.

After the tiring heroic campaigns, the poem says, the universal figure changes his identity, and takes the form of a friend – but he is not even present at the feast, although he is supposed to be there and is eagerly awaited. The commander becomes the friend of the people celebrating peace. But who is it that bends a knee? "doch / Beugt fast die Knie das Hohe", writes Hölderlin in verse 2/20. Is it a noble one who bends the knee in the face of the Prince's majesty? Or is it the Exalted, the High One himself, the Prince of the feast, who almost bends the knee in the face of the peace that is being celebrated? The German phrasing allows for both, and perhaps it is the author's intention to keep this ambiguity open. The translation interprets and negates the ambiguity: "Almost it bends our knees, such loftiness" (verse 2/20). What is irritating about the identification of Napoleon with the prince of the feast is that the narrator now confesses:

"Nothing in / Your presence I know; but one thing: mortal you are not." ("Nichts vor dir, / Nur Eines weiß ich, Sterbliches bist du nicht." Verses 2/20–21) Napoleon is a human being, and as is well known, mortal. One might think that even in Hölderlin's time, Napoleon as a hero was considered immortal in terms of the deeds and convictions he stood for and the hopes people associated with him. But the following verses 2/22–24 read:

"A wise man could elucidate much for me; but where / A God as well appears, / A different clarity shines." ("Ein Weiser mag mir manches erhellen; wo aber / Ein Gott noch auch erscheint, / Da ist doch andere Klarheit.") Not only here, but more often in the poem there will be talk of a god, one of the gods. Can the immortality of a hero, celebrated by humanity, be elevated, even temporarily, to the status of a deity? In a monotheistic world of faith, this would be blasphemy. But Hölderlin speaks from the horizon of a mythological cosmos of gods. The famous *Ältestes Systemprogramm des Deutschen Idealismus* (*The Oldest Programme for a System of German Idealism*) speaks of a new "mythology of *reason*", of a new "*sensible religion*" that is to be founded (N. N. 2009 [around 1797], 342). There is much to suggest, without my being able to elaborate on it here, that Hölderlin played his part in these thoughts written down by Hegel's hand (N. N. 2009 [around 1797], note 390).

It should be noted here that the prince of the feast was also identified with other figures – God the Father, Christ, Saturn, the God of peace, to name a few (MA 3, 206/207; see also Szondi 1970).

I am in favour of superimposing the different interpretations, as Hölderlin did in other poems when he addresses mythical deities in one as Christ, as Dionysus, as Zeus or others. This might seem far-fetched, but it is not, as I have just indicated. One thing is certain: In the 156 lines and 12 stanzas in total, there will neither be any arrival of this prince of the feast, nor will his identity become clear.

It is still important to take a closer look at the third stanza, which reads:

Yet not sprung up today, nor unproclaimed he comes
And one who did not balk at either flood or flame
Not without reason astonishes us, now that all is quiet,
Dominion nowhere to be seen among spirits or mortals.
That is, only now do they hear
The work that long has prepared them, from Orient to Occident,
For now immeasurably, fading away in the deeps,
The Thunderer's echo, the millennial storm

> Rolls down to sleep, intermingled with peaceful music.
> But you, grown dear to us, O days of innocence,
> It's you, beloved, that bring this feast-day too, and round us
> The spirit flowers, vespertine in this quiet;
> And, friends, I must advise you, though
> Our hair had turned silver-grey,
> To see to garlands and banquet, now like men immortally young.
> (Verses 3/25–39)

The God, the All-Known, is not "unproclaimed", is not only expected by the lyrical narrator-I, the host of this poetically sung celebration of peace, but by everyone. His arrival is expected, he is a hero "who did not balk at either flood or flame", and his arrival comes at a time when domination is not to be seen, not to be recognised, as formulated in the poem. This may reflect the post-revolutionary change of power in some European countries as well as the open power relations at the onset of peace in general after the end of a war.

It is precisely such a dying away of war in the explicit sense of the word and the dawning of peace that Hölderlin shapes here in a deeply impressive way: "For now immeasurably, fading away in the deeps, / The Thunderer's echo, the millennial storm / Rolls down to sleep, intermingled with peaceful music." ("Denn unermeßlich braußt, in der Tiefe verhallend, / Des Donnerers Echo, das tausendjährige Wetter, / Zu schlafen, übertönt von Friedenslauten, hinunter.") The sounds here are composed most artfully: It is an immense roar combined with a thunderous echo, probably of cannon shots, of the war drum encouraging battle and of fanfares that one might perceive with the inner ear. But this loud noise fades into the depths, falls asleep, as the words expressly state, in order to free and open the soundscape for something else: "The Thunderer's echo, the millennial storm", the Europe of the centuries-long, indeed over a thousand years of war noise, now transforms into cadences of peace that drown out the earlier desolate din. What a wondrous vision. One might also say that the banquet hall – built into nature, projected into it – is set in the very place where the warring enemies used to destroy each other, even if Hölderlin does not explicitly reflect this in poetry. With peace comes silence, a soothing stillness, another sound characteristic that, as we know, belongs to music like acoustic pauses. But silence also enables inner focus, concentration, in which the spirit blossoms, as some say.

Noteworthy, too, is the wording that the "days of innocence", also bring the feast today, too: "auch heute das Fest". That means, the feast may take place today, but also in the future or in the past. The openness of time is lost in the English translation: "But you, grown dear to us, O days of innocence, / It's you, beloved, that bring this feast-day too, and round us / The spirit flowers, vespertine in this quiet". ("Ihr aber, teuergewordne, o ihr Tage der Unschuld, / Ihr bringt auch heute das Fest, ihr Lieben! und es blüht / Rings abendlich der Geist in dieser Stille", verses 3/34–36).

Peace has not come for the first time, it is being celebrated now and today, as it has been many times before, with the difference, of course, that a thousand-year storm is now abating– that is, there is the prospect of establishing lasting peace, after the French Revolution and, before that, the American Declaration of Independence, reaching entirely new dimensions politically. A few years earlier, Kant had also put the vision of eternal peace into writing, in a covenant, with his peace treaty with humanity.

The first three stanzas of this peace hymn by Hölderlin take the reader and listener into the events of the feast; the place, time and occasion are now known and made tangible, the celebration can now begin with all the "loving guests", who have gathered for the evening hour.

"now that all is quiet, / Dominion nowhere to be seen among spirits or mortals"

This turn of phrase in verses 3/27–28 draws attention to a passage of text Hölderlin addressed to his friend Isaac von Sinclair on December 24, 1798, during a stay in Homburg (today's Bad Homburg). He writes in this letter:

> [...] it is a good thing, and even the first condition of all life and all forms of organization, that no force is monarchic in

heaven or earth. Absolute monarchy will always cancel itself out, because it has no object; in the strict sense it has never even existed. Everything is interconnected, and suffers as soon as it is active, including the purest thought a human can have. And properly speaking an *a priori* philosophy, entirely independent of all experience, is just as much a nonsense as a positive revelation where the revealer does the whole thing and he to whom the revelation is made is not even allowed to move in order to receive it, because otherwise he would have contributed something of his own.

Anything made, every product, is the result of the subjective and the objective, of the individual and the whole, and the fact that the share the individual has in a given product can never be completely separated from the share the whole has in it shows once again how intimately every individual part is bound up with the whole and that together they make up *one* living whole which, *individualized through and through as it is, consists of parts which are entirely independent* but *at the same time intimately and indissolubly interconnected.*

Hölderlin ends his letter with the reflection:

Of course, from any one *finite perspective* one of the independent forces in the whole will be the dominant one, but it can only be regarded as temporarily dominant, a matter of degree. (Hölderlin to Isaac von Sinclair, Homburg, December 24, 1798, Hölderlin 2009a, 117–118)

"Absolute monarchy will always cancel itself out" Hölderlin emphasizes. As the context makes clear, this is a philosophically metaphysical consideration that at the same time and inevitably brings up the question of political forms of government. The context in which absolute monarchy was literally abolished, or at least radically questioned, is of course the French Revolution, an event that is also in the back of Hölderlin's mind. There is no mention of law or politics in the rest of the letter to Sinclair, which has only survived as a fragment. However, just one week later, at the turn of the year 1798/1799,

Hölderlin wrote a letter to his half-brother Karl Gok that is remarkable for the context at hand in several ways. Several times in it, he addresses the bond between philosophy, politics and poetry: he got caught up "into all sorts of thoughts about the interest the Germans currently have in speculative philosophy and in reading matter of a political nature and also, but in smaller measure, in poetry" (Hölderlin to Karl Gok, 31.12.1798/1.1.1799, Hölderlin 2009a, 119) He also notes the "beneficial influence philosophical and political reading matter is having on the development of our nation", the Germans. He is annoyed by the "the affected talk of heartless cosmopolitanism and inflated metaphysics" among Germans. He sees a remedy for this in the acquaintance "with the constitutions and philosophers of the world" (Hölderlin to Karl Gok, 31.12.1798/1.1.1799, Hölderlin 2009a, 120), but also in the development of interest in the general, which is able to put aside short-sighted and one-sided personal interests, customs and opinions and to question their meaning where this is necessary for the better progress of humanity.

"Kant is the Moses of our Nation", as Hölderlin writes, morally as unconditionally as pragmatically far-sighted, leading us out of the desert, making philosophy a political study; just as, in general, philosophy and politics, duty and law, have to go hand in hand, supporting and accompanying each other, as Hölderlin thoughtfully notes on January 1, 1799. Although, according to Hölderlin with great clairvoyance, people adhere "too one-sidedly towards the great autonomy of human nature, still it is the only possible philosophy *for our time*". Hölderlin emphasises:

> For all that, the interest in philosophy and politics, even if it were more general and serious than it is, falls far short of being sufficient for the education of the nation, and it would be a good thing if there were at last an end to the boundless misconceptions that lead to art, and especially poetry, being devalued by those who practise and enjoy it. So much has already been said about the influence of the arts on the education of man, but it always came out as if it wasn't meant to be taken seriously, and that was quite natural, because they didn't reflect on what the true nature of art, and especially

poetry, is. (Hölderlin to Karl Gok, 31.12.1798/1.1.1799, Hölderlin 2009a, 121)

Poetry is not a superficial pastime or distraction, but gives us a sense of tranquillity that is a source of vitality, a view shared by Hölderlin and Friedrich Schiller. Several of these reflections bring to mind Schiller's concept of aesthetic education as well as that of active determinability in the essay *Ueber die ästhetische Erziehung des Menschen in einer Reihe von Briefen* (*On the Aesthetic Education of Man in a Series of Letters*) from 1795. It is the central task of art to stimulate in people a state of active determinability that makes them open and receptive to beauty and all that aesthetic education seeks to awaken in the sensual and spiritual forces: Morality, freedom, responsibility, for oneself and for others, and more generally a sense of the common good in society (see Waibel 2013). Like Schiller, Hölderlin prescribes a "philosophico-political cure", a "political and philosophical education" for the Germans (Hölderlin to Karl Gok, 31.12.1798/1.1.1799, Hölderlin 2009a, 123).

The people of that time, including Hölderlin, lived in a fever of revolution, of renewal. It is a philosophical attitude of the spirit that is guided by the idea of renewing oneself from the individual, of questioning, of becoming actively active, of making a difference. These are the basic elements of Kant's and Fichte's philosophy, and the postkantian writers, including Hölderlin, tended to follow them.

With his book *Hölderlin und die Französische Revolution* (*Hölderlin and the French Revolution*), published in 1969, Pierre Bertaux made a decisive contribution to bringing the political dimension of Hölderlin's poetic work into view.

At the same time, it is clear that the orientation of the philosophers and poets of this time towards subjectivity does not mean retreating into an inwardness, but rather that it is clear that the renewal, opening up, transformation emanating from spirited individuals must also be a transformative event for society as a whole. The vision of a new beginning is consequently one that must ultimately have an effect on politics and that, with the philosophical and spiritual new beginning, an opening for the new must take place. The openness that Hölderlin so powerfully sings about has attracted many interpreters.

Openness is here in Hölderlin's philosophy another word for freedom. It speaks to the horizon of possibilities to be grasped in thought and action, but also to the need and responsibility to shape where matters of life are not yet fixed. Openness is a freedom in which one is placed in order to become active, to take responsibility if necessary; or also in order to endure and cope with the uncertainty, unpredictability, the very openness of life.

Freedom is a commodity that must first be understood by the individual in its singularity as well as in its generalisability, that must be created as a value in order to then have an effect on the world through action. Freedom has many facets, sometimes also that of creating openness because prevailing norms and values are questioned. The French Revolution of 1789, but also the American Declaration of Independence of 1776, was experienced and recognised as such a turning point at the time, and still is today. It is very gratifying that the ideas of freedom, equality, citizenship and peace have their historical place and that some of them have been realised. The fact that these ideas still hold a great deal of potential for future developments, that what has been achieved covers up some blind spots – after all, what does equal rights for women, people of a different gender or people of colour mean today – is a great aspiration that demands realisation, in our minds, in education, in culture, in politics.

Hölderlin studied numerous writings on the political philosophy of his time by Rousseau, Fichte, Kant, and was probably involved in discussions with Hegel and his questions on the philosophy of law. He was familiar with Schiller's intention not to make literature an instrument of politics, but nevertheless to articulate central convictions in it. Hölderlin's *Celebration of Peace* is a song, but a song that paints a picture of a more beautiful humanity.

It is astonishing and worth emphasising that Hölderlin very clearly testifies to an anti-monist and anti-hierarchical position both in his letters around the turn of the century and in the poem *Celebration of Peace*. He is obviously very serious about celebrating a peace that not only means the end of wars, but aspires to a social peace that brings real freedom and equality into view and allows them to be expected.

"Much, from the morning onwards, / Since we have been a discourse and have heard from one another, / Has human kind learnt; but soon we shall be song"

These important verses are found at the beginning of stanza 8 (verses 91–93). Here we are talking about the morning, whereas in the first stanza the guests of the peace celebration have gathered at the evening hour. This could lead one to equate the *Celebration of Peace* with the events of a day. It may be a world-day, but it is certainly not a day in the literal sense. In Hölderlin's thinking, morning can be associated with the Orient, the East, Asia and Greece, from where the Scriptures, the Bible, found its way to the West, to the Occident. Biblical content is alluded to several times in this poem, which I will not go into here. It should be mentioned that in stanza 4, Jesus is mentioned without being explicitly named. He is one of those whom the host-narrator would like to invite to the feast: "And many there are I would invite, but you, / O you that benignly, gravely disposed to men / Down there beneath the Syrian palm-tree" (verses 4/40–42). The friendliest young man, kindly and earnestly ("freundlichernst"), a word composition characteristic of Hölderlin with his fine linguistic sensibility – this young man under the Syrian palm tree is Jesus Christ. The poem goes on to speak of the "beam" (verse 4/48), the beam of light that Jesus' words brought to humankind. The poet, of course, laments the "deadly doom" that befell Jesus on the cross, and at the same time, with an enjambment of stanzas, offers the consolation that this death, this doom, was not in vain:

But oh, more darkly, even as you spoke,
And dreadfully determining a deadly doom overshadowed you there.
That's heavenly fleets on; but not for nothing;

For sparingly, at all times knowing the measure,
A God for a moment only will touch the dwellings
Of men, by none foreseen, and no one knows when. (Verses
4/5/49–54)

Napoleon was already described as a youth in the poem, now Jesus
is spoken of as a youth under a Syrian palm tree. This is evidence
that there are different identities to be assigned to the prince of the
feast. Hölderlin refers several times, and also here, to the fact that
the gifts of the gods, the divine signs, including those of Jesus, can
only be borne by humans to a small extent, according to their capacity for comprehension. So, obviously, many signs, many small gifts
from the gods are needed in the long world-day, from morning to
evening, from the Orient to the Occident, through which the heavenly ones gradually send Goodness, Beauty and Truth to humankind,
since humankind again and again proves incapable, even unworthy,
of recognising, grasping and holding on to the divine gifts.

Jesus is preacher and spokesman on the morning of the world-day
of Christianity that begins with him and his word. The Church has
kept the conversation with him alive. Where religion is actively experienced and practised, it can be said that "we have been a discourse
and have heard from one another," (verse 8/92), again a linguistic
turn of phrase that is deeply touching and a call to examine if where
people are in conversation, we really listen to one another: "Seit ein
Gespräch wir sind und hören voneinander"! In this world day, this
day from the morning, in which the "Thunderer's echo, the millennial
storm", or in German, "Des Donnerers Echo, das tausendjährige Wetter," Hölderlin sings, roared over Europe, the West, humankind has
experienced much. Having experienced much includes the Enlightenment hope of having become wiser from the disasters, of having
learned. The promise is that soon we will be singing – "but soon we
shall be song", "bald sind wir aber Gesang" (verse 8/93). Moses, Jesus,
Kant let us hear their word, have initiated turning points in time. But
the poet Hölderlin counts himself among the singers, like Homer or
Pindar or Plato, whose vision is that not only songs resound and fade
away, but that it is a WE, a community, that IS singing. A great word,
a bold hope.

Speaking and listening on the one hand, and singing, alternating with a chorus, the we of speaking and listening, the we of singing – Hölderlin had a deep awareness that literature, that the poetry he sought to create, had to be a mirror of the whole, more beautiful, better human being. He distinguished philosophy from this. He developed a procedure according to which he assigns to the poetic imagination and fantasy, in all its immediacy, as much its place as to the many other things that need to be shaped in a significant work of poetry. He gives an idea of this in a note he made on the occasion of his translation of Antigone by Sophocles. In 1804, he explicitly states what can already be observed in earlier works as well:

> The rule, the calculable law [...] is one of the various sequences in which imagination and feeling and reasoning develop according to poetic logic. For whereas philosophy only ever treats one of the soul's capacities, so that the presentation of this one capacity makes up a whole and the mere hanging together of the parts of this one capacity is called logic, poetry treats the various capacities of the human being so that the presentation of these various capacities makes up a whole, and the hanging together of the – more autonomous – parts of these different capacities may be called a rhythm (in a higher sense) or the calculable law. (Hölderlin 2001 [1804], 113)

The consideration that "imagination and feeling and reason develop according to poetic logic", "Vorstellung und Empfindung und Räsonnement, [sich] nach poëtischer Logik, entwikelt" (MA 2, 369), and that these different faculties are linked in poetry, while philosophy develops only one sequence, namely that of reason, or better, résonnement, reveals Hölderlin's highly reflective awareness of the problems of poetic, artistic activity. The logos of imagination concerns the choice of fable, story or object of representation. The deliberation of sensation refers to the musicality, rhythm and metrics of language as well as the sensation of feelings, or the creation of moods ("Stimmungen"). The deliberation of reflection refers to the layer of reflection present in the work of art, but not to the poetological reflection, which is a meta-reflection of the work of art.

Composing the poetic whole, and thereby combining different levels such as the feeling, the content of the object, the musical rhythm into a whole that passes through very different parts, is not only a central concern in the main poetological writing *Wenn der Dichter einmal des Geistes mächtig ...* (*When the Poet is once in Command of the Spirit ...*) but is also reflected several times in the *Frankfurter Aphorismen* (*Frankfurt Aphorisms*), also called *Sieben Maximen* (*Seven Maxims*). Hölderlin states about the work of the poet that he must find the right measure of enthusiasm and sobriety, must sound out the right emotional state in himself and in the work, in order to then also emphasise how much he expressly thinks in musical dimensions when composing a work as a whole, that is, he understands the "song", the "Gesang", of poetry and the poet quite literally:

Altogether he [the poet] must accustom himself not to wish to achieve the whole that he intends in the individual moments, and to suffer that which is momentarily incomplete; his desire must be, that he surpasses himself from one moment to the next, to *the degree and in the manner that the object demands it*, until finally the main tone of the whole profits. But under no circumstances should he think that he can only surpass himself in a *crescendo* from weakness to strength, he will thus become untruthful, and overstrain himself; he must feel that he gains in lightness that which he loses in significance, that stillness replaces intensity, and thoughtfulness replaces verve in a beautiful way, and thus in the continuance of his work there will not be a necessary tone that does not to a certain extent surpass the one before, and the dominant tone will only be dominant because the whole is composed in this and in no other way. (Hölderlin 2009b [1789/1799], 241)

The singer is a composer, a composer who wants to present a highly complex whole, and who reflects on this in the most precise way in terms of production aesthetics, work aesthetics and reception aesthetics, in order to take these reflections over into the production process, which at the same time must free itself from wanting to plan everything, in order to allow creative freedom its appropriate place.

This consideration of poetry as composition, as music, as song, is an appropriate moment to address Theodor W. Adorno's famous essay, which he entitled *Parataxis*. One of Adorno's central concerns is to put Heidegger's readings of Hölderlin into context. With his contribution, Adorno created a new caesura in the reception of Hölderlin in the 1960s, which was oriented, among other things, towards Walter Benjamin's reception of Hölderlin. Adorno sees an openness at work in Hölderlin's poetry that orients its form to music. "Great music is a conceptual synthesis; this is the prototype for Hölderlin's late poetry, just as Hölderlin's idea of song [Gesang] holds strictly for music: an abandoned, flowing nature that transcends itself precisely through having escaped from the spell of the domination of nature." (Adorno 2019 [1963–1964], 394) Adorno linked this to his observation that Hölderlin's poetry is paratactically ordered. That is: "Dispensing with predicative assertion causes the rhythm to approach musical development, just as it softens the identity claims of speculative thought, which undertakes to dissolve history into its identity with spirit." (Adorno 2019 [1963–1964], 396) This is clearly turned against Heidegger's interpretation of Hölderlin, its metaphysical appropriation of his being and against the tendency to dissolve poetry into philosophy, as Adorno states in clear polemics in the first sections of his essay (Adorno 2019 [1963–1964], 380–381; Kreuzer 2011, 183–192; Bayerl 2002, 110–118). Adorno goes on to say: "Once again, the form reflects the idea as though it were hubris to fix the relationship of Christianity and antiquity in propositional form. It is not only the micrological forms of serial transition in a narrow sense, however, that we must think of as parataxis. As in music, the tendency takes over larger structures." (Adorno 2019 [1963–1964], 396) In the paratactic equation of linguistic formations, Adorno sees a linguistic gesture at work that has normative significance.

What is said is placed next to each other on an equal footing, forming an open sequence that can be broken off, but does not culminate in a supreme one. The hypotactic sentence architecture, on the other hand, creates subordination and superordination. The paradigmatic meaning for what is said therefore also designates the one who says something. The paratactic gesture obviously also includes dispensing with predicative assertions, since they also imply hierarchy. The serial principle of parataxis, which Adorno identifies as an outstanding feature of Hölderlin's poetry, and in which he already recognises an essential form of musical composition in Hölderlin's poetry, has obvious traits to the twelve-tone technique, which Adorno himself studied, explored and applied during the years of his own composing.

Adorno not only reflected on Hölderlin's poetry in the 1960's, but also made Hölderlin's late poem from the so-called Tower Period, namely *Die Linien des Lebens... (The Lines of Life...)* the basis of one of the 6 compositions in the context of the *Sechs Bagatellen für Singstimme und Klavier op. 6 (Six Bagatelles for Voice and Piano op. 6)* that he composed. The Bagatelles were written in the years 1923–1942 (see Klein/Kreuzer/Müller-Doohm 2011, XV). All six bagatelles refer to texts, something rather untypical for this genre, which, influenced by important compositions such as those of Beethoven, Bartók and Webern, rather suggests small, cyclically unbound instrumental pieces (see Waibel 2017).

At the time of composing the 6th Bagatelle on Hölderlin's poem *Die Linien des Lebens... An Zimmern (The Lines of Life... to Zimmer])*, from 1934, Adorno probably did not yet have all the insights he elaborated on Hölderlin in his contribution *Parataxis*. And yet it is most remarkable that this piece of Adorno's compositions is the one that is most strictly composed according to the principles of twelve-tone technique. Clearly, a direct line leads from this composition to what Parataxis contributed, even though there are more than 30 years between them. Hölderlin's poem reads:

The lines of life are various; they diverge and cease
Like footpaths and the mountains' utmost ends.
What here we are, elsewhere a God amends
With harmonies, eternal recompense and peace. (Hölderlin 1998c [1812], 329)

Back to the song *Celebration of Peace*, which Hölderlin introduces with the remark: "But if, nonetheless, some should think such a language too unconventional, I must confess to them: I cannot help it. On a fine day – they should consider – almost every mode of song

[Sangart] makes itself heard; and Nature, whence it originates, also receives it again." (Hölderlin 1998b [1803], 209)

The style of singing, as Hölderlin lets the reader know, breaks with conventions. Beautiful days, of course, promise open hearts of listening, openness to engage with the new, openness to a style of singing that breaks with conventions to make possible a new dwelling, a new spirit, a new we. This singer relies, in keeping with Kant, on his inner nature, which gives art its new rules: "Nature, whence it originates, also receives it again."

Kant stipulates in a famous definition of the artist-genius, that must have been binding for Hölderlin:

> Genius is the talent (natural gift) that gives the rule to art. Since the talent, as an inborn productive faculty of the artist, itself belongs to nature, this could also be expressed thus: Genius is the inborn predisposition of the mind (ingenium) through which nature gives the rule to art. (Kant 2000 [1790], AA V, 307)

In stanza 6 of the Celebration of Peace, we hear talk of the All-Glorious One, the Father of all existence, whose Son is addressed here as the "Ruhigmächtiger" ("quietly powerful"). The holidays are days of song, are days of joy, are days on which the high spirit draws near to the people. Hölderlin's verses read:

> Yet to the All-Living from whom
> Many joys and songs have sprung
> There's one who is a son, and quietly powerful is he,
> And now we recognize him,
> Now that we know the Father
> And to keep holidays
> The exalted, the Spirit of
> The World has inclined towards men. (Verses 6/71–78)

In stanza 8, there is a turn of phrase that juxtaposes conversation and song and differentiates them from each other. The idea continues with an enjambment in stanza 9. The context of verses 91–117 is:

Much, from the morning onwards,
Since we have been a discourse and have heard from one
another,
Has human kind learnt; but soon we shall be song.
That temporal image too, which the great Spirit reveals,
As a token lies before us that between him and others,
Himself and other powers, there is a pact of peace.
Not he alone, the Unconceived, Eternal
Can all be known by this, as likewise by the plants
Our Mother Earth and light and air are known.
Yet ultimately, you holy powers, our token
Of love for you, and the proof
That still you are holy to us, is the feast-day.

The all-assembling, where heavenly beings are
Not manifest in miracles, nor unseen in thunderstorms,
But where in hymns hospitably conjoined
And present in choirs, a holy number,
The blessèd in every way
Meet and forgather, and their best-beloved,
To whom they are attached, is not missing; for that is why
You to the banquet now prepared I called,
The unforgettable, you, at the Evening of Time,
O youth, called you to the prince of the feast-day; nor shall
Our nation ever lie down to sleep until
All you that were prophesied,
Every one of you Immortals,
To tell us about your Heaven
Are here with us in our house. (Verses 8/9/91–117)

Celebration of peace, feast, banquet, reminiscent of Plato's Symposium, – it is the poet's song that grants hospitality in a distinctive
way. Hospitality, one is reminded of Kant's world citizenship, human-
itarianism, which Kant admittedly addresses in a very sober philosophical and at the same time demanding way in the peace treaty,
demanding because hospitality ("Wirthbarkeit") is not grace, not
philanthropy, but a *right*.

The appeal to what reason and enlightenment demand in Kant's perspective is one thing. The other, however, is a renewed and higher Enlightenment, as conceived by Friedrich Hölderlin or Friedrich Schiller or, as the Enlightenment of the Enlightenment, by Georg Wilhelm Friedrich Hegel. In a more explicit sense than Kant, these call for the education of the whole human being, that is, not only of the rational but also of the sensual and emotional human being. In the *Fragment philosophischer Briefe* (*Fragment of Philosophical Letters*) Hölderlin therefore not only speaks of a higher context that must be formed and shaped as opposed to the mechanical course of human life, but he even speaks "of the duties of love and friendship and kinship, of the duties of hospitality, of the duty to be magnanimous towards one's enemies" (Hölderlin 2009c [around 1796/1797], 237). If the concept of duty points to Hölderlin's readings of Kant's moral philosophical writings, which he admittedly interprets beyond Kant, the idea of the duty of hospitality and magnanimity towards enemies points to a reading and interpretation of Kant's peace essay.

> A condition of peace among men living near one another is not a state of nature (*status naturalis*), which is much rather a condition of war, that is, it involves the constant threat of an outbreak of hostilities even if this does not always occur. A condition of peace must therefore be *established*; for suspension of hostilities is not yet assurance of peace, and unless such assurance is afforded one neighbor by another (as can happen only in a *lawful* condition), the former, who has called upon the latter for it, can treat him as an enemy. (Kant 1999a [1795], AA VIII, 348/349)

The state of peace is not a state of nature. Therefore it must be "established"; "Er muß also *gestiftet* warden", Kant tells the readers of his essay *Toward Perpetual Peace*.

The poet invokes song, a banquet hall in nature, a well-composed soundscape in which the thunderous noise of war descends, fades, falls silent to make way for the sounds of peace, a clear breath that proclaims joy and hope, as stanza 10, the beginning of the final triplet, ends with Mother Earth now knowing that she must not drag what is not yet ripe into the light before its time in order to keep the peace.

The vision of peace:

Winds lightly breathing
Already announce you,
The vapour that drifts from the valley
And the ground still resounding with thunder,
But hope now flushes our cheeks,
In front of the door of their house
Sit mother and child,
And look upon peace,
And few now seem to be dying;
The souls of the oldest even
Held back by a hint, a promise
Conveyed by the golden light. (Verses 10/118–129)
Translation: Linnea Gustavsson

Literature

Adorno, Theodor W. 2019 [1963–1964]. "Parataxis. On Hölderlin's Late Poetry." In *Theodor W. Adorno: Notes to Literature*, edited by Rolf Tiedemann, translated from the German by Shierry Weber Nicholsen, 376–411. New York: Columbia University Press.

Friedrich Hölderlin. 1998. Celebration of Peace. In *Selected Poems and Fragments*. Translated by Michael Hamburger. Edited by Jeremy Adler. With a new preface and and introduction by Michael Hamburger. Penguin Books. 208-216.

Friedrich Hölderlin. 1998. Friedensfeier. In *Sämtliche Werke und Briefe* (MA), 3 Vol., ed. Michael Knaupp. Darmstadt. MA 1, 361-366.

Hölderlin, Friedrich. 1998a [1803]. "Friedensfeier." In *Friedrich Hölderlin: Sämtliche Werke und Briefe* (MA), Vol. 3. Edited by Michael Knaupp, here: MA 1, 361–366. Darmstadt: Wissenschaftliche Buchgesellschaft.

Hölderlin, Friedrich. 1998b [1803]. "Celebration of Peace." In *Friedrich Hölderlin: Selected Poems and Fragments*, translated by Michael Hamburger, edited by Jeremy Adler, with a new preface and an introduction by Michael Hamburger, 208–216. London: Penguin Books.

Hölderlin, Friedrich. 1998c [1812]. "Die Linien des Lebens ... An Zimmern (The Lines of Life... to Zimmer)." In *Friedrich Hölderlin: Selected Poems and Fragments*, translated by Michael Hamburger, edited by Jeremy Adler, with a new preface and an introduction by Michael Hamburger, 328–329. London: Penguin Books.

Hölderlin, Friedrich. 2001 [1804]. "Notes to Antigone." In *Friedrich Hölderlin: Hölderlin's Sophocles. Ödipus & Antigone*, translated by David Constantine, 113–118. Northumberland: Bloodaxe Books.

Hölderlin, Friedrich. 2009a. *Essays and Letters*. Edited and translated with an introduction by Jeremy Adler und Charlie Louth. London: Penguin Books.

Hölderlin, Friedrich. 2009b [1789/1799]. "Seven Maxims." In *Friedrich Hölderlin: Essays and Letters*, edited and translated with an introduction by Jeremy Adler und Charlie Louth, 240–243. London: Penguin Books.

Hölderlin, Friedrich. 2009c [around 1796/1797]. "Fragment of Philosophical Letters." In *Friedrich Hölderlin: Essays and Letters*, edited and translated with an introduction by Jeremy Adler und Charlie Louth, 234–239. Penguin Books.

Kant, Immanuel. 1999a [1795]. "Toward Perpetual Peace. A philosophical Project." In *Immanuel Kant: Practical Philosophy*, translated and edited by Mary J. Gregor, 315–351; The Cambridge Edition of the Works of Immanuel Kant, Cambridge: Cambridge University Press; cited as usual, AA VIII, 341–386.

Kant, Immanuel. 1999b [1797]. "The Metaphysics of Morals." In *Immanuel Kant: Practical Philosophy*, translated and edited by Mary J. Gregor, 353–603. The Cambridge Edition of the Works of Immanuel Kant, Cambridge: Cambridge University Press; cited as usual, AA VI, 203–693.

Kant, Immanuel. 2000 [1790]. In *Immanuel Kant: Critique of the Power of Judgment*. Edited by Paul Guyer, translated by Paul Guyer and Eric Matthews. The Cambridge Edition of the Works of Immanuel Kant, Cambridge: Cambridge University Press.; cited as usual AA V, 167–484.

Kant, Immanuel. 2006 [1798]. In *Immanuel Kant: Anthropology from a Pragmatic Point of View*. Translated and edited by Robert B. Louden, with an introduction by Manfred Kuehn. Cambridge: Cambridge University Press; cited as usual AA VII, 117–333.

N., N. 2009 [around 1797]. "The Oldest Programme for a System of German Idealism." In *Friedrich Hölderlin: Essays and Letters*, edited and Translated with an Introduction by Jeremy Adler und Charlie Louth, 341–342 and note, 390. London: Penguin Books.

References of Research

Allemann, Beda. 1955. *Hölderlins Friedensfeier*. Pfullingen: Neske.

Bayerl, Sabine. 2002. Von der Sprache der Musik zur Musik der Sprache. Konzepte zur Spracherweiterung bei Adorno, Kristeva und Barthes [From the Language of Music to the Music of Language. Concepts of Language Expansion in Adorno, Kristeva and Barthes]. Würzburg: Königshausen und Neumann.

Bertaux, Pierre. 1969. Hölderlin und die Französische Revolution [Hölderlin and the French Revolution]. Frankfurt a.M.: Suhrkamp.

Brandt, Reinhard. 2011. "Vom Weltbürgerrecht." In *Immanuel Kant. Zum ewigen Frieden*. Klassiker Auslegen, 1, edited by Otfried Höffe, 95–106. Berlin: Akademie-Verlag.

Höffe, Otfried. 2011. "Einleitung: Der Friede als ein vernachlässigtes Ideal." In *Immanuel Kant. Zum ewigen Frieden*, Klassiker Auslegen, 1, edited by Otfried Höffe, 1–18. Berlin: Akademie-Verlag.

Hölderlin-Jahrbuch 1955/56. 1957. Beiträge zu Hölderlins 1954 neu aufgefundener 'Friedensfeier' von Paul Böckmann, Meta Corssen, Else Buddeberg, Lothar Kempter, Walter Bröcker und einer Bibliographie der bisherigen Literatur zu Hölderlins 'Friedensfeier', 1–109, Tübingen: J.C.B. Mohr (Paul Siebeck).

Kersting, Wolfgang. 1996. "Weltfriedensordnung und globale Verteilungsgerechtigkeit." In *"Zum ewigen Frieden": Grundlagen, Ak-*

tualität und Aussichten einer Idee von Immanuel Kant, edited by Reinhard Merkel, 172–212. Frankfurt a.M.: Suhrkamp.

Klein, Richard, Johann Kreuzer, and Stefan Müller-Doohm, eds. 2011. *Adorno-Handbuch. Leben – Werk – Wirkung*, Stuttgart/Weimar: J.B. Metzler. Werkübersicht und Siglenverzeichnis, X–XVI.

Kleingeld, Pauline. 2011. "On Dealing with Kant's Sexism and Racism." *SGIR Rewiev* 2(2): 3–22.

Kreuzer, Johann. 2011. "Hölderlin: Parataxis." In *Adorno Handbuch. Leben – Werk – Wirkung* [*The Adorno Handbook. Life – Work – Impact*], edited by Richard Klein, Johann Kreuzer, and Stefan Müller-Doohm, 183–192. Stuttgart/Weimar: J.B. Metzler.

Lefebvre, Jean-Pierre. 2011. "Guerre et paix autour de Friedensfeier." *Ètudes Germaniques* 66, 2: 239–263.

Patzig, Günther. 1996. "Kants Schrift 'Zum ewigen Frieden.'" In *"Zum ewigen Frieden". Grundlagen, Aktualität und Aussichten einer Idee von Immanuel Kant*, 1st edition, edited by Reinhard Merkel und Roland Wittmann, 12–30. Frankfurt a.M.: Suhrkamp.

Szondi, Peter. 1970. "Er selbst, der Fürst des Fests. Die Hymne 'Friedensfeier.'" In *Hölderlin-Studien. Mit einem Traktat über philologische Erkenntnis*, edited by Peter Szondi, 62–92. Frankfurt a.M.: Suhrkamp.

Waibel, Violetta L. 2013. "Die Schönheit als zweite Schöpferin des Menschen. Schillers Idee des 'Spieltriebs' und der 'aktiven Bestimmbarkeit' in den Briefen 'Über die ästhetische Erziehung'." Contribution to the Festschrift of Konrad Liessmann's 60th Birthday in April 2013. In *Intellektuelle Interventionen. Gesellschaft, Bildung, Kitsch*, edited by Katharina Lacina and Peter Gaitsch. Wien: Löcker Verlag.

Waibel, Violetta L. 2017. "Adornos Sechs Bagatellen op.6 im Ausgang von deren Dichtungen." In *"Durchaus rhapsodisch". Theodor Wiesengrund Adorno: Das kompositorische Werk*, edited by Gabriele Geml and Han-Gyeol Lie, 49–71. Stuttgart: Metzler.

2005. "Frankreich (France)." In *DIE Zeit. Das Lexikon mit dem Besten aus der ZEIT in 20 Bänden*, Vol. 5, Flue-Gram, edited by Zeitverlag Gerd Bucerius GmbH & Co. KG, 77–95, Hamburg: Zeitverlag.

Thinking, Evaluating, Enjoying
On the Aesthetic Materiality of Thought

Soumyabrata Choudhury

Introducing a Heideggerian Resonance:
Thinking at the Place of the Unthinkable

Anyone familiar with Martin Heidegger's works will hear the resonance of one of his well-known titles in that of the present essay.
"Thinking, Evaluating, Enjoying" will no doubt remind the reader of
the German philosopher's text "Building Dwelling Thinking". Let me
spend a little time on Heidegger's 1951 lecture to enrich and amplify
the resonance if not for any other more substantive reason.

Heidegger presented "Building Dwelling Thinking" in 1951 as part
of a colloquium on the theme of "Man and Space". This was apparently
a forum to discuss the scope of architectural thought. But Heidegger's
own contribution goes in a somewhat different direction. A preoccu-
pation that he had since the days of his seminal essay "The Origin of
the Work of Art" and going beyond the 1950s to the late Heideggerian investigation of the question of technology; the philosopher, in
his 1951 lecture, looks at the status of "the Thing" as other than an
instrumental or manipulable entity. This includes the status of the
"architectural thing". So instead of treating the so-called architectural
entity, which is the building, as something to be constructed and
utilized, Heidegger already grounds the essence of such an architectural project in something more primordial that he calls "dwelling".
The technological project of constructing a house, a bridge or any
other unit of public space must already strive to belong to the idea
of dwelling. Clearly, at the level of conceptual thinking, this order of

ideas is unusual if not counter-intuitive because according to this direction of thought, the very purpose of constructing or "building" which is to dwell, is already presupposed to have been realised in the thought of the architectural project: there is always already dwelling. So, strictly speaking, according to the demands of thinking causally, the idea of "dwelling" is *unthinkable*. But what is even more interesting in Heidegger's presentation is that this reversal of the direction of thought is not expressed in the slightest philosophical jargon. In fact, the entire lecture is delivered with a certain sense of being very close to the movement of *common language*, that is to say, the speaker addresses his listeners with an attitude of sharing the experience of language at its most non-specialized and secular usage. Yet, no one will deny that Heidegger's own use of language is strikingly – and sometimes disconcertingly – original and uncommon. The question that arises then is: how is this uncommon effect produced out of an apparently common and shared material? The answer to this is no doubt provided by Heidegger himself in several of his lectures and essays, particularly the ones dealing with language, art and technology: the most uncommon effect produced by language in its universal common movement takes place in *poetry*. And it is the poetic reconfiguration of common language instead of philosophical jargon that makes a presentation like "Building Dwelling Thinking" so public and so singular.

In the text itself, we read the emergence of the German words for building and thinking, as more and more defamiliarized from their accepted architectural and spatial senses. I will not enter into the actual deepening of the roots of these German words – that in any case is not within my competence – but even at the level of a translated text, this so-called etymological movement does not at all enable an interpretative or philological consolidation of the institution of meaning. It is not that we merely get to know deeper meanings of the common words that building and dwelling are; we are, instead, invited to *listen* to these words in a kind of self-dilating movement.[1]

---

1   For this exercise in deepening and dilating the German words *bauen* and *wohnen* (in German for building and dwelling respectively) in their intertwinings, see Heidegger 1993, 348–49.

Like in poetry, the displacement of words is not towards new meanings but towards a certain unexpected *appearance* of the word itself – even though the latter is totally familiar to everyone and no one expects anything new from it. It is in this sense that Heidegger lets "building" and "dwelling" appear in a way that is so unthinkable according to their referential or conceptual orders that the effect is one of being present to language itself in a new way.

Heidegger says that dwelling is not, in its primordial self-movement, being housed in a building. Dwelling is to dwell on earth. To that extent, the word is coextensive not with the architectural enclosure of space but with the existential co-dwelling with mortals as they exist on the earth (Heidegger 1993, 350). The architectural project of building can only respond to the call of this primordial sense of dwelling. Hence, Heidegger says, building must belong to dwelling (ibid., 362). And the only so-called demonstration of this reversal of the order of the architectural proposition is the poetic self-movement of language. However, in presenting this self-movement in its most singular, unexpected turn of appearance, Heidegger also pronounces a kind of historical verdict on the language of the present, the very language he uses and reconfigures. His verdict is that the originary meaning of words today has been forgotten. This is enormously and curiously significant because exactly when Heidegger himself lets language appear in a new way, in that very act he announces the forgetting of language's primordial power to appear.

A logical path to take in the wake of Heidegger's verdict would be the historical one. One could then enquire that when was it that, or in which historical epoch, the originary light of language fell into "oblivion".[2] In the several Heidegger texts that pertain to this question, we will never find a univocal historical answer because in Heidegger's view, the very horizon of history opens with this forgetting. Even the great Greek opening to what Heidegger calls the "history of metaphysics" takes place with a split in the world of Greek thought; divided between its historical calculus or technology of propositional thought and its immemorial presence to language's

---

2   "The proper sense of bauen, namely dwelling, falls into oblivion." (Ibid.,
      350)

proximity to things.[3] In this sense, it is difficult to distinguish between the originary Greek forgetting and the contemporary German
oblivion. But the paradox is that Heidegger himself speaks in and
through the present whereby he makes language enact new unforeseen effects. This then leads to the extraordinary result – that the
most singular poetic effects of language felt in the present are in
the service of the forgetting of language's originary poetic essence.
More exactly, Heidegger wants to announce this forgetting but he
must do so in the punctual historical present of his own times and
he can do this only with the abstract authority of a specialized philosopher. This is the shattering paradox of the Heideggerian act of
language.

If I may be so bold as to say, this is also a kind of "symptom" of
Heidegger's "forgetting of history". Let me try to substantiate this
point. In Heidegger's text, there is a very interesting ambiguity about
the relationship of language and temporality. At every moment of the
text Heidegger speaks of the paradoxical presence of the originary
forgetting that language carries up to the present of its usage. At the
same time, as a philosopher, he is able to subject to thought this very
moment when all of the "history of metaphysics" comes to a threshold
of self-exposure or even end – which Heidegger calls the threshold of
an "end of philosophy". So, Heidegger's voice is placed at that delicate
threshold from where the history of forgetting must both be recalled
and returned to its place of the originary split. So, the split itself is
redoubled at every moment of the history of metaphysics continuing
up to the point where Heidegger's own philosophical authority is located. It is for this reason that Heidegger himself must perform the
delicate task of deauthorizing philosophy in a philosophical voice;
while the very propositional and prosaic "sound" of philosophy must
now be recomposed or even re-sung as the call for a poetic ear to
lend itself to philosophy's newfound but equivocal resonance. Now,
at the level of the common experience of language at its most universal amplitude, one would trace this call to the innermost capacities

---

3   "As a form of truth technology is grounded in the history of metaphys-
     ics, which is itself a distinctive and up to now the only perceptible phase
     of the history of Being." 'Letter On Humanis'. (Ibid. 244)

of a "common", a "people" – but it is not certain that Heidegger does not return the capacity for a poetic ear to the exceptional attunement of the philosopher, even now at the limits of the institution of philosophy.[4]

Towards the end of 'Building Dwelling Thinking', Heidegger says that man's homelessness today in its attendant misery should not be reduced to the difficulties of modern-day housing projects that genuinely plague the working population (ibid., 362–63). Man's homelessness is the very unconcealment of the originary forgetting of the meaning of dwelling on earth that finds some of its most acute manifestations in contingent historical situations. But the situation itself must not be confused with the essence of the truth of "homelessness". Peculiarly, this warning by the philosopher gives the effect of alerting us not to confuse the truth of homelessness with the situation of the homeless. Instead, echoing his extraordinary analysis of 'The Peasant Shoes' in Vincent Van Gogh's paintings in "The Origin of the work of art", Heidegger here again asks us to lend ourselves to the *sensation* of rural peasant "dwelling", somewhat removed from the corrosion of industrial life. Even within the history of forgetting, there is as if a neighbourhood or even a sensation of enjoyment that peasant life unconsciously disposes itself towards in still being able to truly dwell, that is to say towards the thinking of the truth of dwelling.[5] It is by this hierarchical evaluation of historical sites within the *same* conjuncture that according to my argument, Heidegger disavows the task of thinking the truth of modern industrial capitalist life at its most uninhabitable and unthinkable place.

---

4   Though I cannot perform the task here, it's interesting to speculate how Heidegger's poetic rarefaction of common language compares with Franz Kafka's dictum "literature is an affair of the people."

5   See 'The Origin of the work of art' Ibid. 139–212. also see 361–362. Also see in this context the brief editorial introduction to the English translation of this text in which it's pointed out that one of the associated earnings of the German words *wohnen* for dwelling invokes the sense of "delight", a reconciled and harmonious type of *enjoyment* (ibid., 345).

The Sensation of Thought and a Trace
of the Unthinkable

There will be occasion to come back to the "symptom" surfacing out of the Heideggerian resonance of this essay and to recuperate its disavowed historicity. But before that, it is crucial to clarify that Heidegger is far from being a theoreticist or positivist anti-historical thinker. It is in this context that one might consult Jacques Derrida's 1976-77 lectures at École Normale Supérieure given in the wake of the tremendous impact of Louis Althusser's thesis on the epistemological break in Marx's writings, between a historicist, humanist phase and the construction of a true scientific object. Interestingly these lectures are published under the title *Theory & Practice*. Derrida interposes Heidegger and Aristotle, among other figures from the history of philosophy (particularly Kant) in the mainstream Marxist intellectual sequences starting from Marx himself up to Althusser. The chief motivation in this exercise is Derrida's desire to displace and complicate the classical division and hierarchy between what is called "theory" and "practice". The larger conclusion that comes out of these heterodox investigations is that both theory and practice are already part of the widest generality one confers upon the word Reason. This is also the absolutely essential reference to Kant but in this essay, I will not render it explicitly. But how does Derrida arrive at this conclusion – which instead of closing the relationship of theory and practice, opens it up towards new directions?

One of the key Heidegger texts that Derrida analyzes is 'The Question Concerning Technology'. The expected correlation between a theory of science and the epoch of technological domination is precisely where Heidegger makes his philosophical intervention. The classical understanding of "theory" being the knowledge of objective reality is, in Heidegger's singular move of a kind of linguistic recollection, refers to the Greek origins of the word "theory". Heidegger dilates the solid sense of the word "theory" into its Greek construction as a combination of verbs. One of these verbs itself has its roots in the Greek word *theia* – which means in the exact theatrical sense, the appearance of the aspect of something that is rendered present.[6] Derrida shows that here Heidegger is already dismantling the abstraction of theoretical knowledge towards an *existential* emphasis on the theoretical relation being one that arises out of a "concern" with things. But what is the concern? Here Derrida's own marginal notes suggest a fascinating series of associations that ally concern with value or dignity or even to intensify this style of thinking, a kind of "attachment" (with all its unconscious and even libidinal connotations that Derrida himself does not mention).

In other words, the theoretical moment of science or knowledge is already an existential involvement with what Heidegger has repeatedly called "things". Things are not the same as the objects of knowledge; they are, as already shown in "Building Dwelling Thinking", the sites for the *experience* of thinking that the poet responds to with a more delicate and attuned ear than the specialised philosopher. So, at this existential level, poetry is not the opposite of theory or more generally of knowledge; it is its primordial site of attachment or a kind of "concernful" attachment.

During this discussion arising from Heidegger's text, Derrida notes a little reference to Aristotle's Nicomachean Ethics which the German philosopher doesn't elaborate. Derrida himself, in this particular lecture, spends some time on this marginal reference, specifically the Book 6 of Aristotle's text. Here Aristotle is speaking of the domain of what in Greek is called logos – commonly translated as Discourse or even Reason. But in this enquiry Aristotle is not merely concerned with the intellectual capture of what he calls invariable things which do not allow for the thought of change. Instead of this rigidly scientific domain for the logos, Aristotle speaks of the ethical mobilisation that logos allows for in the pursuit of virtue (arate). This is interesting because the ethical search for virtue must itself be constituted out of the intellectual faculties that otherwise are imagined

---

6   For Derrida's investigation into these Heideggerian deconstructions of Greek philosophy see particularly the fifth lecture in Derrida, 2019, 80–83. My own discussion to follow from here is based on the material which Derrida cites and analyses in these three critical pages. This material consists of texts from Heidegger, Aristotle as well as marginal references to Plato and Kant.

to be dominated by the stakes of purely scientific research. Derrida outlines the process of this logistical mobilisation of reason (logistikos) that again proceeds from an existential concern with "things".

The point is that these things are nothing if not *historical* and woven from the fabric of contingency. Before I conclude this section with making a remark or two on the aspect of this contingency let me recapitulate Derrida's own outline of Aristotle's text.

The real interest of Aristotle's ethical system is the traversal from something like the most granulated trace of the sensible encounter of the human animal with things – to the threshold of a properly humanised question of choice (prohairesis), which synthesises the sensible experience of things with the thought of the thing when mediated by the properly human event of a "desiring choice". This is the expansive work of the logos in the history of society or historical societies (logos echon). Nevertheless, the question will have to be asked whether the stage of desiring choice completely assimilates the sensation of thought – which Aristotle calls aesthesis and at the strict level of its meaning as an animal encounter of the human being is unthinkable? This is the precarity of contingent or deliberative rationality that I am also calling the historicity of thought. On the one hand there is, this point onwards, a great anthropological project that western philosophy rationalises leading up to the doctrine of faculties and a general formula of Man = Sensation + Desire + Reason. On the other hand, the entire movement of thought between Heidegger and Derrida is the dismantling interrogation of this doctrine of anthropological metaphysics. In Heidegger's own trajectory, particularly in his late works the signs of such dismantling are most vividly seen in poetic fragments whether belonging to poetry or Heidegger's own philosophical prose. Derrida himself raises the issue of Heidegger's relationship to Marx through the text of 'The Question Concerning Technology'. Evidently to Heidegger, Marx despite his strong anti-theoreticist rejection of philosophy (particularly in his Thesis on Feuerbach) still belongs to the history of metaphysics or the anthropological dogma. In Derrida's lectures this relationship of the two thinkers with their respective announcements of "the end of philosophy", is rendered productively indeterminate. The Aristotelian perspective in fact permits the more fundamental question that if the Greek thinker instituted "man" as the principle or the measure of the flickering values that arise in historical and contingent situations – which are as much temporal as spatial – and this very institution is shown to be an anthropological metaphysics, then what effect does such a dismantling or decentering have? One of the effects is already evident in Heidegger's extraordinary extractions from poetry and other works of art as the very liminal signs of an end of metaphysics with their residual "saving power" in the absence of the arrival of any "gods".[7] But at the end of this section, I would like to indicate a second regime of effects, briefly drawing it out of another Aristotelian text.

In the Book 8 of his Politics Aristotle uses the Greek term katharsis for a kind of degraded, even animal enjoyment that the "labouring classes" experience in the theatre which is to be distinguished from the more cultivated delights of the upper social strata when enjoying the art of music in their leisure.[8] The criterion for this distinction is that the cathartic enjoyment, strictly speaking is unthinkable – if thought is to be understood as a logos which institutes measures and principles by which the proper works of human society are to be evaluated. In his lecture, Derrida has already pointed out that Aristotle is concerned with the work (ergon) proper to each stage of man's traversal of the logos: the aesthetic, the intellectual, the desiring. By the argument of the Book 8 of his Politics the aesthetic-cathartic enjoyment still does not lend itself to a proper anthropological capture of measure or principle (arche). This is the crux of the matter: at every stage of the traversal of thought or logos, there is a precarity and divisibility because no stage quite escapes the living memory of the unthinkable animal or aesthetic experience of the cathartic stage. At the same time, Aristotle in Politics says the cathartic experience is not the exclusive degraded potential of those literally treated as animals in human society – slaves, women, immigrants comprising the

---

7   For Heidegger's extraction of Hölderlin's original phrase "saving power" as inscribed in his *Patmos* see 'The Question Concerning Technology' (Heidegger 1993, 333).

8   For the relevant citation from *Politics* Book 8, see Ford 1995, and my own earlier essay on this question: "Ambedkar Contra Aristotle. On a Possible Contention about who is Capable of Politics" (Choudhury 2018, 199–231).

"labouring classes". The cultivated classes are equally capable of this enjoyment that constitutively falls outside the "scene" of value – in that sense is not constituteable as a form, hence is unthinkable. But precisely because everyone including the upper classes are in danger of falling below the level of anthropological institutions of value and "thinkability", everyone must be governed. So, Aristotle instructs the continuous monitoring and vigilance of the upper classes particularly its youth, so that the work proper to these classes does not get irredeemably corrupted by the animal-aesthetic habit (hexis).[9] This is the shattering paradox at the heart of Aristotle's philosophy which institutes the measure of all thinkability according to principles from which follows the evaluation of works proper to man and this very act of institution, at every moment, carries the hazard of falling into a sub-institutional or anti-institutional scene of cathartic enjoyment – in that sense im-proper ob-scene enjoyment. In political terms this implies the Aristotelian instruction towards the continuous government of an ungovernable human habit. Would it be a scandal to suggest that this kind of enjoyment which carries the oblivion of thought as principle and measure of value at its heart, resonates with Heidegger's favour for an immemorial enjoyment of "dwelling"? Conversely, one could ask the speculative-historical question that will there ever have been a thought of enjoyment? What will have been its historicity?

---

9   This Greek word *hexis* is a complex ensemble of meanings. On the one hand it means something like aptitude or capability which can be externalised into *ergon* or work. This is only possible with education, cultivation and eventually socialisation of the human animal. But as "habit" hexis connotes something automatic and unthinking. If *katharsis* in the basic Greek sense means physical relief from pathogens or toxins (or a virus, why not, speaking from within the thick of the time I'm speaking), then the analogy of purgation applied to aesthetic enjoyment reduces the latter to a repeatable form of response to the medicinal-artistic stimulant. In this sense the aesthetic material of a repeatable *hexis*/ habit is indispensable for the thought of art as form and deliberate construction but does not qualify *as* thought which is the constitutive power of hexis understood as aptitude.

Is There a Thought of Enjoyment?

Earlier we saw Heidegger opening the scene of history along the contour of a split or a division – between forgetting and the history of the disclosedness of that very forgetting. This is the same as the history of philosophy determined as metaphysics. While even in Heidegger there is a keen awareness of the anthropological support of this metaphysics, the primary site of the mode of human existence where this metaphysics and the history of forgetting that resides at its heart is played out, is *language*. At the same time, language is also the site of the redoubling of the split that opens the scene of history. In that sense language is never univocal and propositional; it is equivocal and poetic where the very manifestation of an inapparent forgetting is also the act of the disclosure of this truth of forgetting. Poetry ceaselessly exchanges the passivity of an effect of language arising out of an inapparent oblivion with the felicity or delight of something like a surplus possibility which language projects into the future. To this extent Heidegger's use of the word "oblivion" (or "forgetting") is essentially an extraction from language just as the salvational name "God" is the futural promise of language itself. The Heideggerian "symptom" of language is precisely that while it contains in its depths the several contingent associations and displacements of meaning, it also insists in the present, of its application on the essential necessity of a metaphysical determination. Heidegger distributes the symptom between the ambiguous poetic effect of the immemorial presence of truth (which Heidegger calls "dwelling" in the essay discussed above) and the propositional reference to a historical society (technology as the overwhelming empirical reality of industrial society evaluated by Heidegger's thought as a metaphysics).

What is interesting in Aristotle's position within the history of philosophy is that while he provides the inaugural paradigm for a scientific and theoriticist thinking he also opens up the *logos* to a logistical or contingent intellectual challenge. In that sense he is also the first thinker of *historical* societies insofar as history is the domain of a kind of precarity or divisibility that logos must constantly deal with; bringing into play not just theoretical reasoning but also subjective faculties like sensibility and desire. Nevertheless, Aristotle's own "symptom" is seen to be the equivocity between a hierarchical division of capacities and faculties articulating the animal, the slave, and the human proper to society, and the anthropological universalism of man as the measure or principle of all social and civic value. So, with reference to the corporeal meaning of the word *katharsis* in Greek which indicates the physical relief of being freed of the body's illnesses (*pathe*) implying a purely negative sense of "enjoyment", being also articulated with an aesthetics of higher cultivated civic delights (*diagoge*, cultivated leisure) Aristotle commits nothing if not an *anthropological inconsistency*. If Heidegger's site of philosophical equivocity is language, the site of Aristotle's anthropological inconsistency is the *body*. He, on the one hand institutes the doctrine of property or propriety with regard to what the human being must externalize at each stage of his process of thinking (*logos*) as the work (*ergon*) proper to that stage, and on the other hand, every stage is threatened by the unthinkable cathartic enjoyment: the threat being political insofar as the social and civic value of work is threatened by a negative and cathartic enjoyment unworking the very anthropological measure of all values and producing a trace of *ungovernable* obscurity (or even stupidity usually associated with any form of life reduced to the brute body of the organism) in every constituted and transparent form of thought. That is why Aristotle's *Politics* at this level is neither a political theory nor an organized praxis; it is a continuous government of contingency and precarity prescribing ceaseless vigilance towards this trace of anthropological inconsistency at the very dawn of the civic and political Man. Alternatively expressed, this "symptom" is the contradiction plaguing the thought of philosophy in a class society where class is the point of obscurity or unthinkability staining the transparent glass of theory and practice, which Derrida pointed out were on the same side of philosophical history. Curiously, this point of contamination which class and stratified society condenses in itself is also a point of enjoyment. Thus, insofar as the history of philosophy is as much a history of symptoms thought is accompanied by an obscure enjoyment, which itself is constitutively unthinkable. To which the question follows: is there a possible thought of enjoyment within not so much the history of philosophy as the larger space of a history of society? We could also call this Marx's question heard in several texts including in *The German Ideology*. And waiting in hope for a certain affirmative thought of enjoyment in Marx one must further wonder – what will be the site of such an affirmation given that the site of obscurity or inconsistency in the chronicles of great philosophers makes for either a certain melancholic triumphalism of the past or a skeptical government of the present?

In January 2016, at a public forum in Berlin, Alain Badiou and Jean-Luc Nancy carried out what was eventually inscribed as a text with the title *Dialogue on German Philosophy*. In the course of the conversation, the two French maestros arrived at the name "Marx". Both agreed that Marx can't be said to quite belong to the history of philosophy and that he does not confirm to the universal figure of "the philosopher". In fact, Badiou sets up a kind of test for what a true philosophical sequence in history might be: is a philosophy able to extract a universal value from the contingent historicity of a situation? (Badiou and Nancy 2018, 25) If so, how is it possible?

Though not responding directly to this test, Nancy actually suggests that Marx does offer a new value to be subjected to the universalizing thinking process in the concrete situation of the middle 19th century. According to Nancy, paradoxically this universal value is the value of "enjoyment". Nancy recalls Marx's texts in which the author, when advocating the abolition of private property, asserts that with such an abolition, the form of collective property, or property *as such* would also be abolished. This double abolition would be the event for the thinking of a new form of individuality. So, Nancy wonders, what would such an individuality consist of? Again he remembers a part of Marx's *Economic and Philosophical Manuscripts of 1844*, where the author speaks of the workers' "enjoyment" as it is revealed to be an essential stake of his/her production. The worker enjoys himself/herself in the very act of production in the mode of a certain recognition or dignity (or even attachment). In this sense, the production of value and the event of a kind of self-enjoyment are indiscernible. Now Nancy of course uses the French word "jouissance" as a translation of Marx's own German word(s) for "enjoyment" in the 1844 text (ibid.,

27).[10] I don't want to elaborate on the issue of *jouissance* – again it is not in my competence as I am not a speaker of French – but a short parenthesis on the equivocity and possibility of this word is in order.

In so far as jouissance refers to sexual pleasure, it brings up the perspective of an experience which is both intense and finite. To this extent, the linguistic challenge is to think in the word jouissance any kind of universal value to the extent that its primary reference is to the particularity of the sexual act. What is interesting in this discussion is that often in the general imagination of an infinite enjoyment, whether conceived of in the sphere of aesthetic or religio-mystical enjoyment, the measure of such an infinite experience still remains the irreducible real of sex. This of course leads to a logical impasse because the very measure is incommensurate with an infinite horizon of experience. This impasse is also reproduced in the relationship of the commodity with the consumer in capitalism. On the one hand the commodity is the object of "enjoyment" sought to be infinitely reproducible and on the other, by virtue of being an ephemeral object of utility, the jouissance of the commodity must always end. Capitalism's challenge is not dissimilar to the challenge of art or religion insofar as it seeks to measure an infinite circuit of enjoyment by the real of an irreducible but finite – or even more precisely instantaneous – pleasure/jouissance. That is to say, the commodity is relentlessly sexualized in the capitalist projection into the consumer's imaginary. Nancy's invitation is to think of a universal value of jouissance beyond and against this series of logical impasses that in his own words actually foreshadow the death of jouissance (ibid., 27).[11]

---

10   The implication of the workers' relationship to his/her production as enjoyment is surely the very ground on which the real historical analysis of workers' alienation in industrial capitalism can be carried out. After all, alienation is either the deprivation of an original capacity for enjoyment or even more disturbingly a perversion of the generic capacity for enjoyment into a specific form of *alienated enjoyment.*

11   Which is not to say that there are no significant differences between the spheres of aesthetic enjoyment, religious epiphany and the so-called consumer satisfaction in relation to the measure of sexual pleasure. It seems to me that religio-mystical experience has an ambiguous attitude

Historically speaking Marx is indicating something which is in the order of a kind of philosophical future. And as Nancy and Badiou separately refer to, this future is most vividly imagined in scenes of a society to come where the human being would work in the morning, fish in the afternoon and play the violin after sundown.[12] The philosophical infinity of this imagination consists not anymore in the image of an exceptional but banal "natural" experience (that is to say the sexual experience) but in a reconfiguration of the very ground on which human beings constitute their common forms of life. So, the form of life of a communist future here seems to be imagined as a zone of indiscernibility between labour and leisure, value and enjoyment. But we must note that while on the utopian side, this scene referred to by the French philosophers from Marx's *German Ideology* is an index for what Badiou called a future "Marxist anthropology", such utopia is strictly based on a critique of both the anthropological universalism of Man as the measure of what is the proper of individual human externalization into work/value (*ergon*) as well as of political economy which takes individual men as units of ownership of property both as objects of value and enjoyment (ibid., 29).

Two questions follow from the above analysis: firstly, how is the transition or change from the critical side to the utopian side to be thought? What is the *principle* of this thinking that itself cannot be

---

towards imagining itself in sexual terms. In religious narratives mystical transformations are often depicted through erotic imagery even while the eros itself is turned into a spiritual affair. Artistic thinkers in the modern times have often refused the analogy of their jouissance with sex. For instance, the theatre thinker Antonin Artaud violently rejects the hypothesis that the animating force of art can in any way be reduced or compared to the automatism of a sexual energetics. It seems to me capitalism is the most receptive entity to being sexualised. That is why Nancy's pronouncement of the death of the jouissance of value in capitalism is so significant. Also, for a reference I will not explain see: Jacques Lacan's verdict "capitalism, that was its starting point: getting rid of sex" (Lacan 1990, 30).

12   This shared invocation of the scene of the future from *The German Ideology*, among other things, leads Badiou to wryly remark that he and Nancy are finally agreed on one subject: Marx. Wouldn't this agreement also constitute a "symptom"? (Badiou and Nancy 2018, 27)

completely materialized by the historicity of the critical present nor be totally left to the clouds of the imagination? Secondly, what will be the political form of such a possible change from critique to affirmation? What will be its organized temporal strategy? These two questions in a way cover the greatest amplitude of Marx's project and the Marxist practices to come. However, the rudiments of this massive history are to be found in a text which is as brief as it could be from a year after the 1844 *Economic and Philosophical Manuscripts*. This is Marx's text called *Theses on Feuerbach* from 1845. In conclusion I will make a few notes on this text but before that let me close this section by reminding ourselves that in the 1845 work Marx explicitly raises the question of the philosophical institution. Badiou and Nancy are of course keenly concerned with what will be Marx's position, given that he is not interested in an abstract philosophical counter system to the established philosophical institution(s), but what is also of great interest is that the explicit object of Marx's thinking in the *Theses on Feuerbach* is not determined by the conceptual terminology of political economy that he is otherwise so preoccupied with. He does not ever mention the word "labour" in this text but poses the general problem of *practice*. It is this general level of enquiry that one had already seen in the 1844 text with the thinking of the form of what Marx calls "generic humanity" as opposed to the work of producing specific or specialized values through labour (ibid., 27). If in the 1844 text, generic humanity is not the description of either an anthropological or a politico-economic form of activity but a principle or even an *axiom*, then in the 1845 *Theses on Feuerbach*, does Marx have any further accompanying axioms to wager? And if to wager an axiom is a philosophical act par excellence, then what is Marx's "position" when he speaks of "human sensuous activity" in the 1845 text? Is it an anthropological or a political position – or a philosophical one?

Concluding after Marx's Eleventh Thesis on Feuerbach: The Transvaluation of Human Sensuous Activity as the Materiality of Thought

In the first thesis on Feuerbach, Marx reproaches Ludwig Feuerbach, the firebrand atheist Left-Hegelian, with not being able to think of "human sensuous activity" as itself an object of thinking. Feuerbach is only able to think of the products of human sensuous activity in the form of the external "object" or "reality" or even "thing". He is not able to think the thing that is human sensuous activity. He is not able to *think things*.[13] In this respect, Marx is tantalizingly close to Heidegger and both these thinkers, in their respective times and contexts, take a resolute distance from philosophy as merely conceptual represen-tation. It's a different matter that Heidegger in *The Question Con-cerning Technology* himself reproaches Marx for falling back on a metaphysics and anthropologism of "labour". My intervention at this point remains that Marx does not paraphrase "human sensuous ac-tivity" as labour in the 1845 text. He does not even oppose theoreti-cist or scientific thinking of external reality with practical-historical thinking. He asks the question *in principle*, as the very materiality of all possible thinking – isn't the thought of human sensuous activ-ity the inescapable self-reflexive dimension of all practice? To that extent, the pertinent problem is not whether thinking is practical or theoretical but rather that isn't all practice that is to say human sensuous activity internal to the very "act" of thinking. Marx distin-guishes between Feuerbach's contemplative materialism from what he himself espouses to be an active materialist practice but this prac-tice is not the same as the labour which produces external works and values; it is the "subjective" (Marx's word in the Thesis I) attachment to the very thing that triggers thought and from which the material-ity of thinking cannot be distinguished.

So, a precise and bewildering problem arises that if human sen-suous activity is to be taken in its subjective existential upsurge and not evaluated as the "object" produced by this activity, then by what

---

13   See the first thesis in 'Theses on Feuerbach' (Marx and Engels 1969, 13–15).

material reality – the real, as it were – will this subjective activity be measured. In the first thesis, Marx gives a somewhat idiosyncratic if problematical indication of what is at stake: he asks his addressees to desist from taking human sensuous activity in its "dirty-Jewish form of appearance" (Thesis 1). It seems to me that Marx is alluding to a precise historical situation where the "dirty-Jewish form" is dominantly received by society as a dirty-Jewish *enjoyment* (with all the overdetermined meanings that the French word jouissance has with its transgressive and surplus sexual connotation). The 19ᵗʰ century majoritarian anti-semetic Europe was constantly posing the anxious question: what is the Jew doing in his "dirty" corner? What secret enjoyment does he take in his hole (with all the animal connotations of a rat's hiding place as well as the subhuman ghetto)?[14] Marx, in his polemical figure, alludes to a very particular reality or real of his own historical situation that the name "Jew" both condenses as a point of blockage or obscurity of social rationality; and as also the point through which a vertiginous series of imagined enjoyments pass. They pass as "appearances" as do shadows in a theatrical play of light and darkness with only the audiences thrilled stupefaction to vouch for its ephemeral reality.

In the theses that follows, Marx does not at all abstract the so-called enjoyment of human sensuous activity into a new theoretical object of thought. He seeks to think this activity at the level of its subjective enjoyment – if enjoyment is to be taken as attachment or recognition not just by the other but as self-evaluation within the practice – towards a critical-analytical horizon as well as an affirmative-revolutionary one. Underlying both these horizons is a concrete materialist question: who enjoys the human sensuous activity as its subject? Who is the subject of enjoyment? The critical analytical refutation of Feuerbach is that the subject is not the isolated natural-anthropological individual, who according to Feuerbach is the victim of religious delusion or alienation. One could also call this

---

14   This anxiety with appearance or dissimulation today applies to the figure of the muslim on a global scale. Again its as if the question whispered deafeningly lingers in the air: what is the muslim doing? What secret *terrorist* enjoyment is s/he taking in her Islamic corner/ghetto/Nation?

Marx's refutation of Feuerbach's theory of religious enjoyment. For Marx the alienated consolation of religion is itself the product of a contradiction that is internal to human sensuous activity at the level of society or "social relations". So social relations are determined by their specific historicity rather than being the sum total of the institutions governing the activities of natural individuals. The subject of enjoyment is already a self-divided subject insofar as society is the battleground of contradictory enjoyments. In the tenth thesis, Marx calls this the battleground of "civil society". From the standpoint of civil society, the natural attitude of treating the social space as a test case of the secular demystification of religious delusions ultimately puts every individual to this scientific or theoreticist test at his/her own isolated level. From this standpoint, one is not able to see that even delusional enjoyment is an affair of social circulation and not an object of individual therapeutics. This is Marx's exhortation to the passive materialism of Feuerbach to self-politicise itself, that is to say, to risk a certain new political enjoyment.

However, if this exhortation is not towards any kind of adventurism (anarchist terrorism) or sensationalism (aestheticization of politics), then even this new enjoyment must base itself on a critique of class-and social politics. Feuerbach only sees individuals who belong to the two objective "worlds" – the delusional religious and the scientific secular. He is unable to see these two worlds/objects/values-systems as themselves involved in a contradictory social relationship lived out by the sensuous activities of "human" society. It is this new standpoint of a human society in opposition to civil society that Marx affirms as the possible ground of a "new philosophy". This is the crux of the matter: even while human society is, in Marx's historical present, a contradictory battleground of civil society – as well as the State, something I will not deal with here – as a new generic standpoint, it already promises a future. But the crucial prescription at this point is that for such a future to be realized, the present has to be changed in practice, which is impossible without the human sensuous practice of thinking this change, here and now.

Who will think this change? Or, how is it possible to think "change" itself as a universal value when the only material sign of change is a certain enjoyment or enthusiasm for the thought of change in a contradictory present?[15] In his eleventh thesis on Feuerbach, Marx dismisses the "philosopher" as the possible agent of thinking the thing called "change". The thesis reads "The philosophers have only *interpreted* the world in various ways; the point is to *change* it." (Marx and Engels 1969, 15). What is to be noted in these two momentous lines is that there is nothing in the second sentence as following from the first one which implies that the philosopher is obliged to change the world. At the same time the thesis delivers the imperative of change as an undisavowable philosophical blow. So, it is clear that Marx does not enjoin the philosopher to change the world. He simply rejects the office of old philosophy as passive and scholastic. The revolutionary force of change is a matter of historical contingency and precarity – which becomes the object of Marxist strategies of organization. But the universal newness of change or revolution as a value and enjoyment is the affirmation at the site of a new philosophy without any need for the old philosopher. Marx doesn't seem particularly interested in whether the vehicle of this new philosophy is the political militant or the poet of the future. He is not interested in replacing or extending the severe authority of the philosopher with the warm tones of a poetic voice or the terse injunctions of an organisational discourse. Something more this-worldly, non-specialised and rare is at stake with the thought of change: a new *capacity* for thinking, evaluating, enjoying is born and exactly at this birth, when the mirror of philosophy is cracked beyond repair, Marx utters the word philosophy as part of common language but with a new and uncommon

---

15   While enthusiasm reminds one of Immanuel Kant's choice of affect that the thought of the French Revolution produces in his text 'The conflict of faculties', we must remember Kant still thinks of this affect as arising in a kind of spectatorial imagination (see Kant 1979). The spectator is an abstract theatrical figure who sees as if the revolutionary events appear and pass through his/her "mind" as an objective neutral presentation rather than a historical sequence with divided and partisan subjective stakes. For Kant no partisan universalism is possible in real history. For Marx only a partisan universalisation of values and enjoyments arising in history can vindicate the truth and force of a materialist philosophy. The epic question for the future that Marx does not give the slightest trace of an answer to is: *Who will be the philosopher of this new philosophy?*

effect. Would it be archaic, or in bad taste, or an invitation to a secret, almost obscene enjoyment – or would it be an act of universal, public solitude today – to call this effect "communist"?

Literature

Badiou, Alain, and Jean-Luc Nancy. 2018. *German Philosophy. A Dialogue.* Edited by Jan Völker, translated by Richard Lambert. Cambridge MA: The MIT Press.

Choudhury, Soumyabrata. 2018. *Ambedkar and Other Immortals. An Untouchable Research Programme.* New Delhi: Navayana.

Derrida, Jacques. 2019. *Heidegger: The Question of Being and History.* Edited by Geoffrey Bennington. Chicago/London: University of Chicago Press.

Ford, Andrew. 1995. "Katharsis. The Ancient Problem." In *Performativity and Performance*, edited by Andrew Parker and Eve Kosofsky Sedgwick, 109–132. London: Routledge.

Heidegger, Martin. 1993. *Basic Writings.* Edited by David Farrell Krell. New York: HarperCollins.

Kant, Immanuel. 1979. *The Conflict of Faculties.* Translated by M. J. Gregor. Abaris Books.

Lacan, Jacques. 1990. *Television. A Challenge to the Establishment.* Translated by Denis Hollier, Rosalind Krauss, and Annette Michelson. New York: W. W. Norton & Company.

Marx, Karl and Friedrich Engels. 1969. *Marx/Engels Selected Works, Volume One.* Moscow: Progress Publishers.

The Balloon Universe

Tanja Traxler & Reinhold A. Bertlmann

Abstract: *Space is a highly relevant research topic in contemporary physics, as it tackles the unification of general relativity and quantum theory. In physics, space is a very special research topic: the traditional method to isolate the studied object is not possible. Thus, physical investigations into space need to be accompanied by philosophical considerations. In this paper, conceptions of space will be addressed from a multidisciplinary perspective ranging from physics and philosophy to arts-based research. In particular, the geometry of the universe, especially the Balloon model, will be examined in accordance to recent experimental findings.*

Prologue

On September 14th, 2015, only a few scientists noticed that this was the start of a new era in astronomy. Months later, after rigorous testing, it was published in February 2016 that the first direct observation of gravitational waves had been achieved by the Laser Interferometer Gravitational-Wave Observatory (LIGO) (Abbott et al. 2016). The finding is significant due to multiple reasons: at last, a century old prediction derived from Albert Einstein's theory of general relativity could be proven experimentally. Even more so, gravitational waves open a new window into the cosmos and offer an unprecedented opportunity for sensing and making sense of the universe.

Ever since humans started to observe the sky, the only resource of data was electromagnetic waves, mostly in the visible spectrum. In the course of the 20th century the frequency spectrum of cosmic inquiries broadened, e. g. when taking radio waves into account.

Eventually, a second resource of cosmic information was established but remained much less important than electromagnetic waves: cosmic particles. The dawn of gravitational wave astronomy allows for studying astronomical objects that remain largely obscure to electromagnetic waves and particles, such as black holes. As gravitational waves encode gravity-based information about the universe, their detection raises physical as well as epistemological issues (cf. e. g. Bunge 2018).

When the concepts of spacetime are at stake, the traditional method of the physical sciences to isolate the studied object fails. Thus, Einstein himself championed interdisciplinary scholarship such as the history of science when inquiring the very concept of space:

> In the attempt to achieve a conceptual formulation of the confusingly immense body of observational data, the scientist makes use of a whole arsenal of concepts which he imbibed practically with his mother's milk; and seldom if ever is he aware of the eternally problematic character of his concepts. [...] He [the scientist] will however, be grateful to the historian if the latter can convincingly correct such views of purely intuitive origin. (Jammer 1993, xiii–xiv)

While since Kant's *Critique of Pure Reason* the concept of intuition is most relevant for the philosophical discourse when addressing space, when Einstein refers to "views of purely intuitive origin", he appears to not use "intuition" as a technical philosophical term but rather as a synonym for instinct.

It is our hypothesis that cross-disciplinary explorations such as philosophical inquiry, historical analysis, and arts-based research are most valuable contributions to the physical investigation into concepts of space and time and vice versa.[1] The following analysis of conceptions of space and time, the origin and genesis of the universe, and the nature of reality will be accompanied by dialogues in the tra-

---

1   See performance by Jyoti Dogra, *Black Hole* (2018). Available at: https://www.youtube.com/watch?v=DQPlGg89TWU (Accessed: July 23rd, 2024).

dition of a Platonic symposium from a three-act play as presented in a lecture performance by the authors in October 2019.[2]

The Beginning of All Beginnings

Is space a substance that acts as an absolute container within which material objects are placed? Or is space a relative quality which refers to the relational status of objects and does not possess any independent physical reality? Questions like these, spanning between Isaac Newton's absolute and Gottfried Wilhelm Leibniz's relative conception of space, set the intellectual stage for Immanuel Kant's investigations of space. In his *Kritik der reinen Vernunft* (*Critique of Pure Reason*) of 1781, Kant contrived to develop a theory of space that would consider elements of both the absolute and the relative conception (Kant 2009 [1781, 1787]). This unification came at a price: no longer is space conceived as a phenomenon that is accessible by observation, but according to Kant's critical philosophy the structure of space itself is inscribed into the human subject as an a priori intuition. Thus, scholarly knowledge of space is inseparable from the means of representing space to ourselves by experience (DiSalle 2006, 56). This means that space is a problem of both, of consciousness and of our bodily embeddedness in space: one needs to be in space to be able to imagine empty space (Böhler 2024).

In 1755, decades before the publication of *Critique of Pure Reason*, Kant anonymously published a thin monograph which went almost unnoticed: *Allgemeine Naturgeschichte und Theorie des Himmels* (*Universal Natural History and Theory of the Heavens*). During the printing of the book its publisher went bankrupt, therefore no more than just a few copies were circulated (Kant 1955, 10). The book re-

---

2   A video of the lecture performance "Das Universum ist ein Luftballon!" (German) by Tanja Traxler & Reinhold A. Bertlmann in the course of the Globart Academy 2019, on October 4th, at Essl Museum in Klosterneuburg, is available at: https://www.youtube.com/watch?v=joliWeOzynk (Accessed: June 20th, 2021).

ceived hardly any attention despite its monumental contribution – to cosmology and far beyond.

In *Universal Natural History and Theory of the Heavens* Kant presented an original theory of the genesis of the cosmos, in which the formation and evolution of stars, planets, and among them, Earth, were not guided by a supernatural power but solely by the physical behavior of matter. Evidently, mathematical techniques and empirical findings have evolved dramatically since Kant, but nevertheless his proposed nebular hypothesis comes in large parts close to modern explanations of the formation of celestial objects as outlined by the so-called solar nebular disk model.

Intriguingly, before Kant, inquiries in natural history were mainly concerned with evolution in space, while human history dealt with changes over time. Kant's *Universal Natural History and Theory of the Heavens* brought the scope of the latter into the scholarship of the former and thus paved the way to framing natural history as an evolution in time. This fundamental shift was hardly noticed, even less cherished by his contemporaries and successors. Early credit came from dialectical materialism: in *Dialektik der Natur* (*Dialectics of Nature*) Friedrich Engels referred to Kant's *Universal Natural History and Theory of the Heavens* as the "point of departure for all further progress" (Marx and Engels 1987, 324).

Fueled by advances in astronomical measurement techniques, plenty of empirical evidence could be contrived which set the foundation for Kant's philosophical analysis: by and large it had become clear that the surface of the moon is much bumpier than previously believed. Even more so, with his changing appearance through the seasons, Mars seemed to be a world like earth. Through the comparison of old and more recent star charts in the beginning of the 18th century it was revealed that presumably fixed stars had changed their positions. Also, the discovery of supernovae called into question the unchangeable and unmovable character of stars. However, most relevant for Kant's reasoning was the observation of blurred astronomical objects which Thomas Wright believed to be huge assemblages of distant stars (Kant 1955, 9). At that time, the term "nebulae" referred to diffused astronomical objects of any kind. Only later the notion was exclusively reserved for interstellar clouds of dust, hydrogen, helium, and other ionized gases, but not for distant galaxies.

Based on these observations, Kant proposed the idea that Earth, the solar system, and even the fixed stars were created by natural processes from primitive matter such as nebulae. Within the framework of this nebular hypothesis, the planetary system did not require a creator, as it did according to Newton's understanding. The only action that Kant left to a supernatural being was the creation of some initial matter in the distant past, from which everything else has developed through natural processes alone.

Thus remained the question how and why the beginning of the universe took place – unless the universe has been there forever. While Kant favored the idea that initial, unstructured matter took over from pure nothingness, later scholars retrieved Aristotle's eternity of the cosmos. The 20th century brought a major shock to the believers in an eternal universe: by help of yet even more powerful astronomical observation technologies, Edwin Hubble proved that many astronomical objects classified as nebulae were not clouds of cosmic dust but galaxies beyond the Milky Way. On top of that, Hubble provided evidence that all these nebulae appeared to recede from Earth. To account for this fact, it was useful to assume that the universe was expanding, alas distant galaxies do not actually travel away from Earth, but through the expansion of the universe space itself is swelling and the distance between remote galaxies increases with by the overall flow.

How could believers in the eternal cosmos save their cosmogony in the face of these findings? Steady-state model was the name of their last resort, which was proposed by Fred Hoyle, Thomas Gold, and Hermann Bondi. Inspiration came from the movie *Dead of Night* of 1945, which was a favorite of these three scientists. *Dead of Night* served as a metaphor that something can be dynamic by being unchangeable, like an evenly flowing river (Clegg 2012, 188ff.). Analogously, the steady-state model suggested that even an expanding universe could be eternal, assuming that its density remained unchanged due to a continuous creation of matter. It was thus a physical theory to account for eternity – yet the final nail in its coffin was already waiting around the corner, within our own galaxy.

Figure 1: This composite image of the Orion Nebula, retrieved by the Hubble Space Telescope and the Spitzer Space Telescope, shows gaseous swirls of hydrogen, sulfur, and hydrocarbons that hold a collection of infant stars. (Credit: NASA/JPL-Caltech STScI)

Figure 2: Tanja Traxler & Reinhold A. Bertlmann during the lecture performance "Das Universum ist ein Luftballon!" at Globart Academy, October 4th, 2019. (Credit: Zentralbibliothek für Physik der Universität Wien)

The Curvature of Space and Time

Jamming signals or pigeons' shit? Those were the options that Arno Penzias and Robert Wilson faced in 1965 when their high precision measurements by help of a radio telescope showed a faint background noise which they were unable to get rid of. After rigorous testing, both interference signals and feces could be ruled out, and fortunately colleagues of Penzias and Wilson offered another explanation – of extraterrestrial origin. As it was established by Hubble's measurements that the universe expands, two rival theories were left to provide a proper description of cosmogony: the steady-state model and the Big Bang theory.

As George Gamov had first realized, if the Big Bang theory was correct, then space across the universe should be filled with remnant photons from this creation event. The calculations placed the frequencies of these photons in the microwave spectrum. Eventually it turned out that it was exactly this cosmic microwave background that Penzias and Wilson had accidentally detected (Penzias and Wilson 1965, 419). According to Stephen Hawking, the discovery of the cosmic microwave background served as the "final nail in the coffin of the steady-state theory" (Hawking 2002).

By addressing most remote astronomical phenomena that are entirely alien to everyday physics, both Hawking and his colleague Roger Penrose made major contributions to our understanding of how the universe has evolved ever since its fulminant beginning. Among their favored objects of inquiry were black holes. So, what is a black hole?

A region respectively an object[3] in spacetime is called a black hole if the gravity there is so strong that nothing – no matter, no light – can escape. According to Einstein's Theory of General Relativity which predicts that a sufficiently large mass can curve spacetime so much as to form a black hole, such regions do exist. A black hole can be the final stage of a star when it is massive enough. The star after

---

3   Depending on perspective, a black hole can either be conceived of as a region in spacetime which is extremely curved through gravity, or as an object with sufficiently large mass to curve spacetime.

its explosion to a supernova collapses under its own gravitation and forms a black hole. The boundary of the region from which escape is impossible is called the *event horizon*. In the center there is a *singularity*, a point with infinite density, see Fig. 3.

However, a black hole is not entirely black, the quantum field fluctuations allow the black hole to emit radiation – the so-called *Hawking radiation*. Thus, a black hole evaporates. While the *Hawking radiation* still needs to be experimentally verified, there is broad agreement that it exists, and there are several attempts to detect it by help of laboratory systems (Robertson 2012).

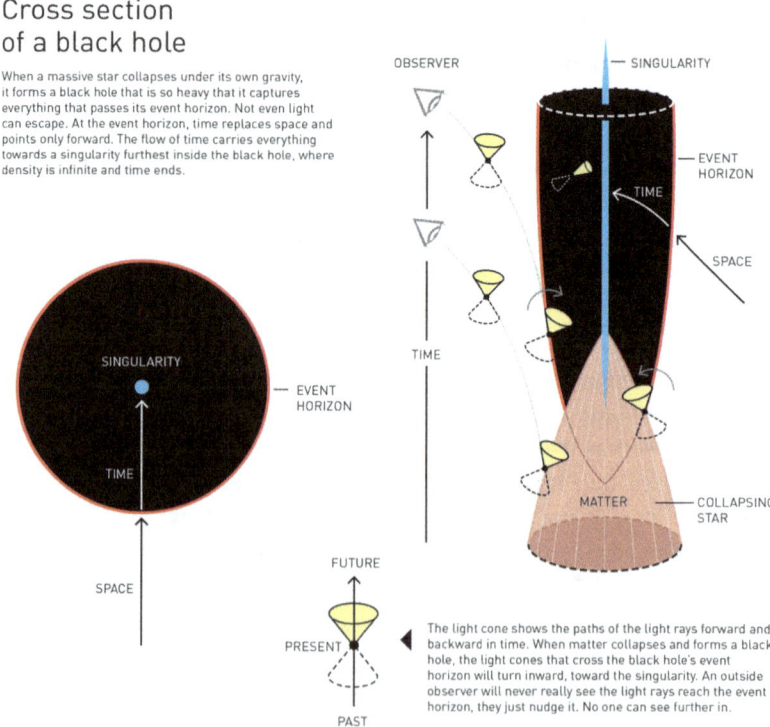

Cross section of a black hole

When a massive star collapses under its own gravity, it forms a black hole that is so heavy that it captures everything that passes its event horizon. Not even light can escape. At the event horizon, time replaces space and points only forward. The flow of time carries everything towards a singularity furthest inside the black hole, where density is infinite and time ends.

OBSERVER   SINGULARITY

EVENT HORIZON

TIME

SPACE

SINGULARITY

EVENT HORIZON

TIME

MATTER   COLLAPSING STAR

TIME

SPACE

FUTURE

PRESENT

PAST

The light cone shows the paths of the light rays forward and backward in time. When matter collapses and forms a black hole, the light cones that cross the black hole's event horizon will turn inward, toward the singularity. An outside observer will never really see the light rays reach the event horizon, they just nudge it. No one can see further in.

Figure 3: The graphics to the left display a black hole with the singularity in the center and the event horizon. To the right, the evolution of a collapsing star is presented, time is in the vertical, space in the horizontal. (Credit: Nobelprize.org)

In a nutshell, the physics of black holes implies that spacetime is curved substantially in the presence of massive astronomical objects. However, there remains the question of the overall curvature of three-dimensional space across the universe.

Until the 1800s it went without saying that it is possible to mathematically describe physical space by means of Euclidean geometry. This assumption was called into question by a mathematical discovery by Carl Friedrich Gauss, János Bolyai, and Nikolai Lobachevsky: these three mathematicians discovered independently that there were other logical possibilities for a uniform three-dimensional space. Unlike Euclidean space, the geometries presented by Gauss, Bolyai, and Lobachevsky lead to spaces that are not flat but curved.

To make sense of curved spaces it is useful to image two-dimensional surfaces within three-dimensional space and draw a triangle on these surfaces. For a positively curved space, which can be imagined e.g. as the surface of a sphere, the angles of the triangle will add up to more than 180 degrees. For a negatively curved space, which may look like the surface of a saddle, the sum of the angles will be less than 180 degrees, while for a flat space the sum will be exactly 180 degrees.

The radical insight by Gauss and others was that space can be curved all by itself, even if it is not the surface of an object. This proposition remained purely obscure until Einstein proposed his General Theory of Relativity which allows physical space to be curved in the presence of massive objects. However, General Relativity does not give an answer to the question whether the universe as a whole is curved positively, negatively, or flat – so how to resolve this cosmic puzzle?

ACT TWO: The main characters encounter an obstacle.

Physicist: As density increases and space shrinks when approaching the Big Bang, the laws of classical physics are no longer valid, but those of quantum physics apply. In quantum theory, the uncertainty relations play a major role: the deviation of energy multiplied by the deviation of time equals approximately the

Planck constant. For extremely short durations, the energy can grow almost infinitely. Thus, the Big Bang may have evolved from quantum fluctuations.

Philosopher: But what preceded the Big Bang? How can there be a deviation of time if there was no time at all? In Plato's Symposium, Socrates makes a surprising conviction: he states that the only subject he can claim to know about is love (Plato 2008b, 8). This is what the Symposium, the universe and everything, is all about: a kind of love which perceives the intellectual by the sensual and which respects the sensual without getting lost in it. This kind of love is philo-sophia, the love of wisdom. And there is no one who could tell us more about it than Socrates.

Physicist: What preceded the Big Bang? For the universe to come into existence, two ingredients are necessary: space and energy. Space and energy have both evolved during the Big Bang and space has expanded ever since. At least three dimensions are needed that living beings can evolve. With only two dimensions it is not possible to obtain a digestive system and all those things. From energy, matter was derived and from matter galaxies evolved. Within those there are stars and planets, but also extremely massive objects, such as black holes. It happens time and again that two black holes orbit one another, they become closer and closer and eventually merge abruptly. This process results in a strong shaking of the fabric of space and time. Such gravitational waves can be measured here on the earth.

Philosopher: Aristophanes reminds us that love is the power that brings the greatest happiness to the humans (Plato 2008b, 22). Initially, humans had a completely round form, with four arms, four legs, two faces exactly alike set on a round neck, and there were three sexes: male, female and a combination of the two (cf. ibid., 22–23). Because of their attempt to attack the gods, Zeus split all humans into two. Since this time, everyone is longing for his or her lost half. "After the original nature of every human had been severed in this way, the two parts longed for each other and tried to come together again. [...] We are all continually searching for our other half." (ibid., 23) Thus, love is always the love for something, so it needs what it longs for. But what is love when its essence is desire?

Physicist: When approaching the Big Bang, gravity increases. As we know from Einstein, time is not a constant, but it slows down with increasing gravity. This means that when approaching the Big Bang time slows down and down and down until it stops. Before the Big Bang there was nothing, not even time, not even space. When there is no time, there can be no cause and no effect. Thus, there is no cause for the Big Bang.

Philosopher: What concerns the creation of all living beings, Agathon states: "And who will deny that it is by the wisdom of Love that all living things are begotten and born? Do we not know that in the practice of craft any man who has this god for a teacher will turn out to be brilliant and famous, while the man untouched by Love will remain obscure?" (ibid., 31)

Physicist: In quantum field theory, nothing does not exist. All of space is filled with fields. When space evolved during the Big Bang, also fields emerged. The ground state of these fields is called vacuum, but because of the permanently fluctuating fields, quantum vacuum is quite large, practically infinitely large.

Philosopher: Well, what to do about infinity?

Physicist: We need to regularize it! By the means of mathematics, we can extract something finite from these infinities.

Is the Universe an Expanding Balloon?

Imagine you are an ant. Your body is quite flat, and you spend your life on a two-dimensional surface. Eventually, you might wonder what the overall curvature of the space you inhabit is. This is a simplified version of pretty much the situation we humans face when thinking about the geometry of the universe. The task is: draw triangles and determine the sum of the angles. The trouble is: the triangles need to be really, really huge in order to retrieve any meaningful information.

To determine the curvature of the universe, again the cosmic microwave background radiation serves as a crucial tool for investigation. As the universe does not look the same everywhere (there are stars and galaxies here and there, and emptiness in other regions), it was assumed that there are fluctuations in the cosmic microwave background radiation. And indeed, those temperature fluctuations could be detected (Mather et al. 1990; Smoot et al. 1992).

The peaks in the microwave background radiation also allow for retrieving the desired cosmic triangles to determine the curvature of space: if physical space were curved like a spherical surface, the angle covered by each microwave-background peak would be bigger and thus shift the peaks in the power-spectrum curve to the left. On the other hand, if space had a negative curvature, the peaks would look smaller and would be shifted to the right (Tegmark 2014, 78).

By measuring the cosmic microwave background radiation with increasing accuracy, various independent experiments such as WMAP, BOOMERang, and Planck have confirmed that space is flat, the margin of error could be reduced to only 0.4 percent by 2013 (NASA 2014). In the years after, the most precise data has been provided by the Planck ESA-mission and allowed for the conclusion that the universe is flat, with an accuracy of 0.2 percent (Aghanim et al. 2020). However, recent studies (Park and Ratra 2019; Di Valentino et al. 2020; Handley 2021) come to a different interpretation, claiming that the universe is not flat at all but positively curved. While the established view is that the universe is flat, discussions are heating up.

But what does it actually mean to state that the universe is flat respectively curved? The mathematics of General Relativity refer to four-dimensional spacetime, which can be flat or curved, depending on the mass distribution. As discussed above, the more massive an object is, the stronger is the resulting curvature of spacetime. Experimentally, the universe is the observable universe. For a specific instant of time it is possible to obtain a three-dimensional slice in the four-dimensional spacetime. When astronomers conclude that the universe is flat/curved according to their observations, this statement refers to the three-dimensional space of the observable universe.

Obviously, the geometry of four-dimensional spacetime exceeds human intuition. Yet sense-making in scientific terms requires more than 'just' mastering mathematics. As physical theories are grounded in mathematical descriptions, scientists have always thrived to offer intuitive analogies to communicate their findings and push the frontiers of knowledge. Inevitably, such intuitive images can never fully capture the mathematical description of a theory. Still, they may prove valuable for highlighting certain aspects of a physical theory.

In this sense, we consider the balloon analogy of cosmology insightful, as it alludes to two main features of the universe – the curvature of space and the expansion of the universe. More precisely, the analogy refers to the two-dimensional surface of an inflating balloon (not the three-dimensional balloon itself): if an ant is crawling on the surface of a large balloon, the ground would appear flat to the ant. Yet, global geometry is a positively curved space. In addition, if the balloon is being inflated and there are several ants on its surface, the distance between the ants increases; the further the ants are apart, the faster they are moving away from one another. This is essentially what happens to galaxies in our universe.

Besides the debate concerning the Planck data on the curvature of the universe, it needs to be considered that experimental data is only accessible for the observable universe. If the entire universe is sufficiently large, it might well be that despite actually being curved, data from the observable universe suggests that it is (nearly) flat.

Further investigations will be required to address the question of the flatness respectively curvature of the universe. As the results depend crucially on energy density and the amount of dark energy in the universe (Tegmark 2014, 83), experimental methods sensitive to gravity such as gravitational waves may be valuable resources.

So, what about gravitational waves? As mentioned above, according to Einstein's General Theory of Relativity, gravity arises as a geometric property of spacetime. More precisely, the *curvature of spacetime* is determined by the energy and momentum of matter and radiation (Rogers 2017). When massive objects accelerate, they cause changes in the spacetime curvature which travel outwards at the speed of light in the forms of waves – these are known as *gravitational waves*. In essence, gravitational waves are ripples in spacetime caused by accelerated masses.

When such a gravitational wave passes by, it distorts spacetime, and an observer could – in theory – experience this distortion. This very tiny effect can be observed by help of most sophisticated detectors based on laser interferometry. Even tiniest differences in the path lengths of the interferometer can be retrieved by detecting interference fringes. This effect is used by the Laser Interferometer Gravitational-Wave Observatory, in short LIGO: two interferometers with arm length of about four kilometers are placed in Hanford and Livingston (US), see Fig. 4. The LIGO collaboration was first able to detect gravitational waves in September 2015. The waves were caused by two black holes with 29 and 36 solar masses, which orbited each other and finally merged about 1.3 billion light-years away. The mass of the new, merged black hole was 62 solar masses, thus the energy equivalent to three solar masses was emitted as gravitational waves, see Fig. 4.

GRAVITATIONAL WAVES FROM
COLLIDING BLACK HOLES

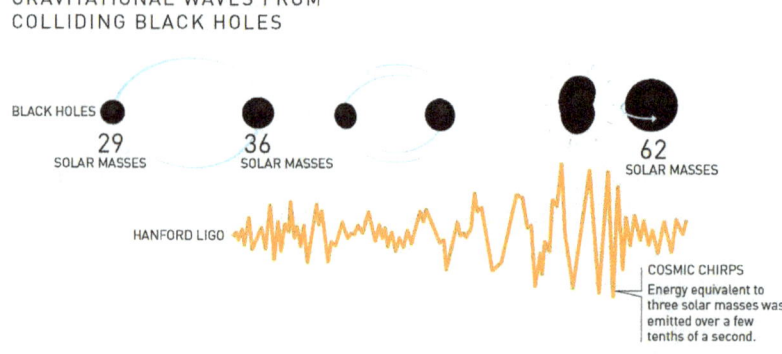

Figure 4: The spiralling and merging of two black holes with masses of 29 and 36 solar masses to a black hole of 62 solar masses is shown together with the corresponding LIGO signal. (Credit: Nobelprize.org)

As Gamov was the first to predict, after the Big Bang the universe was filled with plasma. While cold hydrogen gas is transparent and invisible, hot hydrogen plasma is opaque and glows brightly – just like the surface of our sun. For this reason, it is not possible by help of electromagnetic waves to see further back than about 400,000 years after the Big Bang. However, for gravitational waves the initial state of the universe is not opaque but transparent. Therefore, by way of gravitational waves it might be possible to uncover what precisely happened, and we might be able to gather information about the Big Bang, the most bizarre prediction of Einstein's Theory of General Relativity, where all matter, energy and spacetime originates from.

ACT THREE: The climax occurs as well as the resolution.

Philosopher: If the universe expands and everything recedes from us, will it not be that one day we can see no more stars?

Physicist: Yes, I fear so. I am also not satisfied with this outlook, although this will take place only in billions of years from now. I would love to be still around in 500 years, when humankind will have much more advanced technology and will thus have been able to entirely revolutionize our understanding of the universe. 1000 years ago it was believed that angels move around the stars like little light bulbs. Maybe our contemporary conception is just as naïve compared to what humans will know in 500 or 1000 years from now – assuming that humankind will last until then.

Philosopher: Speaking of this, I am reminded of Chaerephon. Already as a young man he was a friend of Socrates. As the latter reported, Chaerephon was not shy to ask the Oracle of Delphi if there was someone who was wiser than Socrates. The Oracle replied that no one was wiser than Socrates. Based on this information, Socrates concluded: "I am wiser than this man [an unnamed public man of Athens, note by the authors]; for neither of us really knows anything fine and good, but this man thinks he knows something when he does not, whereas I, as I do not know anything, do not think I do either." (Plato 2005, 83)

Physicist: In the beginning, the universe was extremely hot. Only through expansion the universe cooled down, and only then the different interactions appeared, which had before only been some kind of soup. One second after the Big Bang the temperature of the universe was one thousand times higher than the temperature of our sun today. At that time electrons did already exist, as well as neutrinos, photons and the respective anti-particles. But all these particles were free. Only later, when the temperature had decreased again, electrons and positrons met because of the expansion of space – and annihilated one another. The same was true for neutrinos and anti-neutrinos, and this way radiation was created. We can imagine the universe as a balloon that is being inflated: the galaxies, the stars and we humans are sitting on the surface of this balloon like flattened ants. When calculating the temperature of the universe, the universe is conceived as a global container, and an average is derived. Naturally, there are local fluctuations, and these are very important, as they are responsible for the formation of galaxies. When density increases, this has an immediate effect on geometry, and this way expansion is slowed down and gravity increases.

Philosopher: How can we reach the ideal state, this question was intensively discussed by Timaios. Plato wrote down Timaios' considerations on the subject: "the best kind of movement is one that is generated by oneself within oneself, because there's no movement that has more natural affinity with the movement of the thinking part and of the universe as a whole. Somewhat worse than that is any externally generated movement, but worst of all is the one that affects only parts of a supine, still body, and uses substances that are different from the bodily parts affected." (Plato 2008a, 94)

Physicist: Quantum fluctuations are entirely random – it is not possible to attribute any cause or any effect. This troubled Albert Einstein when he stated: God does not cast dice. But when we look at the evolution of the universe, we have to say: God actually does cast dice! The universe can be compared with a large casino. If the universe is large, this means that the dice fell many times. And whenever I cast dice many times, I will obtain an average – this is classical physics. If the universe is small, much less gambling took place – in this scenario the uncertainty relations play an important role, and quantum fluctuations will be substantially large. As the universe has allowed for our evolution, also we are the product of quantum fluctuations in an early universe.

Philosopher: For Timaios, there are cosmic causes of reason for seeing and hearing. We were supplied with vision "to enable us to observe the rational revolutions of the heavens and to let them affect the revolutions of thought within ourselves," (ibid., 38) he states. "That is, the gods wanted us to make a close study of the circular motions of the heavens, gain the ability to calculate them correctly in accordance with their nature, assimilate ours to the perfect evenness of the god's [sic!], and so stabilize the wandering revolutions within us." (ibid.)

Physicist: I need to say one more thing, and this is my philosophical legacy: the universe possesses a directionality. This has been acknowledged by many, also by theologists. I do not believe that we humans are the last stage, but evolution continues to allow for the existence of further and further developed living beings which have consciousness and which perceive the cosmos within which they live and thus also perceive what is behind everything. By seeing the universe within which we live, the universe intuits its own existence. The universe had to let us evolve in order to perceive itself. This is the only thing that makes sense – not in total but at least approximately. When it comes to the question why we live, we have to acknowledge the fact that we are close to a star from which we receive energy. Everything has evolved in a way that planets could form and that through nuclear synthesis heavy elements like iron were generated. Exactly those heavy elements and the radiation pressure from the sun allowed for life to develop. Life in the sense that molecules reproduce. It requires a lot for this to be possible. The natural constants need to be tuned with one another, there is a kind of cosmic architecture. For me, this is the hint that there is a directionality, a kind of "behind", one could say, a "hidden intelligence". The universe is more than mere random chaos.

Epilogue

Modern physics confirmed that Plato was right, after all: for Max Tegmark, both the physical investigation of the macrocosm and of the microcosm changes some of our most basic ideas about reality (Tegmark 2014, 15). He thus states: "If my life as a physicist has taught me anything at all, it's that Plato was right: modern physics has made abundantly clear that the ultimate nature of reality isn't what it seems." (Ibid., 17)

Reality is not what it seems. One reason for this is our so very limited means to explore the world around us. Throughout the history of science, collecting empirical data about the universe was primarily bound to vision. With the increasingly frequent detection and analysis of gravitational waves, this proposition is changing fundamentally – with unforeseeable consequences for our understanding of reality and the universe we are part of.

Acknowledgements

The authors would like to thank Arno Böhler and Susanne Valerie Granzer for their invitation to develop the lecture performance which served at the basis for this publication, for Globart Academy 2019. Many thanks to Veronika Mayer, who conducted a composition for this lecture performance, as well as to Österreichische Zentralbibliothek für Physik, in particular to Daniel Winkler and Viktor Zdrachal for filming and recording and to Alexander Zartl for his support of the project.

Literature

Abbott, B. P., Abbott, R., Abbott, T. D., Abernathy, M. R., Acernese, F., Ackley, K., et al. 2016. "Observation of Gravitational Waves from a Binary Black Hole Merger." *Physical Review Letters* 116 (6).

Aghanim, N., Akrami, Y., Ashdown, M., Aumont, J., Baccigalupi, C., Ballardini, M., et al. 2020. "Planck 2018 results." *A&A* 641.

Böhler, Arno. 2024. "Gilles Deleuze: Kant-Lektüren." In *Immanuel Kant – Freiheit, Vernunft, Sinnlichkeit*, edited by Waibel, Violetta, Brinnich, Max, Geml, Gabriele and Schaller, Philipp. Berlin/New York: De Gruyter, 23. September 2024. https://doi.org/10.1515/9783111386270-015.

Bunge, Mario. 2018. "Gravitational Waves and Spacetime." *Foundations of Science* 23 (2): 399–403.

Clegg, Brian. 2012. *Vor dem Urknall. Eine Reise hinter den Anfang der Zeit*. Reinbek: Rowohlt Digitalbuch.

DiSalle, Robert. 2006. *Understanding Space-Time. The Philosophical Development of Physics from Newton to Einstein*. Cambridge, New York: Cambridge University Press.

Di Valentino, Eleonora, Alessandro Melchiorri, and Joseph Silk. 2020. "Planck Evidence for a Closed Universe and a Possible Crisis for Cosmology." *Nature Astronomy* 4 (2): 196–203. https://doi.org/10.1038/s41550-019-0906-9.

Hawking, Stephen. 2002. "Black holes, relativity and my eureka moment. From a lecture given at the University of Cambridge by the Lucasian Professor of Mathematics to mark his 60th birthday." *Independent*. January 15, 2002. https://www.independent.co.uk/voices/commentators/stephen-hawking-black-holes-relativity-and-my-eureka-moment-9132870.html (last accessed: 12 June 2025).

Handley, Will. 2021. "Curvature Tension. Evidence for a Closed Universe." *Phys. Rev.* D 103 (4).

Jammer, Max. 1993. *Concepts of Space: The History of Theories of Space in Physics*. New York: Dover Publications.

Kant, Immanuel. 2009 [1781, 1787]. *Critique of Pure Reason*. Translated and edited by Paul Guyer and Allen W. Wood. Cambridge: Cambridge University Press.

Kant, Immanuel. 1955. *Allgemeine Naturgeschichte und Theorie des Himmels*. Edited by Georg Klaus. Berlin: Aufbau-Verlag.

Marx, Karl, and Friedrich Engels. 1987. *Collected Works Volume 25. Friedrich Engels: Anti-Dühring and Dialectics of Nature*. International Publishers.

Mather, John et al. 1990. "A Preliminary Measurement of the Cosmic Microwave Background spectrum by the Cosmic Background Explorer (COBE) satellite." *ApJ* 354.

NASA. 2014. "Will the Universe expand forever?" https://map.gsfc.nasa.gov/universe/uni_shape.html (last accessed: 12 June 2025).

Park, Chan-Gyung, and Bharat Ratra. 2019. "Using the Tilted Flat-ΛCDM and the Untitled Non-Flat ΛCDM Inflation Models to Measure Cosmological Parameters from a Compilation of Observational Data." *The Astrophysical Journal* 882 (2).

Penzias, Arno, and Robert W. Wilson. 1965. "A Measurement of Excess Antenna Temperature at 4080 Mc/s." *The Astrophysical Journal* 142.

Plato. 2008a. *Timaeus and Critias*. Translated by Robin Waterfield, With an Introduction and Notes by Andrew Gregory. Oxford, New York: Oxford University Press.

Plato. 2008b. *The Symposium*. Translated by Margaret C. Howatson, edited by Frisbee C. C. Sheffield. Cambridge: Cambridge University Press.

Plato. 2005. *Euthyphro. Apology. Crito. Phaedo. Phaedrus*. Translated by Harold North Fowler. Cambridge: Harvard University Press.

Robertson, Scott J. 2012. "The Theory of Hawking Radiation in Laboratory Analogues." *J. Phys. B: At. Mol. Opt. Phys.* 45 (16).

Rogers, Keir Kwame. 2017. A *Clear View of the Primordial Universe*. PhD diss., University of London. https://discovery.ucl.ac.uk/id/eprint/10044716/1/thesis_KKR_clear_Universe.pdf (last accessed: 12 June 2025).

Smoot, George et al. 1992. "Structure in the COBE Differential Microwave Radiometer First-Year Maps." *The Astrophysical Journal* 396.

Tegmark, Max. 2014. *Our Mathematical Universe. My Quest for the Ultimate Nature of Reality*. New York: Knopf.

Nothing to Fix
Performative Strategies of Incompleteness and the Right to Bodily Integrity

Sandra Noeth

Taking a Breath

Berlin, winter 2021. About a year and a half into a series of lockdowns and various limitations of public life. While negotiating the ever-changing rules and regulations related to the Covid-19 pandemic and their impacts on my own and other people's bodies, new movement patterns emerge. Routines, choreographies, gestures and gazes, translating overall directives into everyday actions and decisions confront us in different ways with questions relating to the security and protection of bodies.

A constituent aspect of our being in the world today is determined by the possibilities available to us to breathe, argues anthropologist Shahram Khosravi (2021), emphasizing that breathing is affected and targeted by socio-political power. This is evident from the fact that our social imagination is dominated by images of people fleeing, suffocating in overcrowded trucks, and choking on pepper spray. Media-generated images and imaginations of new outbreaks of racist police violence against Black people or irreversible environmental damage that perpetuates existing processes of colonization in the Global South come to mind. These are just a few examples of a long history of embodied, structural violence targeting the breath that has inscribed itself in public consciousness and driven civil society protests.[1]

In the context of the COVID-19 pandemic, increasingly high-stakes social dynamics become perceptible by the act of breathing– that vital and inescapable process that so often goes unnoticed. Critically, we can observe on our own bodies that not all people are permitted to breathe in equal ways. As we move through everyday life, we decide how much proximity and distance we allow towards other bodies, which ones we get close to and which ones we avoid. When considerations of health and protection make us hold our breath in proximity to others – when we think we are protecting ourselves in an attempt not to inhale others –protecting our own bodies endangers others by un-protecting them, marking them as a threat. The ways in which we assess other bodies as being "healthy" or "infectious", as being "risky" or "intact", in conversation with the ways we interpret bodily markers of class, nationality, gender or ethnicity, uncomfortably illuminates prejudices and clichés but also fantasies and desires which we not only hold but embody. Judgements ranging from the rational to the moral impact how we categorize the vulnerability of bodies on a personal scale as well as on a legal and political level. Day-to-day choices relating to the placement of the body, situating it in space, provide a visceral understanding of the fact that not all bodies are considered worthy of protection in the first place.

Let's take a breath.

---

1   In recent years, this has been exemplified by civil and political mobilizations such as *Me Too* or *Black Lives Matter* that give expression to a long history of discriminatory and racialized violence, but also by theoretical discussions around necropolitical approaches in border studies, the weaponization of bodies in contemporary warfare and the systemic withdrawal of care in migration politics, for instance. These are but few examples that show how the body is at the heart of these biopolitical, identity-related, humanitarian developments as an agent, target and witness.

On Bodily Grounds. Artistic Investigations

"Protection" here holds several meanings. It pertains to averting physical violence on the material body as well as symbolic-metaphorical attacks on its integrity; it refers to the legal status and corresponding state or inter-state measures that regulate the protection of bodies and their specific needs and experiences; it asks to which bodies we give ethical recognition and value. The privilege of bodily protection is codified in constitutional and humanitarian law, notably the right to bodily integrity, which defines what we can do to our bodies and the bodies of others.[2] However, on the levels of content, scope and application it does not offer any binding definition of what it means for a specific body to be integer, safe or unharmed (cf. Noeth 2024).

In the following reflections I do not aim to trace the legal history of the right to bodily integrity. Rather, I would like to raise the question of how body-based strategies, such as the act of breathing, which might seem mundane, personal and perhaps intimate at a first glance, can take on micropolitical significance. In the context of the unequal protection of bodies, how might a closer look at these strategies contribute to a critical understanding of the notion of bodily integrity? My assumption is that the ways in which bodies are constructed, perceived, staged, performed and interpreted – as vulner-

---

2   The right to bodily integrity is established in the Universal Declaration of Human Rights and numerous derivates. In many sources it is stated as a freestanding, enumerated right that frames other rights, or it exists as a delegated right inherent within some other specific rights (for instance, implied in the right to freedom from torture, cruel, inhumane, degrading treatment; rights related to privacy, health). See: *Universal Declaration of Human Rights* (1948); *International Covenant on Civil and Political Rights* (1954); *Conventions on the Rights of Persons with Disabilities* (2007) (cf. Noeth 2024). Legal theorist Adrian Viens points out that, while bodily integrity is generally perceived as an inherent value by many, there are different and controversial ideas about how the right to bodily integrity differs from other rights (the right to live, the right to liberty, etc.) (Viens 2014).

able or intact, human or nonhuman, for instance – impact their recognition and agency in everyday life and before the law.[3]

In order to approach this process, I draw on arts-based research
developed by practitioners Raquel Meseguer Zafe, Hakan Topal and
Lina Majdalanie[4] over an extended period of time. Offering experience-based approaches, they situate the problem of bodily integrity
within specific geopolitical contexts and on different scales. Through
a series of case studies this text investigates the ways in which their
artistic strategies and processes of decision-making reveal the
structural dynamics underlying abstract notions of security, adversary and risk on bodily grounds. In a wider context, this methodolog-
ical approach seeks to strengthen corporeality and embodiment as
an analytical dimension in the social, political and legal realm.[5]

Lying Down (Non-Horizontal Bodies)

"*I will be your guide. All you need to do is to rest, and listen.*" (Meseguer
Zafe 2021) These are the first words of invitation that choreographer
and performer Raquel Meseguer Zafe addresses to her listeners in an

---

3   The article presents findings from an ongoing research project that
     critically revisits the idea of bodily integrity from the perspective of
     body-based artistic research. The project, for which I shift roles and
     perspectives as a scholar, dramaturg and curator, unfolds in a dialogue
     with artists, activists and scholars from different fields. See: *Bodies,
     un-protected* (with Künstlerhaus Mousonturm, 2021–22, https://www.
     mousonturm.de/en/projects/bodies-un-protected/); (*Un*)*Settled. Per-
     formance, protection, and politics of insecurity* (with HTA-Hessische
     Theater Akademie, 2021–2022, https://hessische-theaterakademie.de/
     en/ringvorlesung/).

4   From a legal point of view, of course, a distinction must be made be-
     tween the different legal frameworks and principles that apply to the
     three examples at stake, notably between civil and national law (regulat-
     ing relationships between private individuals) and international human-
     itarian law (regulating state interference).

5   Similar body-based approaches have been explored in anti-discrimina-
     tion work and conflict resolution and corresponding practices of self-
     care and healing as well as in war and border studies.

audio version of the *Crash Course in Cloudspotting* project in which I participated in summer 2021. The voices we are going to encounter in the subsequent forty minutes are carefully curated and woven together by the choreographer into a multi-vocal, non-linear narrative recounting the experiences of chronically disabled people in public spaces. The stories become part of a much larger archive accounting for experiences of people who live with neuro-diverse disabilities invisible for standard means of representation and which compel rest in public spaces. In doing so, she is careful not to over-interpret the stories shared by individuals or to fall into tragic and heroic patterns into which disabled experiences are often boxed.

Meseguer Zafe describes their – and her – stories of accommodating infrastructure and architecture developed by and for normative bodies as "strange dances." (Meseguer 2021). Not only normative but actively hostile architectural features, accessibility protocols and unspoken rules in cultural institutions or on public transportation that force constant negotiations between disabled bodies and spaces. Social interactions in these contexts range from friendly but intrusive curiosity to verbal and physical violence. All of these forces come together to enforce boundaries between those bodies which are protected and those which are not.[6]

---

6   Challenging normativity, completeness and ableism have been key concerns that critical performance practice and studies have been intensively discussing in the last years. In this context, Raquel Meseguer Zafe's work talks to current debates on care and vulnerability that concern themselves with a strong critique of dominant mechanisms of essentializing, commodifying or objectifying bodies from queer and feminist, de-colonial, and class-related perspectives. As to the specific strategy of lying down, see also the work by artist and activist Liz Crow (Crow 2013).

Figure 1: *Crash Course in Cloudspotting.*
(Raquel Meseguer Zafe)

In *Crash Course in Cloudspotting* participants are confronted with experiences of still bodies in pain and are themselves invited to slow down, pause, and lie down within the installative setting or their respective homes. This unfamiliar experience brings to the fore the fact that, in a western context, the experience of horizontality is reserved for specific cultural spheres and situations. These include the home, the bed, and the hospital and call upon experiences of death, illness, and intimacy. In her live and audio works, Meseguer Zafe moves outside of the normative, ableist framework of uprightness. In doing so, she also rejects the universal claim that the right to bodily integrity upholds alongside other human rights, as it cannot be ignored that they have been designed by and for specific, privileged bodies in the first place. What she proposes is above all a reconfiguration of perspective, a sensorial shift which places visitors or listeners in contact with each other, activating their perception of time and space in alternative and not-always-comfortable ways. Simultaneously, the simple act of lying down in a public space reveals mechanisms of structural inclusion and exclusion. This normative condition largely ignores the relationality of bodies. As performance artist Jeremy Wade states, "(...) the regime of wholeness and all its essentialist baggage is not relational to the needs of different bodies at all." (Meseguer and Wade 2020) His reading focuses on the interpretation of lying down as a gesture of domination. He describes the system of verticality as a system of productivity and hyper-functionality that also reigns the artistic field and risks reducing the body to a commodification and object (cf. Noeth 2024). This conceptualization is also significant for the right to bodily integrity: a right that is anchored in the idea of personhood. This category, which has triggered controversial discussion in philosophy and law alike, links the promise of safety and protection to the register of the subjective, where the individual embodies the human condition per se.

In *Crash Course in Cloudspotting*, being exposed to other bodies challenges the premise of a bound body in a physical as well as in a symbolic sense, allowing for encounter and vulnerability at the same time. "It is only a question of 90° or 180° that disrupts public space," says Meseguer Zafe (Meseguer and Wade 2020), calling attention to the biopolitical disciplining of bodies in the public space and to internalized hierarchies, privileges, and relating mechanisms of censorship. What these temporary communities she convenes around the strategy of lying down offer her is to take the right to integrity beyond the individual and to establish it as a collective demand and responsibility that begins in small, everyday alliances with other bodies that do not belong to our group.

Recollecting Wounds
(Narrating Experiences of Attack)

A wound marks a body and serves as a witness to an experience of intrusion or attack. Next to its physical dimension, it is also a moment of openness to the world in which we are compelled to reorient ourselves, redefine our relations to others, and develop new skills that help us navigate the environments we live in. The wounds that media artist Hakan Topal researches in his *Still Life*[7] project are linked to what has gone viral as the "Roboski massacre," triggering extensive debate and political and activist mobilization around the protection and valuation of bodies internationally. At the heart of the work there are portraits of young Iraqi men who were killed on the night of December 28, 2011,

---

7   The work is based on research conducted between 2012 and 2016 and exists in different formats and media, as a video piece and installation and as a publication. *Still Life* exists in different formats and media, as a video work, installation, and as a publication. (Topal 2012 16)

in an unauthorized Turkish military airstrike. Villagers from Roboski, who routinely – and well-known to local authorities – smuggled gas, cigarettes and daily goods across the Iraq-Turkey border, were targeted that night as suspected terrorists. The mass media coverage of the event was extensive and quick to respond. This type of reporting frequently works with photographic stills, images that, through repetition, become iconic and often exclusive images of an event, easily recognized and classified.

Figure 2: *Still Life*, video still. (Hakan Topal, 2014)

In contrast, Hakan Topal states of his approach, "I always feel as artists we are late to the issues, and (...) I am intentionally late as I want to escape the pre-organization of time as in media coverage of crisis." (Topal and Dewachi 2020). As a counter-strategy, his work *Still Life* relies on video as a durational device to create what he calls "silent monuments." (Ibid.)[8] In one example of this, mothers show framed photos of their lost sons, a performative strategy which opens up

---

8   In the course of the research process Topal visited the border region as well as Roboski village and the families in order to take their accounts. Due to language barriers, silence and non-verbal communication made up a large part of the encounter. Also, he decided to not record the talks, due to ethical considerations (Topal and Dewachi 2020).

"an intimate connection between photography and death" (Ibid.). In their materiality, these photographs are much more than a historical record and acquire agency as they are held, hugged, or used symbolically as political manifestations.

The video portraits that Topal creates are shot in long duration. They shift temporality and scale of perception as they depict subtle movements, delicate gestures of grief, intimate bodily utterances, faces and breathing. On a broader scale, these dramaturgical decisions to accentuate the bodily and performative dimension of loss might be particularly meaningful in the Middle Eastern context, where next to written history, oral, corporeal, artistic, and artisanal practices are important ways of recording and passing on lived experiences. However, the problem of accounting for the lives of marginalized communities that he addresses has structural implications beyond the specific context of the Roboski case, as it reflects on the "impossibility of justice in the aesthetic," as Topal puts it (Topal 2014).

The interaction of law and aesthetics that is indicated here concerns how the experience of the wound is conceived at the intersection of the individual and the collective. Against the backdrop of a global context in which bodies are in ever-increasing numbers the collateral damage of political conflicts (cf. Noeth 2024), Topal's strategy of zooming in on details in *Still Life* counters often generic, anonymized and clichéd accounts that reduce different subjectivities to a generalized victim.[9] These suffocating framings mainly affect marginalized communities and perpetuate structures of colonial inequality. By taking away specificity and situatedness from individuals' lived experiences of grief and loss, representing them as faceless masses and prohibiting them from appearing in their own right, they render them entities to be measured and administrated. Topal's humanization of the victims of the Roboski massacre and their families

---

9   In *Still Life*, Hakan Topal discusses how the question of recognition translates into a complex economy of wounded bodies, where bodies are valued according to profoundly unequal standards. Next to the ethical, political and humanitarian aspects, the economic value that the Turkish government allocated to the Iraqi bodies killed in the Roboski massacre is distinctly lower than comparable condolence payments for western bodies.

in the aesthetic resists these negating forces and returns agency to his subjects. As Topal puts it: "Regarding regimes of visibility, being seen is a political act. [...] Aesthetic justice as a project recognizes, first and foremost, the person in their flesh. It has to start from there. Every victim is an individual victim. There cannot be a victim population." (Topal and Dewachi 2020). His focus on how grief is performed and staged, how it finds affective, symbolic, and embodied expression, and how it is passed on, blurring lines between the personal and the political, offers a durational and dynamic understanding of the wound. A wound that is "travelling" across borders and generations, as Omar Dewachi conceptualizes it, that is a subjective and a social experience at a time (Dewachi 2015).

This transformative understanding of a wound represents aesthetic, political and legal challenges of detecting and accounting for the experience of bodies. It depicts the experience of the wound as a parallel experience of integrity and of integration. This is complicated by the fundamental principle of distinction that is at the heart of international humanitarian law and the right to bodily integrity and which bases the evaluation of the status of a body and its possibility to appear in front of the law on differences and pre-defined categories (such as "civilian" or "military"). As to the example of *Still Life*, some of the distinguishing elements are aesthetic, as they are connected to how a body is performed, represented, recognized and accepted as an integer or a broken body, for instance. Here, artistic practice holds an ambivalent potential to develop visibility, agency and complexity for diverse subjects, while at the same time risking furthering dominant modes of representation or rendering those subjects invisible.

Dead Bodies (Subverting State Protection)

To whom does a body belong after death? Who has access to it, who owns it, and who is responsible for its protection and security? For artist Lina Majdalanie, these questions become very concrete when it comes to what happens to her body after her death. In the lecture performance *Appendice* (2007) she takes us to the Lebanese context, where a number of personal affairs (such as inheritance or marriage, as well as the handling of dead bodies) are not primarily a matter of individual decision-making or basic human and civil rights but delegated to diverse regulatory systems, ranging from the state and communitarian and religious authorities to the medical system. This makes Majdalanie speculate about how to reconcile her wish of being incinerated after her death with the religious laws in place which dictate that her body should be buried.

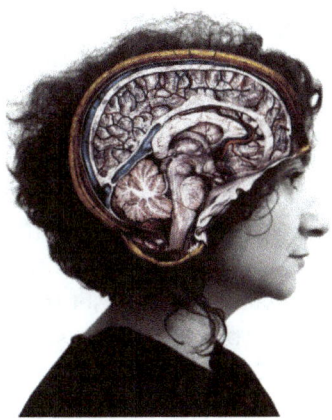

Figure 3: Lina Majdalanie, *Appendice.* (Ghassan Halawani)

In *Appendice* she investigates ways of altering the status of her human, physical body in order to bypass the control of applicable religious and communitarian laws. With reference to the tradition of body art, where the body in its materiality appears as the object and the medium of action, she examines how to potentially dissect her body into parts to be qualified and sold as an artwork and to be ultimately treated according to her will after her death. By voluntarily performing this act of disintegration on her body, Majdalanie explores the question of bodily integrity in biomaterial, symbolic, and legal terms and establishes the dead body as a site of agency in its own right.

In a similar vein, political theorist James Martel refuses to conceive of the dead body as a passive entity subjected to sovereign or state power. Instead, he focuses on the transformative and regenerative forces that dead and unburied bodies hold in metabolic terms, ritually speaking, and in their representational capacities. In his book (Martel 2018) he describes the state's investment in purposefully setting up and staging acts of both vulnerability and intactness on some bodies and its interest in controlling how these acts are interpreted and inscribed (for example in recordings, in news, in archives) as a means of maintaining its authority. Juxtaposing recent cases of racialized police violence in the US-American context with the character of Antigone in Sophocles' play,[10] he demonstrates how dead and unburied bodies turn out to be threatening and uncomfortable for the state. They inhabit the margins of the legal system and escape its mechanisms, interrupting and undermining this carefully woven narrative of protection.

Both analyses show the ambivalences that characterize the right to bodily integrity at its core. Returning to the performative and transformative qualities of the body, they identify moments in which overarching regulatory systems that are set to protect and preserve a body from intrusion and attack turn against it, expelling a body to a legally produced state of unprotection. In contrast, it is a body's immanent potential for disintegration that Majdalanie and Martel identify as a starting point for their projects. Rather than focusing on bodies as objects of protection whose physical integrity needs to be secured and maintained by the state, they examine the withdrawal of dead bodies from aesthetic, political and legal regimes of the state: the more a body decomposes, the more its potential for resistance and subversion unfolds. As Martel has it: "I like to think of our bodies as an anarchist space that we have colonized and controlled from top to bottom, and at least when we are dead it stops." (Martel 2020)

---

10   Martel (2018) discusses in particular the case of Michael Brown, an unarmed Black man who was shot by a police officer and left dead on the streets of Ferguson. Considering this act of police violence, Stefano Harney and Fred Moton describe Brown's body as a body that "refuses to stand", rejecting the framing of this body as a powerless body.

Integrities in the Plural. Keeping Wounds Open

The three examples of body-based research with this chapter is in dialogue with challenge the concept of bodily integrity and its legal articulation in different ways. By emphasizing the entanglement of the individual and the collective in the aesthetic experiences they create, Raquel Meseguer Zafe, Hakan Topal and Lina Majdalanie expose conceptual and ideological aspects underlying the right to bodily integrity and draw attention to moments of ambivalence that are built into the legal system. Though the right to bodily integrity ostensibly pertains to the idea of an individual, complete and autonomous body, their artworks suggest that the law cannot sufficiently capture the diverse protective needs and experiences of bodies in their specificity; it fails to account for the embodied, affective, and sensory experiences connected to physical acts of violence. In other words, it does not respond to an extended understanding of the body and its realities. Furthermore, collective dynamics of inequality and structural non-representation are generated and reproduced in its application. Correspondingly, in her analysis of the connections between international law, warfare and morality, political theorist Banu Bargu points to the fact that the same bodies whose rights are violated are also denied opportunities to give direct evidence of their experience (cf. Noeth 2019). These bodies, she elaborates, are most often not in a position to call for justice and, I would like to add, are most often not in a position to access our theaters, galleries, and performance spaces. This inequality not only applies to the physical bodies that have experienced intrusion and attack, but also to their representations in political lobbying, media, archives and in the arts (Bargu 2016).

In recent years, renewed attention has been given to non-state actors such as artists or activists in the reexamination of political, legal and social issues. The body, here, provides an interstitial tissue between external hierarchies that determine which bodies deserve protection and internalized mechanisms of censorship and consequent hierarchies of embodiment that are handed down over generations. Hence, how we perceive bodies, translate them into movements, images, words and ideas and imagine their integrity is not a purely aesthetic but a political question. Art can allocate vulnerability or empowerment to bodies and is therefore closely connected to the capacity for action which they are afforded on a structural level. Yet, considering legal elements related to bodily integrity from an aesthetic and performative perspective does not come from an over-estimation of art in its capacity to dissolve the realities under discussion. Sometimes a blow just hits too hard.

Indeed, this analysis stays well aware of the fact that aesthetic imagination, performance and experience are immanently part of producing and distributing attention, visibility and value in socio-political, ethical and legal terms. Here, different registers that determine the value of the body collapse: material and monetary value, the symbolic and metaphorical capital of a body, or its capacity to create agency on a political or legal level. Addressing the body as evidence is less inspired by the judiciary evidential paradigm like in classical forensics that is mostly concerned with ascertaining identities. In other words, the body is not approached as a transparent window that provides unmediated access to reality or as the last resort of authenticity and immediacy. Instead, another understanding of "evidence" invites us to consider what a body might be able to tell us – not only by attending to its truth claims but also to its incongruences, dilemmas and gaps, to what it reveals as well as gesturing towards that which is withheld, silenced, and concealed. (Ertem and Noeth 2018, 15).

The cases the artists bring to attention exemplify how much our social, political and ethical relations are defined by aesthetic features. In their arts-based research processes they place relationality at the heart of the debate on bodily integrity, by creating experiences that put us in touch with their own and other bodies in a direct or imaginative manner. Activating body-based strategies such as lying down, recollecting wounds and connecting to the regenerative forces of the body in the legal realm is not about relief or uncritical engagement or empathy, nor is it about equalizing bodies in the first place. It proposes a shift from an abstract understanding of bodily integrity to an experience-based one, attempting to reach a conceptualization of protection that moves outside of the framework of the individual and that is performed and enacted by many bodies. Opposed to a rhetoric that suggests that we need to pull away from others, shield off our communities or close the borders to be safe and protected, this is about exploring possibilities of making the question of bodily integrity a collective concern and responsibility, about training the capacity to respond, when called in a practical as well as in an ethical sense. Thus, what is at stake when bodies become evidence is recognition. This calls attention to the need for better interpretive frameworks outside the universal legal norm, to grasp the complex realities at stake. The goal of revisiting the idea of bodily integrity is not to encourage the ideologies it carries but to acknowledge how ethical calculations, artistic and dramaturgical decision-making and legal consequences are interwoven and to give attention to the fact that no one is born into this profoundly unequal apparatus of distinction but – performatively – transformed into it. Rather than fixing or covering our wounds in a physical, social and legal sense, artistic practice and research might rather be able to contribute to developing strategies to keep them open.

Literature

Bargu, Banu. 2016. "Why Did Bouazizi Burn Himself? The Politics of Fate and Fatal Politics." *Constellations* 23, no. 1 (2016): 27–36.

Butler, Judith, Zeynep Gambetti, and Leticia Sabsay, eds. 2016. *Vulnerability in Resistance*. Durham: Duke University Press.

Cohen, Steven, Lina Majdalanie, and James Martel. 2020. "The Integrity of Dead and Unburied Bodies." Online lecture. Künstlerhaus Mousonturm. May 26, 2020 (unpublished document).

Crow, Liz. 2013. "Lying Down Anyhow: Disability and the Rebel Body." In *Disabling Barriers – Enabling Environments*, edited by John Swain, Sally French, Colin Barnes, and Carol Thomas. London: Routledge.

Dewachi, Omar. 2015. "When Wounds Travel." MAT *Medicine Anthropology Theory*, no. 3: 61–82.

Ertem, Gurur, and Sandra Noeth, eds. 2018. *Bodies of Evidence. Ethics, Aesthetics, and Politics of Movement*. Vienna: Passagen.

Khosravi, Shahram. 2021. "Combat Breathing." Lecture in the framework of *Bodies, un-protected*. Künstlerhaus Mousonturm, Nov. 13, 2021 (unpublished document).

Majdalanie, Lina. 2007. "Appendice." Lecture performance.

Martel, James. 2018. *Unburied Bodies: Subversive Corpses and the Authority of the Dead*. Amherst: Amherst College Press.

Meseguer Zafe, Raquel. 2021. "A Crash Course in Cloudspotting". Audio Performance. Sophiensaele Berlin, July 30, 2021.

Meseguer, Raquel, and Jeremy Wade. 2020. "Dramaturgical Perspectives: Strategies of Non/Productivity". Online lecture. Künstlerhaus Mousonturm, May 27, 2020 (unpublished document).

Noeth, Sandra. 2019. *Resilient Bodies, Residual Effects. Artistic Articulations of Borders and Collectivity from Lebanon and Palestine*. Bielefeld: transcript.

Noeth, Sandra. 2024. "Colder." In *Shielding. Body-based Studies on Integrity and Protection*, edited by Sandra Noeth et al., 50–69. Bielefeld: transcript.

Perugini, Nicola, and Neve Gordon. 2020. *Human Shields. A History of People in the Line of Fire*. Berkeley: University of California Press.

Raimondi, Francesca, and Emilia Zenzile Roig. 2020. "Integrities, in the plural." Online lecture. Künstlerhaus Mousonturm, May 5, 2020 (unpublished document).

Steyerl, Hito. 2008. "Can Witnesses Speak? On the Philosophy of the Interview." *transversal texts*, May 2008. https://transversal.at/transversal/0408/steyerl/en (last accessed: 14 June 2025).

Topal, Hakan. 2012–16. "Still Life". Video work, publication.

Topal, Hakan. 2014. "Collateral Damage, Condolence and the Aesthetic Impossibility of Justice." In *Aesthetic Justice*, edited by Pascal Gielen and Niels van Tomme, 229-245. Amsterdam: Valiz.

Topal, Hakan, and Omar Dewachi. 2020. "Social Wounds." Online Lecture. Künstlerhaus Mousonturm, May 12, 2020 (unpublished document).

Van der Walt, Sibylle, and Christoph Menke. 2007. *Die Unversehrtheit des Körpers. Geschichte und Theorie eines elementaren Menschenrechts*. Frankfurt a.M.: Campus.

Viens, Adrian. 2014. *The Right to Bodily Integrity*. London: Routledge.

Along Each Other. On Shown and Told by Meg Stuart and Tim Etchells

Con-Fusions Between Movement and Linguistic Figures, Between Performance and Critique

Krassimira Kruschkova

Danced and spoken stories contaminate and comment on each other, they collapse into one another in the performance *Shown and Told* (2016) by American choreographer and dancer Meg Stuart and British writer and performance maker Tim Etchells. What shows and tells here are pointedly incomprehensible body and language gestures, as they ironically and melancholically exhibit the incomprehensible itself, perhaps.

In Sheffield in 1984 Tim Etchells co-founded the group Forced Entertainment, transforming the very idea of theatre with every new performance. In 1991 Meg Stuart created her first full-length choreography *Disfigure Study* for the Klapstuk Festival in Leuven, fundamentally renewing European contemporary dance which she still configures differently with each further work. Meanwhile Tim has contributed texts to several of Meg's performances (from *Alibi* in 2001 to *Cascade* in 2021). Since 2016 they have been touring and performing their piece *Shown and Told* together on stage.

Figure 1: Meg Stuart und Tim Etchells, *Shown and Told.*
(Tine Declerck, 2016)

On both Tim's and Meg's homepages we can read:

> *Shown and Told* is a dynamic but fragile performance collage
> *built* from studio improvisation, balancing fixed material and
> possibilities for free-play. Arising from an exchange between
> Meg Stuart and Tim Etchells, it exposes the different practice
> and sensibilities of these two artists, exploring the relation-
> ship between movement, image and performing bodies. Work-
> ing with vivid and surprising images, some of them physical
> some of them linguistic, the two performers develop a con-
> versation that is tough, touching and comical by turns. (Meg
> Stuart and Tim Etchells 2016)

In this collaborative performance Tim improvises text fragments
based on Meg's improvised movement fragments (with every next
performance text and movement becoming more fixed). Or is it the
other way round? They perform without either of them taking the
lead, and we, the audience, cannot stop asking ourselves whether she
is dancing what he is saying or whether he is speaking of what she is

dancing. Then she talks, and he moves… a bit, then they, both of them speaking, show various series of movement fragments.

Thereby the danced and spoken stories seem to escape shown and told non-ambiguity and thus become readable – if at all – only in their mutual con-fusions, in their ambivalence. There is no easy going in this complex translation between accomplice languages, there is rather an uneasy going instead of anything goes. In the deconstructive inversion of the linearity of cause / effect, what is shown and what is told will always have been concrete and abstract at the same time, prospectively and retrospectively at once.

Meg and Tim along each other try to get along with each other, perhaps, and to balance against one another: During this "structured improvisation" (Post 2017), "this thought experiment about taking on something from somebody's practice" (De Meester 2021), as Stuart and Etchells call their work, we are outside their experimental situation and only this way become part of it.

By this ambiguity Meg and Tim abstain from any "shared methodology", as Tim says during a post-performance talk at Kaaitheater (Brussels, December 2016): What they share is "an interest in fragments, in parts of a movement, gesture or state. What it is to work with them as pieces. Assemble them, disassemble them. And it is interesting to see somebody do the same in another language. And thus: doing this performance together is a bit off territory with elements of it that are still mysterious to us."

And in an interview with Eva Decaesstecker in the Kaaitheater program (Decaesstecker 2016) Tim speaks about "working on this space between language as a conceptual force and language as a musical or poetic force." Then, where is this "a bit off territory" between language and movement, but also between "language as a conceptual force and language as a musical or poetic force" – also in all Forced Entertainments' performances?

Where is this territory of dis/assembling pieces? *Are you there?* – Etchells asks during the performance and Stuart replies: *Is that a serious question?* Tim: *It's a 52 % serious one.* Meg: *Is it a philosophical question?* Tim: *More of a political one.* I will come back to this morphing. Tim again in the quoted interview:

The biggest and simplest connection is our common idea of a human being as a kind of meeting point for many different voices, impulses or presences. That might be physically, but also linguistically. For me the connection to Meg's work was always around shape shifting and moving. The instability of the human subject and its presence. The way people are many things in performance but also in the world. Many forces, narratives and possibilities move through us in any given moment. (ibid.)

In their pluralistic duet made of voices, impulses, presences, and (in any given moment) run on forces, narratives, possibilities, Meg and Tim fall again and again into the gap between what is shown / told and what is meant, i.e. they are falling into irony. Irony constantly re-opens this gap, meaning is constantly in suspension as it falls in and out of the shown /told. As if the movement could pronounce and the speaking could dance that which eludes both, that what escapes. Who translates, who embodies, who reveals whom and what here? What and who refers to whom?

Tim comments on Meg's movements by starting every sentence – in anaphora structure – with: It's like ... Meg's later comments are structured in the same way. The rhetoric device of the anaphor, the repetition of a word (or a group of words) at the beginning of successive verses or sentences, shapes the rhythm of the whole structure. It's like ... – as if we could ever spell the elliptic of metaphors, or even spell them out, spelling precisely the difference between similes and metaphors, metaphors as comparisons, but without like or as or as if. Thus, the performance ironically oscillates again and again between the metaphoric and the literal.

While Meg starts and calmly interrupts her highly complex movement sequences, we hear Tim saying: It's like stone steps, like the sound of voices from a faraway room ... you can't hear what they are saying, you wonder what exactly is going on ... It's like the smell of burning, like the way that condensation forms on windows ... The gap between the visible / audible / olfactory / tactile opens up at the very beginning: As if Meg's movements were – synesthetic – sounds, smells etc.

It's like searching for something, searching through rooms, says Tim while performing it. Artistic research in performance is always a re-*searching through rooms*, synesthetic rooms. *Shown and Told is like* this spatial research on representation – especially on the trail of the expressionless. *It's like* Walter Benjamin's formula: "The expressionless is the critical violence which, while unable to separate semblance from essence in art, prevents them from mingling." (Benjamin 1996–2003, 340 [1991, 181])

In performance practice it is not the process only but rather the product too which could appear in an experimental, re-searching mode. Thus, performance problematizes the very conditions of the possibility of re-presentation in theatre and in artistic research. And, as my text proposes, we could go on with this problematizing by cutting the performance parts together-apart, trying to separate their partiture an apparatus, to re-write them through each other, *searching through their rooms*, listening to *the sound of voices from a faraway room*. E.g. to Th. W. Adorno's voice: "It is for this reason that art requires philosophy, which interprets it in order to say what it is unable to say, whereas art is only able to say it by not saying it." (Adorno 1997, 72 [1970, 113])

But how much does philosophy tolerate performance and / as artistic research, how much does it ask "by not saying it"? The melancholy of irony would perhaps be that "critical violence which, while unable to separate" performance from artistic research and both from philosophy, "prevents them from mingling".

Let us have a closer look at the performance: Meg and Tim enter the stage (almost) at the same time. Tim starts to describe – almost simultaneously – Meg's movement by looking at her precisely and tripping along (with) her rhythm, almost. She and he are together and separate at once, almost in a performer / audience situation.

It's – almost – *like* Roland Barthes' *idiorrhythmy* (Barthes 1977) of living together as the occasional synchronization of action rhythms that remain diverging. If contemporary performance practice is often attempted as a figure of togetherness, it is not a utopia of rhythmic, synchronous community, rather an *idiorrhythmic* one. What is on stage and at stake here, is the almost coming together in its precise blurring, the simultancity of the non-simultaneous: As if the performance procedure were a kind of a *broken telephone*-game, slightly shifting / dancing responses and correspondences, failing repetitions.

Or: Tim's tripping along Meg's dancing *is like* the movements of a referee during a boxing match, with Tim at the same time being the other boxer. What does Tim see while he watches Meg dancing? What does she hear while she may dance his words? And what do we see / hear by watching / listening to both of them at the same time?

No, it's not voices – it's more like the sound of the wind, no it's not the wind, it's more like the sound of a kind of machine … You can't be sure … it's like tiny lines, scratches on paper, on glass, on the service of a film. While Tim is trying to speak what Meg is showing, Meg's arms cross hastily – as if they were drawing chiasms, contrasting crossings in the air. As if their chiastic rhetoric tells us: I dance what you (don't) name, and you name what I (don't) dance.

It's like people trying to see with someone else's eyes, echoes Tim. Yes, *it's like* us trying to see what happens on stage with Tim's and Meg's eyes – and them trying to see what they do with the eyes of different audience members, again and again. So, does Tim not speak what Meg dances, but rather how we, the different spectators, may see her dancing? Or how she will have danced?

Either way it will have taken place in the 'Future II', in the future perfect tense – both as a memory of that which never has been present and as re-search, as an opening-up towards something unknown, something *from a faraway room.* For, when we are researching we do not yet know what we are doing – which would be the case especially in *artistic research*: a constellation of words which often rightfully, but sometimes all too inflationarily moves the tongue of contemporary dance and performance (cf. Kruschkova n.d.). A bit *like* René Magritte's pipe which you cannot put into your mouth – except as a word.

So, who is following whom in *Shown and Told*? What follows what – the description following the picture or vice versa? It's *like* the philosophical and performative implications in Heiner Müller's *Picture Description* where every sentence deconstructs the previous one. Tim's suggestions for Meg's movements become more and more intricate:

It's like poems that have been translated from German to Arabic and from Arabic back to German and from German then to Italian and from Italian to Islandic and from Islandic back to Italian and then back to the German – not keeping much from the original sense. It's like Walter Benjamin's *Task of the Translator* which declares the reverse translation impossible. In this context, Benjamin quotes Rudolf Pannwitz who, when translating into German, hopes to *indianize, ingreeze, enenglish* German instead of *Germanizing* Indian, Greek, English (cf. Rudolf Pannwitz in Benjamin 1999, 70–82 [1972, 9–219]).

Or *it's like* Roland Barthes' *Critique et Vérité*: "Would you blame a Chinese (since new criticism seems to you to be a strange language) for the mistakes he is making in French when he is talking Chinese!" (Barthes 1987, 17) This way, Barthes compares and differentiates critique and truth with and from translation: "A critique [...] is not designating a final truth about the image but simply a new image, itself suspended. Criticism is not a translation but a periphrase." (ibid., 36)

Under what conditions are 'French' mistakes in 'Chinese' and vice versa not to be judged but rather to be differentiated (as critique means distinction instead of decision), one might ask? Under what conditions does critique speak sometimes more conceptually, sometimes more poetically, without being just discourse or just art? How to locate the blank space of this 'without', of this melancholic-ironic gap?

In the rift settled in the art / philosophy dichotomy of the occidental world, could critique as a kind of artistic research subvert those oppositions, in order to investigate the conditions under which 'French' misses its 'Chinese' and 'Chinese' misses its 'French', the conditions under which art and philosophy critically "require" (Adorno) or "periphrase" (Barthes) or cut each other "together-apart" (Barad), missing each other as precisely as possible? Or: *it's* simply *like* the game 'Chinese whispers' or 'broken telephone' again.

"Where are the words on the book page?" This is how Jacques Derrida's book Qu'est-ce que la poèsie? / Was ist Dichtung? / What is poetry? / Che chos' è la poesia? begins (a book in four languages, Derrida 1990a). And where are the words on stage? Where are the movements on stage, always already shaped and at once disfigured by discourse? Words and movements on stage – always already

Damaged Goods (thus the name of Meg Stuart's Company, founded in 1994), broken goods and words and promises and hearts. *It's like a broken I-phone,* Meg will later comment on Tim's movement, slightly shifting the game. Or: *It's* always already *like a Broken World* (thus the title of a novel by Tim Etchells (2009)).

We (with our *broken I and worlds*) might also call *Shown and Told* a lecture performance in which the 'we' is co-original with the 'I', *like* in Jean-Luc Nancy's *Being singular plural.* So, it would be a lecture performance only possible as a singular-plural duet, not, as is usually the case, as a solo. Or: *It's like* the confused mathematics, algorithms, rhythms in Heinrich von Kleist's *On the Marionette Theatre* – but who is the marionette and who is pulling the strings? While Meg's crossed arms are waving in the air more and more intensely – in their indefinable definitions, Tim responds: *It's like very complex mathematics you can't understand.* This is where the audience always laughs.

Shown and Told: Past Perfect, retrospectively, in a reverse resonance the *and* in the title insists on the list, listening to the undecidable linearity, causality, hierarchy of listening. Even the spotlights to the right and the neon tubes to the left of the stage (Light design: Gilles Roosen) do not bring more light into the matter – as if they were also only shown and told matters: explicitly exhibited stage lights.

And we – *like* Tim's complex-concrete and at the same time absurd abstract, by no means converging, always alternating descriptions throughout Meg's arms crossings – get stuck in the air, in the movement swarm, in the sign crowd, in the opaque, parallel, broken worlds: *It's like fog in dark or very crowded spaces, spaces that are usually too crowded.* The *usually* overstaffed and over-translated topics and optics remain foggy. Meg is said to dance like the fog over places that are – *usually* – very crowded. How on earth does she do it! Her complex movement is now urgent, now almost bored.

Sometimes *it's like* in *The Last Adventures* (2013), an explicitly choreographic work by Forced Entertainment, where the repeating stanzas of the choir – in their anaphor structure – jump and poetically burst their logic, a tautological thaw of logic:

Sometimes people behave like animals.
Some animals eat people.
Some people eat animals.
Some people act like animals.
Some animals act like people [...]
Some people are awake when they should be asleep.
Some people are asleep when they should be awake.

This chiastically constructed cross-over of words is *like* a foreign language exercise, *like* a (broken) promise of a language. Or: *like* echoes of Peter Handke's early pieces in several of Tim Etchells' performance texts: In Meg Stuart's choreography *Alibi* (2001) he contributes a text (that acts as an echo of Handke's *Self-accusation* (1966)) as a verbally and physically escalating recitative of propositions *like* "I am guilty of looking away", or: "I am guilty of being an American ... I am guilty of ..." etc.

In an interview on her latest piece, *Cascade* (2021), Meg says:

> For instance, when 9/11 happened, we had just started to work on *Alibi*, which deals with violence among other things and when we were working on kinetic energy and its destructive power for *Violet*, the tsunami stuck in Japan, while at the same time the Arabic spring took place. It's spooky! I don't want to mythologize anything or say that I had a vision, it's just really surprising to me that instead of remaining fiction or conceptual, it becomes real. (De Meester, 15)

And the dramaturg Igor Dobricic adds, "that's what happens when you exit linear time."

Back to *Shown and Told*. It's *like crystals, like ice melting*, says Tim – while Meg's movement actually seems to melt, but only very briefly. It's *like* the serially melting ice letters LIVE FOREVER in a video installation by Etchells in Time Square. It's *like people fallen asleep in a subway, or people looking for some lost information*. Or: like Forced Entertainment's *First Night* (2001), which also searches: for lost relatives or lost keys or lost topics: Just *like* a performative artistic re-searching through rooms.

It's *like clocks moving too quickly or too slowly* – when Meg does her circles counter-clockwise while lying on the floor. It's *like people trying to get out of the situation*. Out of this concrete situation? – we ask ourselves immediately, as we watch the confusions on stage, in a performance situation being always already real and fictional at once. It's *like people hiding behind furniture* – while Meg crawls so close to the floor as if she would like to hide under the stage boards.

It's *like wearing someone else's clothes or shoes* – while Meg is busy buttoning and unbuttoning her jacket and pacing back and forth helplessly. It's *like dancing at the end of a party at night when you really, really have to go home* – while Meg's exhausted dancing, while Meg is exhausting dance. It's almost like André Lepecki's Exhausting dance: performance and the politics of movement (2006).

It's *like seeing people for the very first time. It's like seeing people for the very last time. It's like touching people for the very first time. It's like touching people for the very last time*, Tim says coming close to Meg, very close, not touching her and moving away fast.

It's *like questions left on Internet platforms which nobody is replying to*: Like our missing responds lost in Internet translation over and over again: agon and agony of the analogue. And while Meg is stepping back and forth, wondering what her arms are (still) for, Tim's chiastic crossings of anagrammatic body images follow her: *It is more like legs that are more like hands and hands that are more like legs.*

It's *more like falling into deep water, really deep dark water*: It is precisely Tim's over-precision that makes his naming concrete and abstract and absurd at the same time. Meg is very close to the stage edge, to the invisible fourth wall. Tim: *It's more like pushing against walls.* Meg is meanwhile near the stage wall to the left. We notice: a *more* has now crept intensively into the *It's like …* structure: *It's more like …*

What *Shown and Told* is interested in are the over-precise paradoxes of representation, a rhetorical interest in parables that brings the levels of what is shown, told and meant in a relationship that allows these levels to separate just at the moment of comparison – precisely in order to touch each other: *It's more* about the comparably different, about quivering comparisons and tottering touches.

Or it's *like* Peter Handke's motto (a quote from Osip Mandelstam) for his early play *Prophecy:* "Where to begin? / Everything is out of joint and totters. / The air quivers with comparisons. / No word is better than the other, / the earth booms with metaphors..." (Osip Mandelstam cited in Handke 1976, 3). Handke's piece reduces the usual comparisons to meaningless, supposedly predictive tautologies in order to detonate denotations that too are hastily brought back into the familiar. The usual "People will die like flies" swifts into: "The flies will die like flies", which tacitly implies: 'What do we care about flies', up to abysmal tautologies such as "The Jew will haggle like a Jew", in which there glares an inhuman ignorance and indifference, rhetorically camouflaged as a simile (Nägele and Voris 1978, 77).

Meg is now dancing with her arms spread, as if pulled back and forth between two or rather more options: *Like* a scene in her *Alibi*, in which a female dancer is pulled back and forth between two male dancers, hysterically asking herself, asking us: "Left or right! Left or right!", then turning her back on the audience with her shout "Left or Right!", of course completely reversing the directions, the perspective with her arms spread.

Shown and Told – a performance that is pulled back and forth between two or rather more positions or languages, between original copies and copied originals, between prescriptions and descriptions. With the optics of several – aesthetic, ethical, political – un-given options.

Tim: *It's like sending signals over miles and miles, signals in empty rooms, in the night on the edge of a building* – while Meg, with arms up and her back turned towards the audience in desperate decisiveness and undecidability, is faraway, somewhere upstage: A bit *like* – if we keep *sending signals over miles and miles* or are re-searching with *the sound of voices from a faraway room* – the small figure in the distance in Caspar David Friedrich's *Mönch am Meer*.

Or it's *like* giving desperate signs upstage, *like* giving (up) signals. Or *like* Antonin Artaud's definition of the artist as someone who only gives one-off "signs from the pyre" – urgent, still unreadable signs because they can come only once. Or *like* the upstage projection of the small white figure in Meg's *Alibi*, who seems to be giving signals at the airfield with two flags in her outstretched arms.

Or it's more like a kind of light, this kind of movement, Tim is now speaking completely breathless, *or it's more like gunshots.* Or it's *like* the catatonic moving performer pretending to be constantly hit by gunshots, in Meg Stuart's *Alibi* again, the same performer, Davis Freemans, who confessed first: "I'm guilty of looking away..." *Like* a poisoned gift instead of guilt of self-quotation.

We notice: an *or* has now crept explicitly into Tim's *It's more like ...* structure (which is now: *or it's more like ...*), an *or* which by its not given optionality has been implicitly floating from the very beginning. Or: To the undecidability of the *more* (adding an 'm' to the almost homophonic 'or') now an explicit *or* is added. Tim: *Or it's more like embracing yourself to feel OK* – while Meg just embraces herself. *Or it's more like instruments to detect the existence of ghosts.* But which theatre ghosts as visitors only do Meg and Tim conjure or chase away into the void? *Like* in Megs piece *Visitors only* (2003) or in Forced Entertainment's *Void story* (2009). A performative exorcism of the much conjured theatrical presence, a performatively marked absence.

And while Meg has long since been on the ground: *Or it's like people sleeping in hotel rooms for weeks and weeks. Or it's like scientific instruments to detect changes in the weather or in people's memories, like trying to remember what I felt five years ago, five months ago.* Movement and speaking: retrospective and prospective at once: Often the talk is about *remembering of ...* but then also about *learning to ...*: *It's like learning to walk on hot sand or on broken glass.* The *Broken World,* Tim's novel pops up in my mind again. Or: *It's like Bill Viola's video installation Crossings,* in which the same soundtrack evokes water or fire, depending on whether we see the front or the back of the screen showing a figure slowly drowning in water or slowly burning in fire.

Tim: It's more like the sound of births on the end of the telephone line. The telephone again. It's more like triangles or curves or zigzag, like spilt milk – while Meg is 'spilt' on the ground by her movement to pause for a while, and Tim hesitantly points at her and simply says: It's like (short pause) this. After the rapid rhythm of the beginning, speaking and moving suddenly calm down. Do they give up? Give up giving signals?

So, Tim's voice becomes quieter, addressed to the audience, repeating: *It's like ... this*. And after the next moment of hesitation: *It's like ... that*, while Tim's hand flutters back and forth, barely noticeable between Meg and himself, as if he refers to the relationship between the two of them, between what both of them are doing, namely between doing and referring, perhaps.

It's like ... this, Tim says again, while he rolls onto the floor (almost) in Meg's pose and points to or touches the floor with his index finger: *Like* a ballerina would both touch the ground with her pointe shoe and avoid it all at once. Which sore point, which solid base of the references is touched here, which stability is punctured, perforated? Heinrich von Kleist's marionette as well "only touches the ground" – and any ground for being on stage – while pausing for a short moment. A pause, a pose, a point, a touch *like* a peephole through which there flows the moving memory of something that has never been. *Like* the subtle peephole projection in the choreographic installation *the fault lines* (2010) by Meg Stuart, Philipp Gehmacher and Vladimir Miller.

The stage lights are now a bit dimmed. While Tim lingers lying down and rotates minimally around his own axis, Meg stands up. Beginning of the 2nd part. Downstage, on the left stage edge, very close to the audience, Meg starts to speak: *I dance because people ask me to*. The anaphor structure of the sentences comes again, this time a different one: *I dance because it is a good way to seduce people, I dance because I have too much energy, I dance because I like making other people look good*, Meg says with a quick glance at Tim who continues to turn his uncomfortable looping laps on the ground.

I dance because of Iggy Pop and Prince, I dance because I can practice dying and it doesn't seem all that bad, I dance because it keeps me honest, I dance because it is a way to manage my anger, because I can travel forward and backward through time, because it keeps me in shape, I dance because I like to dance next to other sweat bodies all night long, I dance because I can make love with/to the floor all day long, I dance because it never leaves traces. I dance because I wanted to be a magician but I'm not good with stuff.

A bit *like* the paradoxically hesitant magic in Meg's choreography *Until our hearts stop* (2015), that magic of a present absence and lost punchlines. *Or more like* the void loops in Forced Entertainment's *Real Magic* (2016).

Shown and Told works against "the metaphysics of interiority" (a formulation by philosopher Marcus Steinweg in a different context (Steinweg 2016)), against some dance semiotics of the adequately translatable and obtainable. And at the same time the performance works against some rigorous resignations in dance science, claiming a dance which allegedly is discursively completely inaccessible. Instead, *Shown and Told* just leads all undecidability into aporia still working on translation.

Instead of adequate comparison, Meg and Tim propose a complex accomplishment, anticipating art's and philosophy's groundlessness and still re-searching for more (than) grounds and at the same time for no ground, no reason anymore. Again, *like* Kleist's marionette just touching the ground for a moment, nevertheless touching it. Even if we do not dance and show and tell for good reason – or on a stable ground, a ground always consists of multiple grounds.

For this second part Meg Stuart asked choreographers about their reason for dancing and collected multiple answers, different languages. Their monologic assemblages act a bit *like* "more than a language, and at once no language anymore" (Derrida 1990b), as if searching for *plus d'une langue*, probably Jacques Derrida's briefest attempt to define the heart of deconstructive practices. Or: the motivations for dancing are *more like* Roland Barthes' *plaisir* figure: "The pleasure of the text is that moment when my body pursues its own ideas – for my body does not have the same ideas I do." (Barthes 1975, 17 [1973, 30]) In the quoted interview we hear Tim saying: "I think I can articulate about 30-40 % of what we're doing but for the rest, there is not really a language. That means we are sort of blundering – the work is ahead of my ability to describe or articulate it. I like that." I like that too.

The game of broken readability promises, of *remembering* or *learning* (of something that has hardly been shown or told) continues. Meg kneels with her hands on her back, showing her back to the audience. *Like* a scene from Stuart's / Gehmacher's / Miller's *the fault lines* again, that mixes with media execution scenes, while Tim is still stretched out on his side with his head raised uncomfortably. Calming down, pause again. Later, also Tim kneels with his hands on his back – facing the audience. Then he stands up, it is his turn to speak, facing the audience, while Meg looks at him and tries to translate his speech into motion (here the causality is clearer). Beginning the 3rd part:

Tim: *It's like that feeling* (the addition of that feeling ... is new here) *you get sometimes when the train next to you starts to move and you think you are moving, but you are not. Or that feeling when you put all this effort to take off something heavy but it is not. Or when you are coming down the stairs in a building that is not very familiar to you and you think there is another more step but there is not and your food gets* (short pause, maybe also remembering Bruce Nauman saying this once) *disappointed.*

The confused stories of confusions and desillusions, of disappointed feet and pointless jokes, of bodies *searching for something through rooms*, go on: *Or when you look out of the window and see somebody standing down there on the street and you go down but nobody is there and you look up to the window – and you see somebody there.* Again, strange changes of perspectives and of time.

And then time and space move along each other in Tim's stories on moving, pointing and disappointing: *It's like time was coming through walls, walls are making their way through houses, houses moving inside streets, streets are moving through cities, cities moving through countries. It's like* Meg and Tim moving / *searching through rooms* which are also searching.

Moving rooms, which sometimes are looked at under a microscope, sometimes through a telescope, in order to find out what they are *made of* and what they are *run on*: *Cities that are made of memories but run on forgetting, cities build out of forgetting but run on memories. Cities that are made of promises but run on hope, cities build out of hope but run on promises.* The descriptions of the parallel worlds continue to operate chiastically: made of something but run on the opposite.

Figure 2: Meg Stuart und Tim Etchells, *Shown and Told.*
(Tine Declerck, 2016)

Meg is now standing next to Tim, 'translating' into gestures what he says – almost as if in deaf-mute language, but it is not, and that's what this is all about. While Tim evokes *cities made of old books that nobody needs to read,* Meg suggests *cities made of love letters or rainbows, or of Christmas ornaments.* Tim: *cities made of old shoes.* Meg: *cities made of children's clothes, very expensive children's clothes ...* And so on. And already the two seem to be swimming in the same river, in a river that, as is well known, you can only enter once.

So Tim and Meg will 'build' further imagined worlds in rapid alternation: *cities made out of guns, cities made out of blood, or just oil or sweet; or artificial limbs, or used tampons or condoms, or nice songs people don't sing anymore; or skeletons of tiny birds, or limbs of enemies, that have been hacked off* (here also gesturally 'hacked off' by Tim), *or cities made out of hot chocolate, or of picture post cards, or broken I-phones.*

Whereby the whole scene in its broken seriality *is* like – again – a broken telephone game: *Or cities made of feelings, or stories, or eye lashes, or skin, or tiny teeths of snakes, or confetti, espresso cups, regrets, dust, mist, words, just words, just breath, sleep in the eyes in the morning, or nothing, nothing at all.* So, this list, this juxtaposition of our non-classifiable worlds on and on.

It's like the showing and telling of stories along each other beyond causality, rather as a listing that lets commonplaces go to pieces instead of claiming communal availability. The mere listing, serial enumerating of the performative material names nameless differences. Therefore, we often find the hierarchy-less stringing together or 'alphabetizing' of the material in the work of Forced Entertainment.

In the program of Forced Entertainments's 24-hour performance *Who can sing a song to unfrighten me* (1999) Tim Etchells lists the inventory: "Dogs, alphabets, panda bears, fatalities, fairy tales, horror stories, dances, and jokes." (Etchells 2001, Kruschkova n.d.) Listing, especially in processes of artistic research, avoids the hierarchy of terminology, short-circuits parallel levels of articulation. After a theatrical singular *as if* there comes a plural *what if* mode of an exploratory performance practice, which also considers the possibility that scenic presence and linearity might turn into marked absence and *nothing, nothing at all.*

We are dealing with a performative rhythm of heterogeneous listing which ever anew disarticulates fixations imminent with articulation and which is conclusive only if it avoids conclusions. As a continuous de-positioning of dispositives – with an "aggressive humor", with its contaminated, 'con-timed' instead of well-timed lists and levels.

"Humor is something totally aggressive", performer Kristof Van Boven says in Meg Stuart's *Until our hearts stop*, a group work which attempts an enigmatic animality, innocent nonsense und sensual insanity, gamy games, tenacious tenderness – with a sensual nonsensicality and humor, and hesitant magic. "I used to spend my holidays by the Mediterranean. But now I cannot swim in the Mediterranean" – Kristof Van Boven says in this piece, created in 2015, and comments: "Here we transgress all our boundaries." And all the performers and musicians on stage are doing so also literally – by an abysmally comical scenic obscenity which at times seems to go too far, precisely because our intimacy, our coming together can never go far enough (cf. Kruschkova 2016).

In *Until our hearts stop* the dancers come uncannily close to each other in all kinds of constellations – -ménage-à-trois, groups of four, five, six, seven –, before they hastily get out of each other's way (cf. Kruschkova n.d.). Several couples then whirl around vertiginously, each with their counterpart's fist in the mouth, the fist in the other's mouth only holding the rotating couples together. A bit *like* the over-dependence of the couple in *Shown and Told*, only that they cannot hold their mouths.

Or it's like show-and-tell, the school activity in which a child brings an object into the class and talks about it. *Or like* – back to the lists – *Show and Tell* (2013), a 15' long performance by Jonathan Bur-rows and Matteo Fargion which attempts to list some of the artists who have influenced their collaborative works, a list which can never be completed, of course.

In fact, the infected, contaminated lists and levels of humor do not play anything down, provided they are working with their own grounds and abysses, with the non-convergence of motives (*I'm dancing because...*), with the desire for and disorder of the different/iation we all are beholden to.[1] Thus, the laughing dance's sense might go insane but never loses sight of differencing – even threatening thereby to lose its mind, minding understanding, rather "releasing from understanding as a proof of love" (Steinweg 2016).

Instead of just co-understanding, rather problematizing the 'co-', e.g., the audience's unproblematic laughing along. Instead, the sin-gular vibrations of laughter jolt the automatisms of community and identity by continuously laying open new asymmetries. Thus, Tim Etchells instructs performers and audience: "Split the audience. Make a problem of them. Disrupt the comfort and anonymity of the darkness. Make them feel the differences present in the room and outside of it (class, gender, age, race, power, culture). Give them the taste of laughing alone. The feel of a body that laughs in public and then, embarrassed, has to pull it back." (Etchells 2001)

Those instructions suspend hypotactic connections, conjunc-tures and conjunctions, they plead for paratactical instead of order-

---

1   The following section is based in part on material previously published in Kruschkova 2016.

ing listing, which foils the control and relief functions of collective laughter: instead of subordinate conjunction and conjuncture – a conjunctive or subjunctive mood, the mode of possibility in contemporary dance and performance (*or it's more like ...*) and in their theory too, which does not have to take itself too seriously.

The humor in *Shown and Told* focusses on the calculated missing of time, on bad timing, on the rapid standstill of punchlines, on the doubts of language about the body telling, the despair of the body about language showing when body and language upend each other, come across each other, talk at cross-purposes. As an *idiorhythmic* tremor of surfaces, laughter addresses the vibrating aesthetic intervals, *the fault lines* between the parallel worlds to which we, strange humans, funnily enough belong, simultaneously.

It's like that stringing-together instead of the ordering classification of animals by Jorge Luis Borges which Michel Foucault cites in *The Order of Things*. In this precise chaos the humorous, paradoxically short-circuits parallel surfaces of articulation and problematize witless theories of witnessing, affiliation, and community, make them falter by getting stuck within them, in the desiccated theories, *like* in one's throat. *Or more like* Walter Benjamin's definition: "Laughter is shattered articulation." (Benjamin 2002, 32) So bitterly apposite for our time, this chaos of articulation.

The ambiguous, more than obvious and not at all obvious anymore gestures of the comical dis-articulate dance and performance (hi)stories, too, make their academic dryness twitch. The act of listing is about differentiations and con-fusions and chaos: Tim celebrates "the way that Meg orchestrates chaos", as he puts it in the cited interview.

When speaking about lists, about them and through them, we are talking beyond causality. Again: *it's like* a coordinating, paratactic and not like a subordinate, hypotactic conjunction. Meg and Tim 'build' houses, streets, cities, worlds out of words in order to tear them down at once. Whole cities appear macroscopically, made up of smallest particles, micropolitically. In this concrete poetry of onomatopoetic promises all references dissolve, the language becomes an illegible sign (a bit *like* Friedrich Hölderlin's "ein Zeichen sind wir, deutungslos" (Hölderlin 1953, 203), or again *like* Antonin Artaud's giving "signs from the pyre').

Tim intensifies himself more and more into his talking and showing of *nothing, nothing at all*, spreads his arms, takes everything that has been said, danced, and imagined between his hands, quite literally, squeezes it into an imagined package, squeezes it further, the package always becomes smaller, until he swallows it, as if he were letting it disappear into his mouth: What escapes here could be a tongue or language or lingua. Thus, Tim swallows everything that has been said, which can be more than words and no more words anymore. Then he stretches his hand forward – a gesture that will appear again later, more explicitly, I will come back to this. Then he is on the floor, Meg is upstage, both are alone again, solitary, a short pause.

And then – it is no longer possible to count the performance parts which become shorter and start to interfere more and more – Tim's 5-minute voice loop comes: *We let go of each other's hands slipping past each other slowly, very slowly until only the fingers were touching. We let go of each other's hands slipping past each other slowly, very slowly until only the fingers were touching. ...*

Meg comes closer, *it's like* her wanting to save him from the obsessive repetition and at the same moment being magically attracted by its gentleness. The voice loop, the broken record. Remembering Tim's movement at the end of the first scene when he put his finger on the floor – as if the dance floor were his dial and his finger a dislocated clock hand. As if the floor were his gramophone, on which it spins *like* a broken record ... A *bit like* Friedrich Kittler's *Gramophone, Film, Typewriter*.

And then – Meg's and Tim's impossible dialogue, their dialogue on the impossible: *We wanted to say good bye but there was too much noise, we could hardly see each other. / We made plans to travel and send us photos but the camera couldn't focus, the internet doesn't work, we wanted to, we had many ideas ... but some communication problems ... / We wanted to have a beautiful moment ... to sing Rolling Stones, but we thought it would be too much. / We wanted to dance together naked in the rain but there was only sunshine.* The paradoxical overcalculation, the failure, the failed plan: "Our strength is being unable to plan well", says Tim about the work with his group Forced Entertainment (Etchells 2001, 1c).

In our being with, our wit(h)nessing of this iconoclastic performance, nothing remains in the picture, so that we cannot just consume it. Tim continuing the failure list and leading border politics (remembering Meg's *Until our hearts stop*) into an aporia again: *The pictures in our passports looked nothing like our faces, so on the border they said: "No! Would you please step out of the line, Step out of the line please! Step out of the line!"* Tim repeats the instructions of the border police walking backwards, fanatically, louder and louder. These repeated instructions fall out of the previous order of the sentences and paradoxically deconstruct every order.

Meanwhile Meg is in the auditorium, Tim is upstage, repeating obsessively, panicked, *like* a broken record again: *I'm here, are you there? I'm here, are you there? I'm here, are you there?* Is he addressing us? Or Meg? After repeating it several times, the concrete question is: *Are you there, Meg?* A bit *like* the title of a book on Meg Stuart's work: *Are We Here Yet* (Damaged Goods/Stuart 2010). Or *like* Bruce Nauman's *You may not want to be here* (1968).

Or like Forced Entertainment's *Bloody Mess*, in which a performer acting as a clown asks himself several times: "What am I doing here? What am I doing here? On stage, but also in this world." As if we were in this picture puzzle between stage fact and staged fiction too. Meg will soon calm Tim down: *Yes, I'm here*. But it's not that simple, they both know. Tim: *No, I'm here, you are there*. Only a perspective change, again?

Remembering: "Where are the words on the book page?" (Derrida 1990a) And the words and movements on the stage? "They go from being words on the computer screen or on the page to words in a body, in the air. I think, the way I am trying to work with the language is also about how the language sits in my body and how it animates me in space," Tim says in the quoted interview.

Are you there? I'm here! – time and again. Words and moves and spaces and places yet to come. And just before Tim's *here-there*-panic explodes, he just removes another presence / absence dichotomy: *I used to be here, but now I want to be there*. And he moves to another place on the stage. Meg picks up the game: *I was here but now I want to be here.* A 't' runs out of control here and it becomes hard to separate *here* from *'t'here.*

Tim also changes his position – now he is on the ground again *like* at the end of the first scene (the interfering and self-quoting of the single, shorter and shorter performance parts continues), again with his head uncomfortably raised: *Now I want to be here, but I start to regret it, it is not very comfortable, it's like I lost my moment, I'm stuck in this, but it's just a proposition.*

Figure 3: Meg Stuart und Tim Etchells, *Shown and Told.* (Eva Würdinger, 2018)

Are you there? Are you moving? – Tim Etchells asks dancer and choreographer Meg Stuart of all people: in contemporary dance, (non) presence and (not)moving are a topic of course. At that moment Tim, in his uncomfortable reclining position, does not actually see Meg. But we also hear this question in a figurative sense – already being sensitized by what *Shown and Told* could be about: by this floating fictional / real and literal-figurative in every scenic situation.

Are you there? Tim asks again and – as we already know – Meg replies with a question: *Is that a serious question?* Tim: *It's a 52 % serious one.* Meg: *Is it a philosophical question?* Tim: *More of a political one.* "Yes, exactly, there is also a political dimension to this performance not presented as a militant vendor's tray." (Ploebst 2018)

Then a guessing game begins in this performance, which is all along a charade, in the multiple sense of the word, where no guessing can succeed: *Do you remember this hand?* Tim asks with a quick walk forward and (again) with his arm outstretched to the front. After Meg's perplexity, Tim explains his gesture: *Bad news in hospital, when you hear the long peep-signal and see the line on the monitor. Like* the moment in *Bloody Mess,* when two performers, while re-searching for a 'beautiful silence', imagine a peep-life-signal in the hospital room which suddenly stops.

Meg picks up the guessing game: *I have one: Do you know what this is?* Meg seems to be throwing something away, maybe shaking it off, the movement remains of course opaque. *An apology,* she explains her gesture to perplexed Tim. A bit *like* the confuation and intimacy of Philipp Gehmacher's words in his solo *my shapes, your words, their grey* (2013): "I'm done with apologizing."

Now Tim continues the guessing game and lies down – Meg guesses: *It is very minimal, something with water, a river? Or is it a business negotiation? No, a political protest,* says Tim. Now she kneels – like much earlier – with her hands on her back. Tim is at a loss. Meg: *This is classic* (as if quoting again the execution posture in Stuart's / Gehmacher's / Miller's *the fault lines*).

And then Meg brushes the contours of Tim's, then of her own body. (*Like* a gesture in *the fault lines* again, which seems to become 'classic' exactly through this self-citation. Does Meg trace / picture the other's and her own's body counters? Do pictures hurt?

Do we yet *dance because it* does *leave* traces?) So, what is it? *Making friends in a new town,* Tim guesses here correctly for the first time, at least this time Meg does not say 'no' but maybe, because she has to suppress her laughter.

She strokes her face with both slopes, then slightly opens her hands, which are still touching each other at the sides. So, what is that? He does not know. *It's so simple: Facebook!* – she triumphs. Then both of them simultaneously make superimposed wave movements with their hands, surfing in stage instead on the Internet, then they do curves, lines, circles together as if they were spelling their own movements. While Tim makes stomach rotations as if with a hula-horn, Meg guesses: *It's like ritual.* Tim's answer: A *washing machine.*

Figure 4. Meg Stuart und Tim Etchells, *Shown and Told.*
(Tine Declerck, 2016)

We are at the end. Meg: *Do you want us to stage dive but not really do it?* They run towards the audience and stop just before the stage edge. What kind of representability are they at the edge? The irony gap between what has been shown / told / meant explicitly becomes a gap between stage and auditorium, which also can only be overcome ironically.

So, in the end, the two speculate about the possible bending of the edges, just as superimposed waves in physics diffractively bend sharp edges and cause territories to interfere. *Like* in Karen Barads "Diffracting Diffraction: Cutting Together-Apart". *Or more like* Tim's quote about his dis /assembling work with Meg as "a bit off territory with elements of it that are still mysterious to us."

Shown and Told: A text choreography and dance performance that deals with the legibility of our gestures. Gestures which explore and lack their own readability at the same time. They are both microscopic and macroscopic gestures, too big and too small at the same time – as big as if they were about to tear; small enough as if they were not there yet. So, these gestures despair, almost disappear, in all their / our inconsistency (cf. Kruschkova 2016). Gestures which reclaim their complexity and call for new, affective, resistant forms of understanding, also for a challenge of theory *like* Paul de Mans *Resistance to Theory* (Man 1986), *maybe* resistance *against* but also *towards* theory.

Tim in the quoted interview, one last time:

> Language can be a kind of controlling or fixing force in relation to image or to doing, which often seems to be more ambigu-ous and less defined. Something that I have struggled with in my work since the beginning: being in love with language, but also trying not to let it be this controlling, fixing form. To up-set the capacity for closing things down that spoken language has. One of the things that Meg and I are exploring, perhaps, is trying to find ways of working with language and image and language and movement, that allow the language to be open, poetic and on the same level as other kinds of material. I think that this is really important: to allow the language to exist as texture or musicality or energy rather than semantics.

As if the performance were an always shifted correspondence which does not resolve into semantics, just *like* potentiality does not re-solve into actuality. "Some friends of mine call it potentiality [...]. Things waiting to happen", a clown says in *Bloody Mess* by Forced Entertainment, a performance of repeated soundchecks: "One two... one, two, *two*".

"Things waiting *to* happen": we might hear a homophonous short-circuit here between *two* and *to* – in order to destabilize any causality and linearity, in order to subvert any telos, any *to* simply as *two*, as test counting too: *Like* all the lists in *Shown and told* – too multiple to just classify. While things are waiting to happen, the two on stage happen to do other things with /out or rather out of words and moves, as if they were suggesting 'how to do things made out of words and run on moves, and things made out of moves and run on words', to try out a short-circuit with John L. Austin's *How to do things with words* (1962), as confused as it is.

As if philosophy (of language) as well as critique, performance and / as artistic research had to rehearse their problems along each other after all, melancholically-ironically: *One two, two... One two, two...* Speculative and spectral instead of spectacular: *Do you want us to stage dive but not really do it?*

Literature

Adorno, Theodor W. 1997 [1970]. *Aesthetic Theory*. Translated by Robert Hullot-Kentor. Minneapolis: University of Minnesota Press. [Adorno, Theodor W. 1970. Ästhetische Theorie, Frankfurt a.M.: Suhrkamp]

Austin, John L. 1962. *How to Do Things with Words*. Oxford: Oxford University Press.

Barad, Karen. 2014. "Diffracting Diffraction: Cutting Together-Apart", *Parallax*, Routledge, 2014 Vol. 20, No. 3, 168-187.

Barthes, Roland. 1975. *The Pleasure of the Text*. New York: Farrar, Straus and Giroux. [Barthes, Roland. *Le plaisir du texte*. 1973. Collection "Tel Quel". Paris: Éditions du Seuil]

Barthes, Roland. 2002 [1977]. *Comment vivre ensemble. Simulations romanesques de quelques espaces quotidiens. Notes de cours et de séminaires au Collège de France, 1976–1977*. Paris: Éditions du Seuil.

Barthes, Roland. 1987. *Criticism and Truth*. London: Athlone Press. [Barthes, Roland. *Critique et Vérité*. 1966. Collection "Tel Quel". Paris: Éditions du Seuil]

Benjamin, Walter. 1999. "The Task of the Translator." In *Illuminations*, translated by Harry Zohn. London-Sydney: Random House. [Benjamin, Walter. 1972. "Die Aufgabe des Übersetzers". In *Gesammelte Schriften*, Vol. 4.1., edited by Rolf Tiedemann and Hermann Schweppenhäuser. Frankfurt a.M.: Suhrkamp]

Benjamin, Walter. *Selected Writings*. 1996–2003, vol. 1–4. Edited by H. Eiland and M. W. Jennings, translated by E. Jephcott, R. Livingstone, and others. Cambridge MA: The Belknap Press of Harvard University Press, 1. [Benjamin, Walter. 1991. *Gesammelte Schriften*,

under Theodor W. Adorno's and Gershom Scholem's collaboration. Edited by Rolf Tiedemann and Hermann Schweppenhäuser,
Frankfurt a.M., I.1.]

Benjamin, Walter. 2002. *The Arcades Project*. Cambridge MA: The
Belknap Press of Harvard University Press.

Damaged Goods & Tim Etchells. 2016. "Shown and Told." Program
Note. https://www.damagedgoods.be/shown-and-told, http://
timetchells.com/projects/shown-and-told/ (last accessed: 12
June 2025).

Decaesstecker, Eva. 2016. "For Me, Collaboration Is Being Out of Familiar Territory." Interview with Tim Etchells. November 2016.
https://www.kaaitheater.be/nl/duiding/%E2%80%98for-me-
collaboration-is-being-out-of-familiar-territory%E2%80%99
(last accessed: 12 June 2025).

De Meester, Julie. 2021. "Interview with Meg Stuart and Igor Dobricic." Program book of Meg Stuart's Cascade. ImpulsTanz Festival,
Vienna.

Derrida, Jacques. 1990a. *Qu'est-ce que la poèsie? / Was ist Dichtung? /
What is poetry? / Che chos' è la poesia?* Berlin: Brinkmann & Bose.

Derrida, Jacques. 1990b. *Mémoires: for Paul de Man*. Revised Edition.
New York: Columbia University Press.

Etchells, Tim. 2001. "Not part of the bargain. Notes on *First Night*."
Forced Entertainment Contextualizing Pack.

Etchells, Tim. 2009. *The Broken World*. London: Windmill Books.

Foucault, Michel. 1971. *The Order of Things. An Archaeology of the Human Sciences*. New York: Pantheon Books.

Handke, Peter. 1976. *The Ride Across Lake Constance and Other Plays*.
Translated by Michael Roloff. New York: Farrar, Straus and Gi-
roux. [Handke, Peter. 1966. *Publikumsbeschimpfung und andere
Sprechstücke*. Frankfurt a.M.: Suhrkamp]

Hölderlin, Friedrich. 1953. *Sämtliche Werke*. Sechs Bände, Band 2.
Stuttgart: Kohlhammer.

Kleist, Heinrich von. 2012 [1810]. "On the Marionette Theatre." Translated by Kevin J M Keane. https://kevinjmkeane.com/wp-con-
tent/uploads/2015/07/Kleist-On-the-Marionette-Theatre.-Ju-
ly-2015.pdf (last accessed: 12 June 2025).

Kruschkova, Krassimira. 2016. *How Did You Come Together? On Contemporaneity of Dance and Performance.* Keynote lecture, Tanzkongress Hannover. https://2016.tanzkongress.de/files/how_did_you_come_together_kruschkova_eng.pdf (last accessed: 12 June 2025).

Kruschkova, Krassimira. n.d. *Dance Aesthetics as Politics of Friendship.* n.p. https://fabricoftrust.wordpress.com/wp-content/uploads/2017/10/text_kruschkova_013.pdf (last accessed: 14 June 2025).

Lepecki, André. 2006. *Exhausting Dance. Performance and the Politics of Movement.* New York/London: Routledge.

Man, Paul de. 1986. *Resistance to Theory.* Minneapolis: University of Minnesota Press.

Nägele, Rainer, and Renate Voris. 1978. *Peter Handke.* München: Beck.

Ploebst, Helmut. 2018. "Practicing Dying with Ironic Grandeur." November 24, 2018. https://www.damagedgoods.be/EN/about/articles/2018/der-standard-practicing-dying-with (last accessed: 12 June 2025).

Post, Hans-Maarten. 2017. "It's like … He talks a bit and she dances a bit: 'Shown and Told'

(Meg Stuart & Tim Etchells)." Review. *Utopia Parkway* (blog). January 28, 2017. https://utopiaparkway.wordpress.com/2017/01/28/shown-and-told-meg-stuart-tim-etchells/ (last accessed: 12 June 2025).

Steinweg, Marcus. 2016. Discussion with Krassimira Kruschkova in the framework of her talk series *The pleasure of the text. A Discursive Ménage-à-trois* at Tanzquartier Vienna. June 3, 2016.

Stuart Meg / Damaged Goods. 2010. *Are We Here Yet?* Edited by Jeroen Peeters and Meg Stuart. Dijon: Les presses du réel.

Thieme, Barnaby. 2012. "Mnemosyne, by Friedrich Hölderlin." *Mesocosm* (blog). June 6, 2012. https://mesocosm.net/2012/06/06/mnemosyne-by-friedrich-holderlin/ (last accessed: 12 June 2025).

The Feeling of Thinking
Stories on Artists Reading Theory

Veronika Reichl[1]

Abstract: *The following three short stories investigate the experience of artists reading theory. They are based on interviews with artists on their reading. They are part of a broader collection of short stories on students, philosophers and artists reading theory, published as "Das Gefühl zu denken" [The Feeling of Thinking] in 2023 by Matthes & Seitz Berlin.*

Dreaming of cabbage – Sandy reads Heidegger

Sandy is an artist. That means that she takes the form of things seriously. The form concerns every detail of her work: It concerns how Sandy prepares, how she starts and finishes. It concerns the material, the tools and the work space. It concerns how her body moves, how she thinks, and what she intends. And thereby it also concerns her breakfast, her clothes and when to go for a walk in the afternoon. Taking form seriously means taking life seriously. It is not about the results but about every single moment. And that is absolutely true, although every time Sandy beholds one of her finished artworks in all its conceptual and physical beauty she enters a state of childlike, jubilant joy.

Of course, form is also content: Because from all of Sandy's forms one can infer who Sandy is and how she relates to the world. Ideally,

---

1   These stories were previously published in: Veronika Reichl: *Das Gefühl zu denken* © Matthes & Seitz Berlin Verlagsgesellschaft mbH.

all her forms agree with each other in some way and the compliance of all these forms becomes visible in Sandy's art. Yet in the end it is not form that Sandy is searching for. But by searching for the sound form she is also searching for a deep, fundamental thinking, a thinking that becomes possible through and indeed finds its expression by the sound form.

All the important things come to Sandy when she does the work. And she is willing to do it. Reading philosophy is part of it. For example, she often reads Deleuze or Heidegger for half an hour before starting to work artistically. It gets her into the proper mood and it sharpens her intuition. After reading, the sound form for her artworks often comes to meet her, like a friend who unexpectedly rings the bell. For this to happen, the text does not have to be connected to her art project, it just has to be a certain kind of philosophy.

At the moment Sandy is exhibiting in a gallery in Leeds. Her art work consists of sitting in the gallery at a writing desk, reading Heidegger's *Being and Time* and writing it down by hand. It is a testimony to the sheer physicality of the work and also of the physical demands of philosophy. The project seems a little selfish to her, because she is allowed to occupy herself with Heidegger for eight weeks. Copying a philosophical text by hand is a completely different practice than just reading it – it switches something else on and off. It is extremely intimate: The sentences run through her hand and thereby through her brain almost as if it were her own. Sandy often thinks of the monks in the monasteries, who devoted their whole lives to copying sacred texts and how intense and beautiful that must have been.

Right now, the form feels right: The plain, wooden writing desk, the old wooden chair, her simple, dark-blue clothes and the warm socks on her feet. As long as nobody attends, the gallery is a quiet place. In front of her desk the shop window opens the view to the outside, down a tranquil street: enough space for her thoughts to unfold. Time, too, extends before her: hour, days and weeks. Sandy opens *Being and Time* and starts where she left off yesterday. She remembers immediately what the last passages were about. She starts with the next paragraph. She reads each sentence two or three times in a low voice. With Heidegger she often understands right away, at least roughly. When the whole sentence is present in her mind, she writes it down on the paper in front of her in calm letters. Finally, she reads her duplication once more. Right now, she reads and writes:

> Why does understanding always penetrate into possibilities according to all the essential dimensions of what can be disclosed to it?
> Because understanding in itself has the existential structure which we call project.
> It projects the being of Da-sein upon its for-the-sake-of-which just as primordially as upon significance as the worldliness of its actual world.
> The project character of understanding constitutes being-in-the-world with regard to its disclosedness of its there as the there of a potentiality of being.
> Project is the existential constitution of being in the realm of factical potentiality of being. And, as thrown, Da-sein is thrown into the mode of being of projecting.
> Projecting has nothing to do with being related to a plan thought out, according to which Da-sein arranges its being, but, as Da-sein, it has always already projected itself and is, as long as it is, projecting.
> (Heidegger 1996, 136)

Sandy is focused on her work. After thirty minutes she suddenly recognizes a familiar feeling and thinks: *Aha! So, it is working now!* The text exercises something in her brain, it works on her and makes something fundamental happen to her. Everything about her is suddenly in motion. Every part of her is thinking. It is indeed quite physical. Heidegger feels what he is saying. His language is set up in the same way as his ideas. He allows the track of his thoughts to shape the words. Everything agrees with each other and is full of power. Sandy loves Heidegger for searching so urgently for the perfectly apt form for his thoughts. His particular concurring of form and content allows the text to pull not just Sandy's mind but also many other levels of her, some of which are very physical. It pulls them to think.

She would claim that at this moment she comes into full existence. Sometimes it touches her so deeply that she starts to cry.

While reading in this way, she is using a capacity that is not about a skill she learnt in school or anything similar. It is a fundamental capacity. Like when you run. Or when you eat when you are hungry. It is kind of an animal capacity. Using this capacity makes her – it sounds a bit cheesy or esoteric and she does not mean it that way – but that is what happens: it makes her feel the pulse of the universe.

Sandy does not read in order to understand something new or to accumulate knowledge, although of course these things are beautiful things, too. It seems to Sandy that Plato is right when he says: All knowledge is already within us, we just have to re-connect to it. Because that is exactly how it feels: As if reading re-connects her to something that has always been within her and that she still cannot reach on her own. It works best with Heidegger, Agamben, and Deleuze and Guattari.

An elderly lady in a blue coat comes into the gallery and looks around. She does not want to disturb Sandy. Sandy says hello and they start a conversation anyway. Sandy tells the lady that she thinks that art and philosophy are closely related, much more closely than one might normally think. Both are experimenting with ideas and shifting perspectives. Both re-connect the recipients to the important stuff. The lady smiles gently and nods carefully. Sandy continues: *The world needs that too, you know? The world might need other professions more urgently: doctors and farmers and computer specialists, for example – and that's why I sometimes find it difficult to simply draw a rose. And yet there are also very good reasons to draw a rose and read philosophy. You just have to remember them.*

Sandy offers the lady to try copying a bit of Hegel by hand herself. At first the lady laughs and raises her hands defensively. But then they end up sitting next to each other mumbling with concentration. After both of them have written down a long beautiful paragraph, the lady thanks Sandy and walks out into the street with bouncing steps, her copy in hand.

In the first four weeks in the gallery with Heidegger, Sandy grows calmer and calmer. It seems to her that for the first time ever she is actually going slowly enough for these texts to immerse her completely. After five weeks she starts to smell cabbage and earth in her dreams. She often walks across fields under a dim sun. The earth and the air are damp and the colors sparse. She is always wearing heavy leather boots. Sometimes there are cabbage fields, rows and rows of pale green heads as far as the eye can reach. Sometimes there is black, heavy mud, in which her boots sink in deeply. She keeps dreaming that something is written on the cabbage leaves. Often these dreams end with her understanding that it is the dead who write on the leaves. Dead men, dead women and dead children. Sometimes it is the heavy soil itself that writes on the cabbage. The soil writes its being out. As if matter was writing itself. In her dreams, Sandy is part of everything: She is walking and being walked on. She is part of the cabbage and part of the soil, part of writing and part of being written on. She is the angularity of the letters and the smoothness of the cabbage leaves. All this writing happens in German. Sandy does not speak German, she reads Heidegger in English, and yet in her dreams she hears and writes German sentences and is immersed in this German that is written on the cabbage leaves.

Even during the day in the gallery Sandy can now smell cabbage and earth as soon as she opens *Being and Time*. The gallery owner jokes that it is Heidegger's grubby lederhosen that Sandy smells, and maybe it is. It makes Sandy laugh, but it also feels uncanny. After eight days of cabbage, Sandy is fed up. She still loves Heidegger, but it is time to get off the desk, put on some colorful clothes, and lie in the sun. It is time to listen to pop music, eat gummy bears and actually draw a rose. But first she has to get through the last two weeks with Heidegger.

This story is based on an interview with artist Hester Reeve.

Authoritarian cuboids –
Jan reads Deleuze and Guattari

Theory books are authoritarian objects. Closed, compressed, massive. Heidegger. Hegel. Kant. Aggressive cuboids. Written for the chilly air of early mornings, for the progress of civil society, for all the centuries that are to come. Schopenhauer. Adorno. Foucault. Classics. Lifeworks. Male stuff. Nobody can read that!

In any case, Jan cannot. The mere technical process of reading might actually be feasible. But it is impossible for him to ceremonially sit down at a table and open such a book. He imagines this moment of a festive beginning: the cell phone switched off and his teeth brushed; sitting at a blank table, the book in front of him. Then opening the book and beginning with the first sentence of the introduction: Drama of the master's approaching knowledge. The ring of the authors' names and the shape of the books are unmistakable: Jan shall start at the beginning and work through them page by page. Along the way he shall read the ten books that are necessary to fully penetrate the main one. The authority of the books dictates that. Jan cannot do it.

Jan studies fine art in Leipzig. In his seminars he is supposed to read theory all the time. No complete major works – reading them is voluntary – but lots of excerpts and essays. This stuff is almost as solemn as the masters' lifeworks, even on black and white copies. Theory is important at Jan's university. Wherever students think politically, love conceptual art and despise the model of the ingenious artist as being outdated, theory is essential. Jan belongs to this crowd, and he also understands that reading is the right thing to do. He just cannot do it. It has been like this since he was in school: When someone tells him to read something, a steel door clunks – slowly sliding – shut. Then the door is closed. It is a shame, because Jan knows that something important, something he might even enjoy, is locked behind the steel door.

In the end he manages to get a good degree without reading: Jan is a nice person and he is good at what he does, so his profs let him get away with it. After graduating, Jan carries on reading some random stuff every now and then, mostly from magazines. But for his thirty-fifth birthday someone gives him a copy of the small *Rhizome* book by Deleuze and Guattari. It is thin and rickety, so it is just right. The next morning it slips into his backpack almost by itself. On the train it can be opened without any problems and Jan starts reading just for sport. The book bubbles away: It gently rails against the logic of the tree diagram and against everything that is clear, top-down and self-contained. It wants multiplicity and plants and animals and connections and rhizomes. Immediately Jan has hand-drawn, animated films in his mind. The book speaks a lot about Freud and some Anti-Oedipus. Jan does not understand everything, but many things seem surprising and reasonable at the same time. Deleuze and Guattari tell Jan to simply tinker with the ideas in the books. They say that he does not need to read everything, that it is nonsense to want to understand everything, trying that would be completely wrong. Ideally, Jan should rather observe whether something is growing and proliferating between him and the text: herbs or fungi or bacterial cultures or swarms of insects. One or another part of the text might interact with Jan, and maybe they become a machine together that might even produce something. The only important thing is to let something grow, to short-circuit with the texts and to become part of a happy machine. These thoughts are radically new for Jan. They shift something fundamental between Jan and the books.

In the months to follow Jan starts to buy theory books: first a few, then more. He allows titles and covers to seduce him. He particularly likes to order the thin ones with the colorful covers. The books look fantastic on his shelf. Handy, flexible cuboids that perfectly box thoughts. Smooth, white paper. Series of serial letters. Right angles everywhere. Unpretentious minimalism. Books are ideal objects. And finally, Jan can own them. All this wealth is now accessible to him, too. It is a miracle.

The books usually sit around on his shelf for some time while they and Jan get used to each other. Until one day they are at hand and can be tucked into his travel backpack just as easily as a sweater or a notebook. Jan is still unable to sit down at his table to read. That is still too solemn and at the same time too much a luxury. Jan does not have the peace of mind to spend time reading books in his hometown.

He has a project space, a teaching job, exhibitions to prepare and he has kids. But he travels a lot. While the books are in his backpack, their corners scuff in a lovely way. Other books break in the middle or get doodled in. After that they lie more relaxed in his hand. Jan likes to look into shallow things, such as one of Byung Chul Han's small volumes. It puts him in a good mood, even if Jan forgets most of it soon afterwards. Without planning to, Jan sometimes reads books like these from cover to cover, simply because the length of the book fits well with the length of the train ride. The other day he also had a lot of fun with one of the simpler Sloterdijks. The book was full of ideas that matched one of his art projects. Of course, this is male stuff: vain and self-indulgent, yet it babbles so joyfully that it sits quite well with Jan. Sometimes he reads something more complex, something like Niklas Luhmann or Quentin Meillassoux. The more substantial the texts feel, the more important it is to evade the central perspective of their authority. Never to approach them from the front, rather trickle in through a side entrance and read a few sections quickly as if it were an article in a magazine. It is even better to get stuck with a few sentences while flipping through the book, get hooked, and look from there. Sometimes Jan is then drawn into the book. It can be great to find yourself in the midst of dense complexity and conceive some thoughts there. But it can also be the wrong moment, and then Jan shoves the book back into the backpack.

Nonetheless, many books are still unreadable for Jan. Still he is hardly able to touch the central works of great thinkers. A *Thousand Plateaus* by Deleuze and Guattari is one of them. It has been sitting on his shelf for two years now and it is not getting any closer. A *Thousand Plateaus* is a block of some weight. With its bright white, freshly printed pages and the minimalist cover, it is even discernible as a classic from the outside. Awful! Jan's fingers do not want to go there. He also cannot put this book in his backpack for a while and let it tear apart in the bag. Because somehow that would feel wrong with this particular book. In A *Thousand Plateaus* Deleuze and Guattari throw the normal order overboard and ask: Why does everything have to be so compulsive, linear and authoritarian? Let us do it differently! Unfortunately, the size of this gesture gives them an insane authority of its own. The two are obviously outlaws of philosophy, and at the same time they are two of the greatest philosophers ever, and every-one around Jan is reading this, or has read it, or at least wants to read it. But even though Jan would like to finally get to know this almost holy book, he is unable to take it off his shelf and open it. He cannot stand the anti-authoritarian authority of this book much better than the authoritarian authority of other classics.

The feet are not reaching the ground – Annett reads Susan Buck-Morss[2]

Annett has been reading *Hegel and Haiti* by Susan Buck-Morss for two days now. She is enjoying it a lot. She reads on the S-Bahn taking her through Berlin, during the break in the academy yard and at din-ner at home, where she spills a few lentils and some salad dressing on the pages. Buck-Morss writes that Hegel knew about the successful slave rebellion in Haiti and that his reflections on the master-slave dialectic, or more precisely the dialectic of lordship and bondage[3], are closely related to this event. Everyone is reading this essay right now. Annett has to read it too, regardless of whether she decides to focus on fine art or theory in her studies. But there is another reason why Annett reads *Hegel and Haiti*: she is looking for a way to read the great male European philosophers in a feminist, anti-colonial way. Perhaps this can be learned from Buck-Morss.

Annett likes the whole text, but what she enjoys most are the footnotes. Indeed, there are a lot of them – they make up more than half of the text. Annett reads each and every one. The footnotes deal with something additional, and Annett is passionately interested in this additional something. For example, one footnote relates how Eu-rope's growing hunger for sweets fueled the sugar production and thus significantly worsened the conditions for the slaves in Haiti. An-

---

2   This story was not only published as part of Reichl 2023 but also (in a prior version) as part of Potsch 2020.

3   The terms Hegel employs in the German original are *Herr* (master, lord) and *Knecht* (farmhand, bondsman), so the translation *lordship and bond-age* is more apt than the traditionally more common translation *mas-ter-slave-dialectic.*

other footnote explains that Hegel was surrounded by Freemasons and probably belonged to them himself. A third footnote refers to Buck-Morss herself and says that spiritually she feels closely related to Judith Butler, although at a first glance they interpret Hegel's silence on Haiti in opposite ways. All this is super interesting. Annett is also invested in all the footnotes on the titles and places of publication of the books, journals and magazines cited. Because they display a foreign context of its own at which she gets a peek.

Annett briefly researches a few of the references. She always wonders why none of her friends and colleagues seems to do that. Does nobody else care whether the texts and their sources are sound, whether you should believe them or – as surprisingly often – rather not? Do they not mind many authors citing texts arbitrarily and ignoring the context of the original quotations? As expected, in Buck-Morss every reference is viable. Buck-Morss writes about events and people and about what people have said or written. She also writes about which sources reported these events and how trustworthy these sources are and why. Buck-Morss always keeps in mind that she knows things only because someone wrote them down in a specific context. She feels an obligation to all these people. You can feel this in her writing.

The details Buck-Morss reports allow Annett to make contact. As if every detail connects some part of what was previously floating in the background of Annett's mind to specific points in a landscape. Every detail feels a step on solid ground: contact, contact, contact. Each of these contacts is a small, tangible joy. Each makes Annett breathe a little sigh of relief, yet she has no clue what it relieves her of.

Reading Buck-Morss is very different from reading Hegel, which Annett also loves. Hegel, too, makes Annett take steps, but these steps are floating. She can never be sure whether she is hitting the ground or whether she is just tapping on a cloud of meaning. Although she believes that by now she has a handle on Hegel, each of her steps still only creates the possibility of future contact, never the contact itself. Annett loves this tapping on floating meaning: it is as if a shiny space of meaning opens up in front of her. This space is stretched out by Hegel's vibrating texts, and its content goes beyond what Annett can name at the moment. Annett may never be able to enter this room, but she loves to stand at its entrance and glance inside.

For a long time, reading Hegel felt right. By reading him, she absorbed a big chunk of the philosophical canon: her professors (those at the philosophical faculty as well as those at the art academy) liked her engaging with Hegel, and so did her theory friends. After a few months Annett began to write miniatures on Hegel's concepts. It was a semi-literary format that her theory professor at the art academy praised as theoretical prose: A game with Hegel's ideas and his language and an attempt to cut something small and sharp out of Hegel's diffuse texts. It was important to Annett not to use quotations without context, as is often done in the arts, but to refer to Hegel's theses as they might have been meant in the context of the original text. Although her texts were literary and experimental, she also tried to be philosophically thorough. Still, she was not sure that her approach was really allowed. She did not dare showing it to anyone at the philosophical faculty. Something about it seemed suspicious to her.

In the last few months, reading and writing about Hegel felt more and more wrong: Because it is stupid to look for a shiny space of meaning in such an arrogant, authoritarian egomaniac as Hegel; in a white, stately CIS man of all people. By reading him Annett gives Hegel even more influence and he has really had his share. Instead, she should dedicate the stage of her mind to minoritarian authors. In addition, Hegel's thinking is highly speculative – it is no coincidence that often he writes without any explicit references to other authors – and no footnotes. (Although this is probably mostly due to the writing habits of his time.) Hegel spins his ideas mainly from his own mind. If there emerges any contact in reading him, it is a contact to Hegel and only indirectly and strongly mediated by him a contact to the world. Furthermore, Annett suspects that by making her take floating steps Hegel allows her first and foremost to float in her own mind. And she fears that this floating in her own mind might lead mainly to privileged and egocentric thoughts. In this case, her writing might show a lack of solidarity with those who, for economic reasons, have no opportunity to float themselves. It does not help much that her friends like Annett's prose. Annett is also only partly relieved by such clever, political women such as Susan Buck-Morrs, Judith Butler and Catherine Malabou working with Hegel. If all these great women are writing about Hegel, there is a way to read him in a meaningful, ethical and possibly even anti-colonial way. But these women write quite differently from Annett. They do not float with Hegel, instead they relate to a concrete foundation of politics in his texts that Annett can neither fully identify nor address.

Annett stops staring holes in the air and reads on. Buck-Morss talks about a *Minerva magazine* and its extensive coverage of the successful rebellion in Haiti. The journal is important because there is evidence that Hegel read it and therefore knew about the rebellion in Haiti. Reading this passage works immediately for Annett: contact, contact, contact. Annett keeps forgetting the importance of contacts, although it is crucial: in the end, abstract thinking only counts if it touches the concrete world and makes it more accessible. And yet, while Annett thinks and writes, the concrete stuff somehow disappears. She thinks of the moment when she was in Auschwitz for the first time and thought: it's really true, everything really happened! Annett was instantly ashamed of the thought. She had read a lot about the Holocaust; she had seen documentaries and had never even remotely doubted it. It appears constantly in newspapers and in the movies and in literature. It had been an immensely important fact which must always be considered. But it was not until she was standing at the barracks that she realized that in all this time she had not fully understood that it really happened to real people and in real places. As if her feet had not fully reached the ground of this reality. And although at that moment there was strong contact in Auschwitz, even then she could not be completely sure that she had absorbed the full truth of it now.

At the moment, Annett trusts Buck-Morss and the moral integrity of her writing far more than herself. This not-reaching-the-ground might be a fundamental part of Annett's thinking, and it might show up in all her writing. And because it is a fundamental part of her thinking, she will not even be able to perceive it in her own texts. What makes matters worse, is that this not-reaching-the-ground affects her thinking about the things that matter most, as shown by her experience with Auschwitz. Annett cannot go on writing like this.

Suddenly she realizes that she has written very little since her visit to Auschwitz. She was waiting for the problem to resolve itself. But there is no sight of a solution even if she writes like Buck-Morss – constantly referring to sources, constantly striving for contact with the concrete – she cannot be sure that her writing will reach the ground. And working historically like Buck-Morss is hardly what Annett is good at, or would like to do.

Annett feels lonely. Her theory friends have no problem with being in contact with the ground. This question somehow does not apply to what they are doing. For a long time it was them who gave Annett the feeling of standing on safe ground and of being embedded in joint, critical thinking. They started studying art together and discovered theory on the way. Today some of them no longer study art but philosophy, some organize theory parties, others make wild, theory-based films. None of them has a problem with Annett's interest in Hegel. In fact, they approve of Annett reading Hegel, and thereby adding him to the group's expertise, as most of them prefer to read Donna Haraway, Armen Avanessian and Paul B. Preciado.

Two days later Annett is sitting on the S-Bahn with *Hegel and Haiti* again. It is hot, her skin sticks to the seat. Buck-Morss shows that Hegel must have known about Haiti. But he deliberately did not mention Haiti in his texts – most likely for political reasons. He knew that his readers would consider it in this context anyway. Everyone was thinking about Haiti at the time, it was the elephant in Hegel's lordship-and-bondage-room that everyone knew about. But some decades later that was probably no longer the case. Hegel's thinking was received more and more independently of Haiti. It was perceived as ahistorical, purely theoretical thinking. That is how Annett read it, anyway. It had never occurred to her before reading Buck-Morss to ask for the concrete historical context. With nobody any longer knowing about the connection, the rebellion in Haiti became the ghost of the text: something which affects the text and the readers may sense, but they cannot make contact with it. Perhaps such ghostly aspects create a distance between the reader's feet and the ground of the text? Annett puts the book on her lap and thinks about ghosts of texts: There was the European discourse on freedom at

Hegel's time. Yet this theoretical discourse hardly ever mentioned the massive expansion of the slave trade taking place right then. But there was a connection. Just as Hegel never mentioned Haiti in describing the lordship-and-bondage dialectic in which in the end only the bondsman has a chance to develop an independent consciousness by fighting with the master. Today it seems clear that the discourse on freedom and the expansion of the slave trade were inextricably linked. There might be something similar taking place right now: central ideas that occupy our thinking without us naming their concrete background. Maybe partly because we think the background is clear anyway. Or maybe because we are simply not used to talking about it. This idea stays with Annett all day, and so in the evening she asks Helen and Mara and Tim, but they cannot think of anything convincing. There is the inhumanity, the exploitation of the poor around the world as well as modern slavery. But Annett and her friends name these all the time: Annett and her friends are aware of their privilege and that through their consumption and their government they are hopelessly entangled in this injustice. They are also aware that they discriminate against others all the time without wanting to. She and her friends are trying to do the right thing. They are vegans or at least vegetarians, they only fly when they have to, they are involved in political groups, they read and discuss in order to understand what to do. And yet it seems not enough. At night, under her blanket, Annett has the idea that maybe they cannot fully understand all the global suffering as part of their world. The catastrophes are widespread. Even just coping with the knowledge of so many of them is overwhelming. But at the same time, so many of these things seem to take place in a reality somehow separated from Annett's reality. She relates to them in a strangely indirect way. If this is true, she would be a reversal of Buck-Morss' Hegel: Hegel does not mention Haiti and the rebellion there, but he makes them the basis of his thinking and can thus think something new. Whereas Annett constantly refers to all the horrible political, environmental and economic developments she knows about; yet in this moment in her bed it seems to Annett as if somehow she cannot make them the basis of her considerations, as if she is not able to adapt her view on the world accordingly.

The next day, Annett is sitting under the maple tree in the academy's yard again. The weather is still hot and sultry. She has just finished *Hegel and Haiti*. She looks through the beginning of the book once more and finds a passage where Buck-Morss says that the actual subject of her essay is that there is no place in the university for research like hers. She continues: *That is the topic which concerns me here, and I am going to take a circuitous route to reach it. My apologies, but this apparent detour is the argument itself.* (Buck-Morss 2009, 23) Annett is surprised. She missed it the first time. She had firmly assumed that Buck-Morss would tackle everything directly and name everything as specifically as possible. But she claims to make one of her most important points via a detour. Annett feels stupid because she wishes she would not have to construct the argumentative logic of this detour herself. The detour is probably pretty straightforward: Presumably, Buck-Morss simply means that her research speaks for itself and that there should be a place for such research. This idea is quite convincing. But Annett is not sure whether Buck-Morss argument is that simple: To Annett it seems to be somewhat too straightforward for a detour. Annett would love Buck-Morrs to spell it out word for word, so that Annett could be completely certain. Annett also realizes that another central thing is not spelt out in Buck-Morr's text either. It took her a while to find it because the ground of the text is so firm in so many passages. But Buck-Morss does not write on how the perspective on the lordship-and-bondage dialectic must change through the reconnection to Haiti. Either she does not want to determine that, or she thinks it is obvious. Probably it is obvious, but it does not feel obvious to Annett. Of course, knowing about Haiti has already changed Annett's perspective, but she feels that she is missing something and that the change needs to be more decisive. And there is more to it. Everyone keeps saying that you cannot escape Hegel: In a way, everything goes back to him, including all political thinking out there. Annett's personal landscape of thought, the theoretical landscape of the books on her shelves and in her city are directly or indirectly related to Hegel. His thinking made its way everywhere. If the perspective on Hegel must change a great deal, the perspective on all texts which Hegel infiltrated, and also all the texts which these texts infiltrated must change at least a little bit. Changing all these perspectives might provide Annett with more contact to the ground. But she does not know how to do it. Maybe she is already doing it without knowing it. Maybe not. At the moment she does not have a clue.

Literature

Buck-Morrs, Susan. 2009. *Hegel, Haiti, and Universal History*. Pittsburgh: University of Pittsburgh Press.

Deleuze, Gilles & Guattari, Félix. 1977. *Rhizom*. Berlin: Merve Verlag.

Heidegger, Martin. 1996. *Being and time: A translation of Sein und Zeit*. Translated by Joan Stambaugh. New York: State University of New York Press.

Reichl, Veronika. 2023. *Das Gefühl zu denken*. Berlin: Matthes & Seitz.

Potsch, Sandra (Ed.). 2020. *Im Schaum dieser Sprache: Hegel lesen – Texte und Zeichnungen von Veronika Reichl*. Tübingen: Universitätsstadt Tübingen.

Gay Troublemakers
None but Fools[1]

Susanne Valerie Granzer

> The fool doth think he is wise,
> but the wise man
> knows himself to be a fool.
> *Shakespeare, As You Like It*
> Act 5, Scene 1

Under cover …

What is a fool? What hides behind the German word *Narr*, whose origin is etymologically not really known? If, uninhibited by academia, we jump headlong into such questions, a multiplicity of associations, possible readings and concepts stumble over each other. This also applies to the word queer. As today's star, it enters the assembly of words with a mischievous "grin like a Cheshire cat" and makes an impressive cat hump. Then it performs capers on stage, but unexpectedly falls backwards into Alice's mouse hole, where it disappeared. All that remains is an ironic grin of its hype.

But to be more serious. Is the fool just an idiot? Somebody who is not in his/her right mind? A human being with a mental disability? A *"fool by nature"* and not a *"fool by art"*, like the fool character in

---

1 This text was originally published in German under the title "Johnny & Immanuel" in: Böhler, Arno, Susanne Valerie, and Passagen-Verlag. 2018. *Philosophy on Stage: Philosophie als künstlerische Forschung*. First German edition. Vienna: Passagen Verlag.

Shakespeare's dramas, comedies and tragedies? If this was the case, a fool would be a both mentally and physically deformed human who knows and makes the experience of being both psychically and physically – even more powerless than all of us – at the mercy of the world and of him/herself. Abandoned to mishap and disfavour, to scorn and mockery, to glee and humiliation, at best suitable for acting as a powerless scapegoat, for acting out one's own accrued resentment on him/her, because he/she, as already said, is just an imbecile gawk, a goof, a blockhead and a ridiculous oaf. Indeed, a fool who, due to his simplicity, makes us laugh and is laughed at.

Or – on the contrary – he/she is him/herself a jester and giggle, a joker, a rogue, who is laughed at because blatantly he/she makes jokes at the expense of others? Then he/she would be a quick-witted clown making his/her audience look like fools – and of course everybody knows that his/her jokes do not aim at him/herself but certainly always at those others. No question. On the other hand, the jester likes his/her jokes to be rude and dubious. This way he/she may be sure that the audience will laugh, because by way of his/her filthy quotes he/she blatantly "rides the hobbyhorse", as we commonly say. This kind of fun is entertaining and amusing – and it works.

Insofar, in a way the comedian on stage has carte blanche for all kinds of eloquent fun, which he/she presents with the brilliance of an actor. This is much applauded and laughed about, for all of it is just a chimaera, banter and toying with the truth, which is not necessarily believed. Not even if the situation becomes dead serious. Not even if the situation is really urgent – and in Søren Kierkegaard's ironic aphorism this is definitely meant literally:

At a theatre, the props happened to catch fire; the buffoon stepped forward to inform the audience. Everybody believed this to be a joke and applauded. He repeated his announcement: the applause became even louder. This is the way, I think, in which the world will perish, under general applause by funny minds who believe the process to be a joke. (Kierkegaard 1904 [1885], 40)[2]

---

2   English translation from the German edition by Mirko Wittwar.

The conclusion to be drawn from this scene is obvious. One need not believe a jester and buffoon. Not even if obviously he/she speaks the truth. Everything he/she is saying up on stage, what he/she is doing, if he/she is laughing or crying, if he/she gurns or keeps a straight face, all this only serves for entertainment, for the audience's amusement. For, it is down there, in the stalls, where there are all those honourable, scholarly and witty minds who know how to distinguish true from false, not up there, on the stage which is said to be the world. As a passage from a poem by Friedrich Schiller says[3] which has become a winged word, as the educated know.

If we visualise the described situation, at the apron we see an actor wearing the buffoon's dress, desperately struggling for credibility, *as he knows* he is speaking the truth and the whole theatre, with all the audience, will soon be ablaze. By *why* is he not believed? Why? Because this is a buffoon speaking? Because it is clear that everything happening on stage is defined as fiction? Because, according to this conclusion, what he is saying cannot at all be true, not even if it is actually happening at the moment. The stage is the place of fictitious truth. A "temple of lies". And that's that. That's fact. Let the fool jump about like he wants.

In Kierkegaard's aphorism, not the actor is the problem but it is the oh so prudent minds who are dying of laughter about their own approaching deaths, we feel enticed to say. Thus, in the concrete case it is the self-confident audience who think themselves safe because they *certainly know what is true and what is false*, for one thing is fact: on stage, only fiction is negotiated, no facts. This makes the audience blind, and the buffoon's alleged joke has more weight than the deadly seriousness of the situation. Any trace of instinct is lost. No hazy smell of smoke alerts on time, there is no suspicion. From the perspective of a foolish jester, his desperate alarm is read as a

---

3   Cf. *An die Freunde*: "Sehn wir doch das Große aller Zeiten/Auf den Brettern, die die Welt bedeuten,/Sinnvoll still an uns vorübergehn./Alles wiederholt sich nur im Leben,/Ewig jung ist nur die Phantasie;/Was sich nie und nirgends hat begeben,/Das allein veraltet nie!" (Schiller 2004, 421)

slick gag, meant for entertainment – and the more he struggles for credibility, the louder the audience's laughter.

Ha, ha, ha … brilliant that buffoon, spectacular! … ha, ha, ha … he is gesturing as if the devil was in pursuit of his poor soul … ha, ha, ha … now even his voice goes over the top … now he even flushes, and now he gets really pale again … ha, ha, ha … simply great what he is performing up there!

In a fatal way, the actor's *"successful" performance* combines with the deluded idea of the audience which has no doubt that everything happening on stage is masquerade, travesty, sheer *as if*. Consequently, it has no sense for the surprising, improbable which is to come. It has neither eye nor ear. There is no creeping doubt. No *perhaps* finds its way to them. They believe their firm knowledge of *what is true and what is a lie* to be axiomatic. To be definitive. This makes them blind and deaf towards the coming threat. There is no sense of danger. Not even their own will to survive raises the alarm, tells them that in a few moments they are going to miserably burn within a sea of flames. And why? This species cannot be extinct, "like the flea", as is Nietzsche's diagnosis, "the last man lives the longest". So, why be afraid?

Nietzsche's conclusion on the last man fits seamlessly – only that the end is different – to Kierkegaard's sarcastic words when writing: *This is the way, I think, in which the world will perish, generally applauded by funny minds who believe the process to be a joke.*

What is interesting is the fact that at the heart of this aphorism there is a buffoon speaking the truth and not being believed. Does this not suggest another character among the fools? Could it not be that Kierkegaard the philosopher might be read as acting the scorning fool who, by his caustic conclusion, makes fun of preconceptions, leading to deadly disaster into which we blindly run? Is thus a fool – perhaps also – a critic of distinction? A troublemaker, a malicious agent who, for the sake of truth, in a sharp-tongued manner attacks the hidden basements of power, using the weapon of language? An ironic revealer of character, whose perception reaches behind the masks of short-sighted self-confidence, and who, for love of the truth, opens the trapdoors to the understage, to trace down hypocrisy, resentment, and corrupt arrogance? By doing his buffoon job, does he hold a mirror up to both the powerful and the powerless? *Mirror, mirror on the wall* ... Given the mirror's answer, it may well be that the pride is ignited and starts sprawling like weed in the heart, as what the mirror says is the truth. This will not necessarily really set the world ablaze. Or will it? The question is who is going to burn on the pyre then. Or if the hellfire is worldwide, as Kierkegaard the philosopher cynically suggests, should stupid ignorance get the upper hand.

From the prompt box, words can be heard in a low voice, almost whispered, so that one must strain one's ears to understand what is said:

> Be careful. The truth is a hot potato. At all times. Not only in the past. Every time has its own sacred cow. Left and right. – (The voice coughs slightly), Oh, pardon me, now I've almost made a mistake. These days you're easily mistaken. Of course, what I was going to say: reft and light. (Original German Text: "lechts und rinks")[4] – So, one more time, be careful. Not bowing to censorship and attempting to unmask opinions which have become dogmas is dangerous. A pillory is erected with a click – and all licenced fools[5] are no more.

And furthermore, a prudent fool knows – as is the motto if this paper – "*The fool doth think he is wise, but the wise man knows himself to be a fool.*" (Shakespeare [1862], Act 5, Scene 1)[6] That is, he does not

---

4   English translation from the German edition by Mirko Wittwar. Cf. Ernst Jandl: "lichtung: manche meinen / lechts und rinks / kann man nicht / velwechsern. / werch ein illtum!" (Jandl 1997, book back cover)

5   In the past, so called court jesters in their special position had a kind of license which protected them: "In any case, the 'all licensed fool' was, by unwritten law or explicitly, entitled to function as a critic of his master, however also of contemporary life, of society, of the court, in short: of his entire environment, and to hold up a mirror to them." (Langenbach-Flore 1994, 36). English translation from the German edition by Mirko Wittwar.

6   Touchstone asks of William, "Art thou wise?" William incautiously replies, "Ay, sir, I have a pretty wit." This is Touchstone's opportunity, and he retorts: "Why, thou sayest well. I do now remember a saying, / The

just laugh at those others but also, clairvoyantly, at himself. This double art is his own. With it, humiliation and elevation change places without any problem – and in this context, *laughter* is his *weapon, like medicine*. Such laughter serves for being liberated from narrow-mindedness and dogmatism. In the past and today. By way of these tactics, and by help of witty language games, he camouflages his attacks at ignorance and illusions, thus, in the guise of foolishness, blatantly invalidating rules which dominate minds and bodies. Doing so, he definitely proves to be a philosopher who prudently speaks in tongues and ignites flashes of truth which, by way of liberating laughter, are able to strike sparks of the joy of living on a topsy-turvy world.

Such a fool is per se a happy bloke without shackles of morality which make small and limit possibilities. He, who by his witty-mindedness questions the correctness of everything orthodox and does not play by the rules, might be considered a social outsider. He has little use for the lust of resentment, no matter in the guise of which vocabulary it appears. He is driven by a different motivation. Accordingly, he is no square, no bourgeois, no philistine, no hypocrite, and also he does not belong to those who, blinkingly, ask themselves: "What is love? What is creation? What is yearning? What is a star?" (Nietzsche 2005, 16) – because they have forgotten. By his wit, he shoots the arrow of his desire beyond those others *and* beyond himself. Thus, he is anything but foolish, anything but a stupid goof, but much more a *gate to the truth*, a specific truth-teller, a "truth player" (Handke 1989, 24) and "throughway creator" (ibid., 26) who spies the truth he knows to be promised to. In this sense, he might possibly be attributed a *kind of parrhesia practice* (Foucault 2011, 1–22) and be declared a *truth speaker in a fool's dress* whose particular method is the depth and sharpness of his joke, by help of which he makes the audience, by way of laughter, the touchstone[7] for his poisonous

---

fool doth think he is wise, but the wise man knows himself to be a fool." (Ibid.)

7   A touchstone is a testing stone or a try-out stone. In its concrete sense, it serves for investigating the fineness of gold and silver alloys. This method has been used since ancient times. In a figurative sense the

tongue. Among such fools we may file Touchstone from the guild of Shakespeare's fools.

Touchstone: A Shakespearean Jester

Touchstone as the jester is given in the cast of characters of "As You Like It" – probably written in 1599, first published in 1623 – he is one of the *motley-minded gentlemen* Shakespeare created. It is also him who states that a wise man does not only consider others fools but counts him/herself among them. This gives evidence to Touchstone's prudence and humour, based on which he comments on and criticizes what is going on around him, wearing the mask of the goof. His particular name makes us wonder. Why does Shakespeare call him *Touchstone*? Why not *Feste*, like the jester in *Twelfth Night*, or *Costard* in *Love's Labour' Lost*, or *Lavatch* in *All's Well That Ends Well*? He might as well have gone without a name, like the wise jester in *King Lear*. Thus, why Touchstone, of all?

In Shakespeare's time, a touchstone was originally used to determine the measure of gold in a stone (cf. Granzer 2016). A sample was rubbed on a touchstone (mostly black quartz) until it left a visible line, the colour of which was compared to pure gold. Insofar, Touchstone's name may of course be understood metaphorically. For, like the touchstone must show a sufficient degree of hardness to identify the precious metal, quite in the same way Touchstone the jester, by way of his poisonous tongue and prudent jokes, rubs and cuts the audience, to make them aware of the crazed mixture of truth and blindness, of the tragedy and comedy of all life. Intelligently wrapped in wisdom and screwed pun, laughing is allowed in this context. However, while laughing, one or the other is struck by a flash of lightning, shedding light on man's place in cosmos, on time and being, on error and truth, on power and subject – *striking him/ her down to the ground, and suddenly he/she bites a second time into the Apple of Knowledge?*

Cambridge dictionary speaks of a touchstone as an established standard or principle by which someone is touched (Cambridge Dictionary n.d.).

Basking in the forest sun, Shakespeare's fool Touchstone argues with Lady Fortune about her moodiness. Unabashedly, he speaks loudly to himself, as it sometimes happens when we believe to be on our own. However, coincidentally Jacques, the philosophising pessimist, during his stroll through the forest of the Ardennes, hears this motley figure talking – and listens. What he gets to hear makes him burst out laughing, so that he finds it difficult to restrain himself. He is hardly able to utter these words:

> A fool, a fool! I met a fool i' the forest, / A motley fool; a miserable world! / As I do live by food, I met a fool / Who laid him down and bask'd him in the sun, / And rail'd on Lady Fortune in good terms, / In good set terms and yet a motley fool. / 'Good morrow, fool,' quoth I. 'No, sir,' quoth he, / 'Call me not fool till heaven hath sent me fortune:' / And then he drew a dial from his poke, / And, looking on it with lack-lustre eye, / Says very wisely, 'It is ten o'clock: / Thus we may see,' quoth he, 'how the world wags: / 'Tis 'but an hour ago since it was nine, / And after one hour more 'twill be eleven; / And so, from hour to hour, we ripe and ripe, / And then, from hour to hour, we rot and rot; / And thereby hangs a tale.' / When I did hear / The motley fool thus moral on the time, / My lungs began to crow like chanticleer, / That fools should be so deep-contemplative, / And I did laugh sans intermission / An hour by his dial. (Shakespeare [1862], Act 2, Scene 7)

Laughing may have many meanings. Amusement, rejection, realisation, liberation, insight, fright, resistance and much more. It is a power which grasps our mood without being controlled. A power which may get us beside ourselves. Thus, why does Jacques get so much beside himself with laughter when hearing the words of the fool? What does affect him so much when Touchstone, to his "'*Good morrow, fool,' says: 'No, sir, call me not fool till heaven hath sent me fortune*'", to then take a watch out of his pocket and reason about the fugacity of time. Does Jacques the misanthropist read these words about happiness and being a fool as some funny nonsense which makes him laugh so much that he cannot stop for one hour? Is it the silly melancholy of a fool who, precociously and by way of dissimulation and nonsensical banter, moans about Fortuna and life slipping through his fingers? Nonsense, after all. Is it this?

Or, does Jacques the melancholiac overexcitedly burst out laughing given the question about the fugacity of time, which we cannot stop and which, by death, presents us with a last finale in all eternity? Is his unrestrained laughter an attempt to escape this dilemma?

Or is it something completely different? Does, perhaps, Touchstone the fool function as a mirror for Jacques? *What was it again? Mirror, mirror on the wall* ... Is it his intention to make him aware, in a parodistic manner, of his melancholic way of philosophizing? Of his cynical view at the world, where man, through all stages of his/her life, is hit by one mishap, by one disaster after the other, to finally and ultimately dive into complete forgetfulness – today we call it dementia – and that's all?! "*Last scene of all, / That ends this strange eventful history, / Is second childishness and mere oblivion, / Sans teeth, sans eyes, sans taste, sans everything*" (ibid.), this is, a little later, Jacques' bitter and ironical conclusion about the fate of the humans as sheer actors on the stage of the world. Is his disinhibited laughter thus a paradox reaction to the sudden insight into his own dead-end of interpreting the world solely as a blind calamity, interpreting it from its failure and perishing? Does this explain his almost hysterical reaction?

Or, once again, do we have to read Touchstone's passage, where he curses Lady Fortune, who cannot be forced by anything, in yet a completely, completely different way, because in the same breath he is reasoning about man's mortality, who is swallowed up by time? Are, perhaps, the stage of this world and all the colossal fuzz it makes one of the last remaining places where ragtag fools are allowed to caw a melancholic *memento mori* which insists in *for once viewing the world from the perspective of eternity sub species aeternitatis*? (Spinoza 1994, 258–265 [Book 5, Proposition 29–42]) Is that written on the touchstone for the riddle of Fortune which, by such an untimely switch of perspective, may shine in gold – or indeed not? "*And thereby hangs a tale.*" (Shakespeare [1862], Act 2, Scene 7) ...

Johnny:[8] A Contemporary Jester

A leap from Shakespeare's time to the present, to the year 2015, to
Philosophy on Stage # 4, titled "*Artist Philosophers – Nietzsche et cetera*" was a four-day festival which, by different formats, has swapped
the traditional accommodations of the Institute of Philosophy of the
University of Vienna for those of Tanzquartier Wien. One of the protagonists who, on this occasion, appeared on behalf of Nietzsche,
was a late-modern fool by the name of Johnny, a long-standing accomplice and agent of performance artist Barbara Kraus.

High above the heads of the audience, on the balcony of Hall G,
like on the peak of a mountain, there appears a young man, somewhat casually. He is wearing a bright yellow shirt, large checked
trousers, yellow patent-leather shoes, and a red scarf around his
neck. Sunglasses are nonchalant pushed back onto his short, pitch-
black hair, and his upper lip is decorated with a narrow, black moustache. A pencil moustache.

Figure 1: Johnny blinded. (Copyright: Austrian Science Fund (FWF):
AR 275-G21)

---

8   This is a revised English version of parts of the text "Johnny & Immanuel", first published in German ([Granzer] 2018). It is based on the intervention "Out there is a field" by performance artist Barbara Kraus during
the four-days festival *Philosophy On Stage #4: Artist Philosophers–Nietzsche et cetera* (Kraus 2015).

He himself lacks any kind of French elegance. Instead he is drag-
ging his feet, the real provocateur, with a wicked tongue, he speaks
a broad Viennese dialect, behaves badly and unashamedly, and right
on his arrival he has a go at those who are still taking their seats.
They are, he rants, *time monkeys, being late everywhere. Like Kraus,*
he adds. By a "*na hopp, hopp, hopp*" the latecomers are spurred on,
who seem to be embarrassed by being addressed like this in the public. They, he complains, are monkeying about with the time for his
appearance. The time for his *intervention.* Of which, however, he
doesn't know anyway where *to intervene,* he emphasizes in a com-
plaining manner. Then, when right during the first sentence of his
prologue – "*die Kraus hot urndlich vü g'strewert*" *(that Kraus's been
smugging pretty much)* – suddenly, belatedly a spotlight flashes up
right at him, he interrupts himself and stares blinkingly into the light.
Another disturbance. Now, the real cavalier, however with a rebellious undertone, he asks: "*wer hot d i e blendende Idee g'hobt?*" *(whose
bright idea was that?)* – to immediately add that now he was feeling
much more "*pr o – p o t e n t e r, prä-potenter*" *(pro-potent, pre-po-
tent),* or whatever the word was.

   This mocker's sex is unclear. If we look at the moustache, much
suggest that he is a young man in the age of puberty, like sixteen
years old. His voice, on the other hand, is clearly that of a woman.
Now, who is who? Is performance artist Barbara Kraus Johnny's alter
ego? Or is Johnny, the buffoon, Barbara Kraus's alter ego? The identity of these two remains ambivalent. The perfect tightrope walk. A
game without a safety net, played by both in unison and full of verve.
Neither Johnny nor Barbara Kraus care about any possible danger to
fall. Their appearance is an act of radical improvisation. In *his, her,
its* hand *he, she, it* holds a turquoise briefcase, and an exaggeratedly
large bag is heavily hanging from *his, her, its* shoulder, stuffed with
many books, as one is going to see soon. For, one is told, Kraus has
provided him, Johnny, with material for weeks. And this although he
has just been granted half an hour for his intervention. He very much
extends the word i n t e r v e n t i o n, slowly and mockingly he has
it melt in his mouth. – This way, rebelliously the rogue casts his bait,
with a loud mouth, finally he throws himself into a pose, and both
provocatively and narcissistically, definitely in a non moral sense, he

asks: "*Na, wie g'fall i eich da heroben?*" (*Well, how do you like me up here?*) – and with a meaningful look at those sitting down below him he explains: "*Des is nämlich des Podest der P h i l o s o p h e n*" (*For, this is the podium of the p h i l o s o p h e r s*). There is smirking and laughing. Johnny is winning their hearts.

Figure 2: Johnny picks up a bag. (Copyright: Austrian Science Fund (FWF): AR 275-G21)

With his colourfully spotted outfit, the checked trousers and the yellow shirt, equipped with a wicked tongue, always ready for a bold, unashamed extempore – does this Johnny not resemble a showman, a carny? A fool and a jester who through and through belongs to the tradition of the buffoon? Only that he is from the 21st century? But was it not precisely that type of buffoon (Müller-Kampel 2003) Leipzig scholar and Enlightenment philosopher Johann Christoph Gottsched, in the 18th century, wanted to ban from the stages of Germany, to reform them and to raise their educated middleclass quality? The theatre was supposed to teach and educate but not to entertain by way of vulgar jokes and ambiguities, so as to become a source of moral hazards for the audience. Emotions and desires were supposed to be tamed, not to be revealed and discharged. The so called "*Hanswurststreit (Buffoon Controversy)*" began, a struggle for a "clean" theatre, and indeed, in 1737, the buffoon was, in the course of an allegorical play, publicly banned from the stage. However, this intention was met with resistance, most of all in Vienna with its popular tradition of the *Alt-Wiener Volkskomödie (Old-Viennese popular comedy)* – despite Empress Maria Theresia's ban on extemporising of 1752 (Die Welt der Habsburger 2022). *Sic erat scriptum!*

The fool, the freak with rebellious power who, by way of his jokes, confronts the ruling powers, looks back to a long tradition. He is a counterforce to the elements of suppression, of violence, of threat, of the ban, as well as to fear, weakness, humility, hypocrisy and phoniness. He is to be found in antiquity, by the satyr play, which was performed as a liberating aftermath of the tragedies, it is to be found by the institution of the court jester, with the carnival, in Shakespeare of course, as represented by the jester Touchstone, however also by the laughing figures of the Middle Ages which confront this period's subjugating repression and horrifying seriousness (Bachtin 1990, 38–46). This history could be continued until present time Vienna – which has not been subject to any Prussian-Protestant but to a Catholic-Baroque influence – and this city's love of its language games, its specific kind of humour, its Wiener Schmäh (Viennese snide humour). Gimmicks and tricks of everyday life which, by their outrageous linguistic wit, do not "decently" ignore mishaps and mistakes but satirises them with relish. However, after all without any intention of simply humiliating anybody but of dissolving the human, the all-too-human, by way of wittiness and for loosening it by way of humour.

Not self-discipline is pursued, not Freud's delay of instincts, but laughter. You may laugh in a liberating way! For, liberation and freedom are connected to laughter. It is the victory over moral fear, the overcoming of bans and any kind of strictly-by-the-book truth. Quite like in the days of the court jester, when the fool was allowed to appear, in an official function, as the critic of his master. Laughter confronts the power and violence of the rulers, with their frightening servant-tyrant-dynamics. Laughter, on the other hand, tells about the joy of life and about trust in life. In the play of a lustfully intensifying life. It is the affirmation of the becoming, a protection against everything restricting and limiting, against everything terrifying and pretending. It liberates from the black snake of inner censorship and of outward censorship. Did Nietzsche not canonize laughter?

Also, a fool of the post-modern age, a character like Johnny alias Barbara Kraus or vice versa? – this is frequently oscillating, enticing – is such a kind of playful actor, an unmasker and blasphemer. Johnny, who seems to have only superficially and erroneously joined the philosophers, has, as an artist, incarnately achieved a better understanding of Nietzsche than many others by way of their studies. Like his predecessors in the past, also he attacks, makes fun and mocks with the intelligence of a foolish opponent. Also he holds a mirror up to society. In his case, it is no longer the court of some absolutist ruler but it is the high schools, academia, the science business with its flood of congresses, applications and peer reviews, which has traded the books for journals, which sets guidelines and norms which adamantly claim their truth, for example that analytical power is identical with the power of intellect which, with all these issues, celebrates its own masquerades.

Quite in Nietzsche's manner, Johnny doubts all this. "Laughter I have pronounced holy; you superior humans, *learn* from me – to laugh!" (Nietzsche 2005, 259) Only that by this admonition he does not put himself in the balance by way of writing but with the whole weight of his body, from head to toe, by the art of his improvisation, thus risking his skin by his exposed physicality, and not just metaphorically spoken. For, the audience might as well brusquely reject this rogue and his specific fervour by which he attempts to bear down on the spirit if graveness, his arch enemy. They might pursue him with disfavour, they might make him slip during the tightrope walk of his intervention, so that he falls. They might catcall his *Hoppl di hopp!*, they might leave the hall, cheesed off. Or, even worse for a fool, they might react by dead silence to his jokes, to this way make him understand their discontent with this nonsense, with this charade of his.

'The suitor of truth––you?'––thus they mocked me–
'No! Only a poet!
[...]
Only fool! Only poet!
Merely speaking collorfully,
'From fools' masks shouting colourfully,

Climbing about on deceptive word-bridges,
On misleading rainbows,
Between false heavens
Rambling, lurking –
Only fool! Only poet!'[9]

Johnny's art, his freely improvised talk, based on Nietzsche's thought, with its claim to wittiness and humour, in front of a large audience, discusses *a kind of thought which is different* from the traditional, classical way of doing science. It seeks affinity to the arts and their qualities which, according to his interpretation, cannot be labelled as being third class because they just create shadow images but which have self-creative, poietic power. It is a kind of "post-Platonic image of thought" (Böhler 2018, 59–122), making the material conditions of the body the focus of interest and not shrinking back from emotions. For, is not all thought based on desire? (Böhler 2017, 576–603) Emotions inhibited by reflection find their ways out. In subtle and precarious ways. What can be gained by taming them? They have their say nevertheless. Is it not much more about welcoming them as conversation partners? About cultivating them instead of trying to make them obey by way of self-disciplining and to conceal them by way of sham objectivity? – By way of a common adventure of all those participating in *Philosophy on Stage*, this *different image of thought* attempts to make the exposed dimension of the body visible, its ecstatic nature, its haptic intelligence, and the voice of an open body which is touched and can be touched. For it, the skin is not only, in the classical Euclidian sense, solely boundary and fringe but, just the same, a place of extension and touch, and language is not just in the head, so that the voice becomes squashed and thin and loses its volume and power, but it is in the belly and makes the whole body vibrate from hair to toe, far beyond towards those others it wants to reach. Also the ancient word *temper* may be involved and heart does not just refer, cheesily, to pain. Its potential is a protection against

9   Nietzsche, Friedrich. Dionysus-Dithyrambs: Only Fool! Only Poet!
     http://www.thenietzschechannel.com/works-pub/dd/dd-dual.htm
     (last accessed: 24 April 2022)

everything negative which tries to make life small, which would rather like to see it unhappy instead of excessive – and it reaches as far as to the non-sensical which cannot be thought but is the intimacy of thought. It knows about this without "knowing".

By his improvisations with their uncertain outcome, Johnny, by and for this kind of thought, risks himself as an example. He may like it or not, the stage makes sensually visible that bodies act actively and not passively, and quite a few people would be astonished about what the body tells unintendedly and without being noticed. Here now, in the concrete case, Johnny's intervention makes clearly obvious that he does not solely think and act, as a *subject*, through his consciousness, it is not solely his I which is thinking but *it* is thinking within Johnny, he thinks and reacts by his entire *body*. By his head, heart and sex. And – always *it* thinks and acts within in relation to those others. Everything happening by taking the risk of his free play happens only together with the audience, by way of a dialogue with those others. It is inspired and nourished from the resonance of a common *being-with-each-other*. Not without reason, Barbara Kraus calls her intervention *Out there is a field*.

Figure 3: Johnny little ears, Nietzsche. (Copyright: Austrian Science Fund (FWF): AR 275-G21)

Thus, is Johnny not somebody who, by his pertness, knows to be promised to the *great reason of the body*? Might he not say, quite in Nietzsche's words, *Body am I and soul*? Is it not that he took on the coxcomb for the sake of this truth, to this way be able to demonstrate that the body and its great reason: "does not say I but does I?" (Nietzsche 2005, 30) Is it not that his tomfooleries simply serve the attempt to give way to affirming *bodying and living*, quite contrary to the regulations, norms and values which are still predominant with academia, which are basically just travesties of ascetic ideals?

For this purpose Johnny keeps the audience on strings, swiftly declaring the people deputies of *those despising the body*; he tries to wake them up, to make them laugh about themselves, and while doing so he calls a spade a spade. "*Hoppl di hopp!*" he cries out unashamedly, "*I glaub ihr seid z'vü g'sessn. Ihr modert's scho dahin. Unter eurem Hintern is da Moder ... und so kann kaa g'scheits Philosophieren entstehen. Hot nämlich scho da Nietzsche g'sogt: So wenig als möglich sitzen. ... Das Sitzfleisch ist die eigentliche Sünde wider den heiligen Geist. ... Na, i kumm jetzt amoi owe zu eich, i bin da oben v ü z'weit weg.*" (*I think you've been sittin' too much. You're already mouldering away. Below your asses there's moulder ... and this way no good philosophy is goin' to happen. After all, already Nietzsche said: Sit as little as possible. ... The backside is the real sin against the Holy Spirit ... Well, I'm going to come down to you, up here I'm much too far away.*)

Holding a red rose in his hand, after this speech he climbs down the steps, down from his philosopher's mountain, and joins the audience who, sitting down there in Hall G on black cubes or on the floor, welcome him with curious faces, wondering what he is going to do now.

By the praising call "*ihr habt's das richtig erkannt, ihr sitz'st auf da Bühne*" (*you've got it right, you're on stage*) he swiftly chases the spectators from their seats on one of the large pedestals, and while the audience is laughing he starts pushing it, on its rollers, towards the centre of the room. This way he swiftly makes the audience move, and soon he cries "*aufsteig'n, einsteig'n, mitfahr'n!*" (*get on, get in, have a ride!*), that is he surprisingly invites for a ride, circling round with the pedestal, just for the fun of it, just for the sake of making the room feel different, as he says. Some support Johnny with his action, others let themselves actually be shoved. Johnny performs a victory lap, then another one and another one, movement is joy and supports thinking! He takes Nietzsche's demand, which he has quoted himself, literally, while personally integrating those present: "*Sit as little as possible; give no credence to any thought that was not born outdoors while one moved about freely – in which the muscles are not celebrating a feast, too. All prejudices come from the testiness. The sedentary life – as I said once before – is the real sin against the holy spirit.*" (Nietzsche 1989, 239–240) At last he has reached a position he likes, for now it is possible for everybody to sit down around his playground in a circle. However, *come closer please, cozier,* this is how he likes it, *even closer! after all, his own bum is not glued to the seat,* he provokes those hesitating, and he keeps on and on until everybody has actually taken their seats close to the edge of the pedestal, in the midst of which the red rose is lying.

Figure 4: Johnny and the audience push the platform. (Copyright: Austrian Science Fund (FWF): AR 275-G21)

Figure 5: Johnny pushes the podium with the audience. (Copyright: Austrian Science Fund (FWF): AR 275-G21)

By all this to and fro, and to and fro, Johnny moves ever closer towards the audience, who obviously have much fun with this. Now he can take the opportunity. Now, he says, he may go on with freely associating, "*durch Nietzsche und durch mi selba hindurch*" (*through Nietzsche and through myself.*) This is the keyword for outing himself: "*I bin nämlich, – jetzt hob' i's endlich verstonden, wer i bin, – i bin nämlich des Alter Ego von da Kraus Barbara*" (*For – now finally I've got it – I'm the alter ego of that Kraus Barbara*), he admits discreetly and, moving closer to the face of a female spectator, he asks: "*Host mi?*" (*Got me?*) Laughter. As a reaction to her affirmative nodding, he really acts the fool and thumbs his nose, replying: "*Den Schas glaubst ma?*" (*You believe that shit?*) Laughter. Immediately after this he tells her, in a reconciliatory tone, that his 16th birthday has been just in July. "*Des host, i bin in da Pubertät.*" (*That is, I'm in my puberty.*) Renewed laughter. "*Perfect time to make Dionysus, that's the bloke with the small ears, heard,*" he adds while secretively whispering his name to the room. *Philosophy*, he says, *is exciting! Grasping and being grasped*, and, pointing at his body, "*wias aan e i n f a h r t, wos aan h i n t r e i b t*" (*as it c o m e s, that's where one g o e s t o*), entering territory where one has never been before. At *least*, he says, *being a sixteen years old, aspiring junior philosopher, this is his idea of philosophizing.* Only: beware of universities, they, he says, are dry as dust, and beware of too much reading, this is unhealthy, as already Nietzsche had said. "Scholars who at bottom do little nowadays but thumb books [...] ultimately lose entirely their capacity to think for themselves. When they don't thumb, they don't think." (ibid, 253) Always ready for the dissent, just a little later he will take countless books out of his large bag. Volumes on Nietzsche, volumes by Nietzsche, worn down, tattered volumes – and finally he takes out a snow-white wig.

Why, after all, he asks, was Kraus so much afraid of this event? There was no reason for this, he argues, and he lists: "Die Vernunft, die Wahrheit, die Seele, die Hölle, das Jenseits, der Gott – a l l e s obg'schafft. Also wovor muss ma si da no firchten?" (reason, truth, soul, hell, afterworld, the God – it's a l l been abandoned. So, what's to be feared now?) by the way, he says, he is still improvising, even if he is looking like working, he informs the audience, and by the way, during the creative search of his intervention he was feeling "like a blind crab from the sea which is constantly feeling around itself and occasionally catches something: however, he does not feel around to catch anything but because his limbs need movement." (Nietzsche 1988, Band 9, 19)

During all the stages of his intervention Johnny remains the real buffoon. Scorning and ironizing valid norms and values, unashamedly, outrageously, quite like the court jester of the past, whose social meaning was to immediately and publicly announce inconvenient truths, to maliciously refer to certain individuals, to bluntly call them by their names. Doing so, not always he hits the mark. But relentlessly towards himself and towards everybody around, Johnny fights his fight against the predominance and repression of ascetic ideals, against all those images of thought we are entangled with, he unmasks them and does not shrink back from sometimes happily stumbling over his own feet. Does he not mix *and* unite the foolish with the prudent? Does he not create an alliance of lie and truth? This fool, who is wearing his heart on his sleeve, risking parody, ambiguity and boobery, is he not the personified attempt of embodying Nietzsche's philosophy of "immorality", based on a silent hope for a "prelude to a philosophy of the future"?

Figure 6: Johnny: You know you will die. (Copyright: Austrian Science Fund (FWF): AR 275-G21)

"I should only believe in a God who knew how to dance" (Nietzsche 2005, 36), Johnny just quotes *Thus Spoke Zarathustra*, "and when I saw my Devil I found him serious, thorough, deep, and solemn: it was the Spirit of Heaviness." (ibid.) "*Seid's ihr lauter Teifeln?*" (*Are you a bunch of devils*), he quips provocatively, looking sternly at the audience. "*Serious, more serious, most serious, even more serious, more earnest, earnest, Ernestine, Ernest, Enni, Emilia, Erni, Erniberni*". At the same time he warns: "Not with wrath but with laughter does one kill. Come let us kill the Spirit of Heaviness!" (ibid.) – and soon he is extensively flapping his arms and legs. Does he want to make the audience laugh? Or does he want to shake the spirit of graveness, that archenemy of all laughter, off his shoulders? Or, is he indeed a blind crab from the sea whose limbs need movement? For, now Johnny, slapping and swerving his arms and legs, walking through the audience, demonstrates their lust of movement, that fun of bustling and dancing.

Quite in accordance with the classical function of a fool, who had also to remind to the perishability of human existence, from dancing he goes on to death, who is waiting for all of us and may claim everybody any moment. This is the moment when, coincidentally, he encounters somebody who – it may be because of a language barrier, or for whatever reason, Freud's city provides many possibilities of interpretation – comments on Johnny's efforts by quoting Queen Victoria: "*I am not amused*". The opportunity could not be better. This fits perfectly. Any good spectacle needs an opponent, a critic. Even if there is no script in cold print. A carper drives on the action, and this is precisely what is going to happen. Johnny stops short. "*You are not amused?*" he asks, and in a friendly manner, speaking a kind of pidgin English, he explains: "*I just said, how is it for you, that you know, that you will die?*" Loud laughter. Applause. – But his opposite number remains disliking. Johnny's thoughts are flying. One can tell from his face. Quite obviously, he is thinking with lightning speed. Then he rejoices, quite in the Nietzschean, by turning a no into a yes: "*You are not amused? – That was the   r i g h t   answer! Y e s! Me neither. I think it's the meanest thing in this fucking crazy universe, that we are reading all this books – for what use?*" Johnny becomes enraged. "*We are not only reading the books, we are fighting, we are struggling and we say yes to it, yes, yes, yes, yes! You enjoy it.*" Taken away by his *thinking*, Johnny does not forget to say *thank you* – did he even read Heidegger? And as a compensation for all the inconvenience he promises to do his best: "*because you stayed, you will see my Dionysos dancing.*" But still carper is not amused. Also Johnny sticks to his guns and argues by stringent logic "*you see that's what I mean – struggling, fighting, trying your best, giving your best and it's never enough – at the end – you die!*" Great laughter. Everybody likes this fool.

Relieved from the burden of this interlude, Johnny gets back his breath. Vehemently he shakes his body, minces, sprains, like to shake of this burden even physically. As an accompaniment, he roars, the real lion in the desert. Finally, he gets back his speech, he blows up his nostrils and shouts at the audience: "*Wacht's auf, Leit! ... Es geht um   L e b e n   und   S t e r b e n   – und ihr sitz'st da herum wia a f a d e   o i d e   S o c k n !*" (*Wake up, people! ... It's l i f e   or   d e a t h – and you're sittin' around like   d e a d   o l'   s o c k s!*) But this, he says, is no wonder. Life is normed, tamed, disciplined. Everybody was sitting around well behaved, bearing the burden of their duties on hanging shoulders. Tame and obedient. Morally flawless. Everybody knows how to behave. *Even over here,* he stirs up those sitting around him.

Even over here! Repeatedly he criticizes the audience for their civilised bums. This, he says, is not the way of doing philosophy. The urges are tamed; do not step out of line, no extempore, please, this is banned, already since the days of Empress Maria Theresia, thus no lustfulness, not even some minor lust, you better not! woe be to those whetting on the stools to have just a bit more fun. Don't you! – Everybody is sitting tight and waiting, Johnny in his fight against deadness goes on stirring up the audience, simply everybody, no cockiness, no buffoonery, no sly, bad humour, all he is seeing is socially integrated and good people. "For the good – they *cannot* create: they are always the beginning of the end –" (Nietzsche 2005, 185) is his imaginary lamentation, and maliciously he throws himself into a pose. "Hu! Hu! Hu! Hu! Hu!", could it be that they are "Afraid perhaps of an / Angry blond curly-maned / Lion-monster?" (ibid., 270)

After this sermon, which Johnny accompanies with unfitting excursions, quite in line with the tradition of the fools, he asks how much time is left for his finale, the Dionysian dance he has announced. *Five minutes to go?* that is good. Now he is going to dance! Dance everybody to the ground, sphinx everybody to the ground, hex everybody to the ground! Furthermore, he says, he is seeing clearly how the Yes is growing and sprawling out of everybody's heads. So – there will be dancing! But how? How? The audience is amused and curious. Johnny takes off his shoes and socks. Now, he says, he needs naked feet, *and* he needs the physicality of the spectators. While saying this, he bends and extends his body, his arms and legs to every possible and impossible direction, and again he floods those present with obscenities. Suddenly he stops, with a piercing look at the audience, fixating individual persons *"like is only recognized by like"*, and imploringly he raises his arms. Then, with a swift grip, he takes the snow white wig, mutates into a juvenile old man, and while putting it on his head, to everybody's astonishment he has swiftly put one leg on a spectator's thigh, and now one leg is resting on the pedestal while the other one is resting on somebody else's body. Holding this strange position, Johnny is trying to keep his balance and asks himself and the audience what this all has got to do with Nietzsche, after all? "N o *idea*", he admits while the audience is laughing, and continues climbing on and over the shanks and bod ies of the spectators, his hands are clinging to their shoulders and heads, and in a low voice he assures them – *"zu Eurer Beruhigung, i hob des scho g'übt" (to your reassurance, I've practiced that).*

Figure 7: Johnny wig, applause. (Copyright: Austrian Science Fund (FWF): AR 275-G21)

Much, very much laughter and applause during all of his shenanigans. This ragged rogue enjoys the privilege of fools. Finally, he is no longer satisfied with all this, and he stages a ride through the crowd on the shoulders of a spectator. After all, he does not want to dance on his own, he wants everybody to join. True philosophy, he says, happens only by playing, and playing is part of Nietzsche's philosophy, he is just about to explain – when the bell rings. The minutes of the remaining time are over. But Johnny does not allow any interruption, across his imaginary bridge, his bridge made of words and bodies, he tries to reach Krassimira Kruschkova, Director of Theory at Tanzquartier Wien, who loves the blind sea crab so much. To move faster, he calls for a horse, *"another horse! please come on!"*, he looks for and finds a suitable one among those present, and galloping and yelling trium-phantly he arrives at his destination, wearing the snow white wig on his head like a crown. A crown of wisdom, with which this fool, this storyteller and buffoon, this antipode of truth, has crowned himself?

"We have the truths that we deserve depending on the place we are carrying our existence to, the hour we watch over and the element that we frequent." (Deleuze 1986, 110)

Literature

Bachtin, Michail M. 1990. *Literatur und Karneval. Grundzüge der Lachkultur.* Frankfurt a.M.: Fischer Taschenbuch.

Böhler, Arno. 2017. "Immanence: A Life … Friedrich Nietzsche." *Performance Philosophy* 3 (3), 576–603. https://doi.org/10.21476/PP.2017.33163.

Böhler, Arno. 2018. "Philosophy on Stage. Philosophie ALS künstlerische Forschung." In *Philosophy on Stage. Philosophie als künstlerische Forschung*, edited by Arno Böhler and Susanne Valerie [Granzer], 59–122. Wien: Passagen.

Cambridge Dictionary. n.d. "Touchstone." Accessed February 7, 2022. https://dictionary.cambridge.org/de/worterbuch/englisch/touchstone.

Deleuze, Gilles. 1986 [1962]. *Nietzsche and Philosophy.* Translated by Hugh Tomlinson. London/New York: Columbia University Press.

Die Welt der Habsburger. 2022. "Extemporierverbot durch Maria Theresia 1752." Accessed February 7, 2022. http://www.habsburger.net/de/extemporierverbot-durch-maria-theresia-1752.

Foucault, Michel. 2011. "The Courage of the Truth." In *Lectures at the Collège de France 1983–1984*, 1–22. London: Palgrave Macmillian.

[Granzer], Susanne Valerie. 2018. "Johnny & Immanuel. Zwei Lecture Performances." In *Philosophy on Stage. Philosophie als künstlerische Forschung*, edited by Arno Böhler and Susanne Valerie [Granzer], 175–224. Wien: Passagen.

Granzer, Susanne Valerie. 2016. *Actors and the Art of Performance: Under Exposure.* Basingstoke: Palgrave Macmillan.

Kraus, Barbara. 2015. "Out there is a field." Performance in the framework of the four-day festival *Philosophy On Stage #4: Artist Philosophers–Nietzsche et cetera.* Tanzquartier Wien, Halle G, 27.11.2015, 18:45.

Handke, Peter. 1989. *Das Spiel vom Fragen.* Frankfurt a.M.: Suhrkamp.

Jandl, Ernst. 1997. *lechts und rinks. gedichte statements peppermints.* München: dtv.

Kierkegaard, Søren. 1904 [1885]. *Entweder – Oder. Ein Lebensfragment.* Leipzig: Fr. Richter.

Langenbach-Flore, Beate. 1994. Shakespeares Narren und die Tradition des Hofnarrentums, Nordersted: GRIN.

Müller-Kampel, Beatrix. 2003. *Hanswurst, Bernardon, Kasperl, Spaßmacher im 18. Jahrhundert.* Paderborn: Schöningh.

Nietzsche, Friedrich. 1988. *Sämtliche Werke: kritische Studienausgabe in 15 Einzelbänden.* 9, *Nachgelassene Fragmente 1880–1882* (2., durchges. Aufl.). Edited by Giorgio Colli and Mazzino Montinari. Berlin/New York: de Gruyter.

Nietzsche, Friedrich. 1989. "Why I Am So Clever." In: *Ecce Homo.* Translated and edited by Walter Kaufmann, 239–240. New York: Vintage Books Edition.

Nietzsche, Friedrich. 2005. *Thus Spoke Zarathustra.* Translated by Graham Parkes. Oxford: Oxford University Press.

Nietzsche, Friedrich. n.d. "Dionysus-Dithyrambs: Only Fool! Only Poet!" *The Nietzsche Channel.* Accessed April 24, 2022. http://www.thenietzschechannel.com/works-pub/dd/dd-dual.htm.

Schiller, Friedrich. 2004. "An die Freunde." In *Sämtliche Werke in 5 Bänden,* Bd. 1, 421. München: dtv.

Shakespeare, William. [1862]. *As You Like It.* Vol. 2. London and Edinburgh: W. & R. Chambers.

Spinoza, Baruch de. 1994. *A Spinoza Reader. The Ethics and Other Works. Benedict de Spinoza.* Edited and Translated by Edwin Curley. Princeton: Princeton University Press.

List of Illustrations

Tanja Traxler & Reinhold A. Bertlmann

Figure 1: This composite image of the Orion Nebula, retrieved by the Hubble Space Telescope and the Spitzer Space Telescope, shows gaseous swirls of hydrogen, sulfur, and hydrocarbons that hold a collection of infant stars. (Credit: NASA/JPL-Caltech/STScI. https://svs.gsfc.nasa.gov/30775, accessed 14 June 2025.)

Figure 2: Tanja Traxler & Reinhold A. Bertlmann during the lecture performance "Das Universum ist ein Luftballon!" at Globart Academy, October 4th, 2019. (Credit: Zentralbibliothek für Physik der Universität Wien)

Figure 3: The left graphics display a black hole with the singularity in the center and the event horizon. On the right, the evolution of a collapsing star is presented, time is in the vertical, space in the horizontal. (Credit: © Johan Jarnestad/The Royal Swedish Academy of Sciences. https://www.nobelprize.org/uploads/2020/10/fig2-phy-en-cross-section.pdf, accessed 14 June 2025.)

Figure 4: The spiralling and merging of two black holes with masses of 29 and 36 solar masses to a black hole of 62 solar masses is shown together with the corresponding LIGO signal. (Credit: © Johan Jarnestad/The Royal Swedish Academy of Sciences. https://www.nobelprize.org/prizes/physics/2017/popular-information/, accessed 14 June 2025.)

Sandra Noeth

Figure 1: Crash Course in Cloudspotting. (Credit: Raquel Meseguer Zafe)
Figure 2: Still Life, video still. (Credit: Hakan Topal, 2014)
Figure 3: Lina Majdalanie, Appendice. (Credit: Ghassan Halawani)

Krassimira Kruschkova

Figure 1: Meg Stuart und Tim Etchells, Shown and Told. (Credit: Tine Declerck, 2016)
Figure 2: Meg Stuart und Tim Etchells, Shown and Told. (Credit: Tine Declerck, 2016)
Figure 3: Meg Stuart und Tim Etchells, Shown and Told. (Credit: Eva Würdinger, 2018)
Figure 4: Meg Stuart und Tim Etchells, Shown and Told. (Credit: Tine Declerck, 2016)

Susanne Valerie [Granzer]

Figure 1: Johnny blinded. (Photo by the author. Copyright: Austrian Science Fund (FWF): AR 275-G21)
Figure 2: Johnny picks up a bag. (Photo by the author. Copyright: Austrian Science Fund (FWF): AR 275-G21)
Figure 3: Johnny little ears, Nietzsche. (Photo by the author. Copyright: Austrian Science Fund (FWF): AR 275-G21)
Figure 4: Johnny and the audience push the platform. (Photo by the author. Copyright: Austrian Science Fund (FWF): AR 275-G21)
Figure 5: Johnny pushes the podium with the audience. (Photo by the author. Copyright: Austrian Science Fund (FWF): AR 275-G21)
Figure 6: Johnny: You know you will die. (Photo by the author. Copyright: Austrian Science Fund (FWF): AR 275-G21)
Figure 7: Johnny wig, applause. (Photo by the author. Copyright: Austrian Science Fund (FWF): AR 275-G21)

List of Contributors

Reinhold A. Bertlmann is a theoretical physicist and Professor Emeritus at the University of Vienna. His work spans quantum physics, entanglement, Bell inequalities, decoherence, quantum field theory and the foundations of quantum mechanics. He taught and supervised at the University of Vienna, organized conferences and workshops, and authored *Anomalies in Quantum Field Theory* as well as two books with Anton Zeilinger, *Quantum [Un]Speakables I & II*. Bertlmann held research positions in Dubna, at CERN, and in Marseille, Paris-Sud and Orsay.

Violetta L. Waibel was Professor of European Philosophy at the University of Vienna from 2009 to 2023. Her key publications include *Hölderlin und Fichte* (2000), *Spinozas Affektenlehre* (2012), and *Fichte und Sartre über Freiheit* (2015). She organized the 30th International Hegel Congress in 2014 and the 12th International Kant Congress in 2015 and co-edited the five-volume *Natur und Freiheit* (2019). Waibel also organized interdisciplinary Concert-Symposia with Klangforum Wien and Wien Modern and has published widely on consciousness, subjectivity, space, time and aesthetics.

Avital Ronell is the Jacques Derrida Chair and Professor of philosophy at the European Graduate School and Professor of the Humanities at New York University. Her work spans literary studies, philosophy, feminist and trans theory, media, technology, psychoanalysis and deconstruction. Born in Prague, she studied in Berlin, Princeton and Paris with Gadamer, Derrida and Cixous. She has held professorships in US and received major awards and fellowships, among them distinguished French cultural awards. She has appeared in theater and film, including this year's "Surviving Derrida" by Mario Lozano.

Tanja Traxler is a quantum physicist, journalist, and lecturer at the University of Applied Arts Vienna. Her research focuses on the philosophical foundations of quantum physics and the societal impact of quantum technologies. As head of the science department of DER STANDARD she is a leading communicator of science and one of Austria's most established science journalists. She was awarded several prizes for her work in science communication. At the UAAV she combines quantum physics with artistic practices and cross-disciplinary links between science, philosophy and the arts.

Arno Böhler teaches philosophy at the Department of Philosophy at the University of Vienna and aesthetics at the mdw – University of Music and Performing Arts Vienna. He is the Principal Investigator of the PEEK project "Philosophy in the Arts : Arts in Philosophy. Cross-Cultural Research on the Significance of the Heart in Artistic Research and Performance Philosophy", conducted at ARC-mdw and funded by the Austrian Science Fund (FWF). He has been a visiting research fellow in Bangalore, Heidelberg, New York and Princeton, and a visiting professor in Vienna, Bremen and Berlin.

Soumyabrata Choudhury teaches at the School of Arts and Aesthetics, JNU. He has authored Theatre, Number, Event: Three Studies on the Relationship between Sovereignty, Power and Truth, Ambedkar and Other Immortals: An Untouchable Research Programme, Now It's Come To Distances: Notes on Coronavirus and Shaheen Bagh, Association and Isolation and Thoughts of Gaza Far From Gaza.

Sandra Noeth is a professor at Berlin University of the Arts and a practising curator and dramaturge. She specializes in body-based research in the arts, society and politics. Recent projects have focused on the role, status and agency of bodies in bordering processes, on arts, bodies and unequal politics of protection, and on the body in international humanitarian law. She is the author of Resilient Bodies, Residual Effects (2019) and editor or co-editor of several key publications on embodiment and movement. Her work engages critically with artistic, social and political contexts today.

Susanne Valerie Granzer, also known as Susanne Valerie, is a professor emeritus of acting at the Max Reinhardt Seminar at the University of Music and Performing Arts in Vienna, Austria. As an actress, she has performed at state theatres across the German-speaking world. Alongside her acting career, she earned a PhD in Philosophy from the University of Vienna in 1995. Together with the philosopher Arno Böhler, she established the Vienna-based cultural factory *baseCollective* and the festival *Philosophy on Stage*. She is currently a key researcher on the research project "Philosophy in the Arts : Arts in Philosophy. Cross-Cultural Research on the Significance of the Heart in Artistic Research and Performance Philosophy", conducted at ARC-mdw and funded by the Austrian Science Fund (FWF).

Krassimira Kruschkova is a theatre, dance and performance theorist and dramaturge. She teaches at the University of Applied Arts and the Academy of Fine Arts Vienna. Habilitation in 2002; from 2003–2017 head of the Theory Center at Tanzquartier Wien. She curated numerous lecture and performance series and held guest professorships in Vienna, Salzburg, Frankfurt and over several years at FU Berlin. Publications include *Ob?scene* (2005), *Tanz anderswo* (2004), *It takes place when it doesn't* (2006), *Uncalled* (2009), *Wissen wir, was ein Körper vermag?* (2014), and SCORES #0–#7 (2010–2017).

Veronika Reichl is a writer, lecturer, and artist based in Berlin. In 2023, her book Das Gefühl zu denken (The Feeling of Thinking), a collection of stories on reading theory, was published by Matthes & Seitz Berlin. In 2008, she released Sprachkino (Language-Cinema), which explores the interface between theoretical language and pictoriality, published by Merz & Solitude, Stuttgart. She holds degrees in Communication Design and Media Art, and completed an artistic research Ph.D. at the University of Portsmouth.

About mdwPress

The Open Access University Press of the mdw

mdwPress is the open access academic publisher of the mdw – University of Music and Performing Arts Vienna. With this press, the mdw aims to increase the visibility of its research in all its diversity. Free from commercial motives, mdwPress makes research results freely accessible and reusable for the interested public.

The quality and academic freedom of mdwPress are ensured by an academic board whose regularly rotating internal and external members are characterized by distinguished academic achievements. Each proposal for a publication project, including a suggestion for the peer review procedure of the entire manuscript, is discussed and determined by this board.

mdwPress is open to all academic publication formats, including journals and innovative formats, and welcomes inter- and transdisciplinarity. Where necessary, mdwPress relies on external partnerships.

About this Volume

This volume was created as part of the research project *Arts in Philosophy: Philosophy in the Arts. On the Significance of the Heart in Artistic Research* (AR) *and Performance Philosophy* (PP), funded by the Austrian Science Fund (FWF) (Grant DOI: 10.55776/AR822). After the project proposal was accepted by the academic board of mdwPress, the book underwent a double-blind peer review by two reviewers. On the basis of the reviews and subsequent revisions, the academic board accepted the final manuscript for publication.

GPSR Authorized Representative: Easy Access System Europe, Mustamäe tee 50, 10621 Tallinn, Estonia, gpsr.requests@easproject.com

www.ingramcontent.com/pod-product-compliance
Lightning Source LLC
Chambersburg PA
CBHW061603120626
46550CB00004B/1603